# TONY CARR

# TONY CARR

# A LIFETIME IN FOOTBALL AT WEST HAM UNITED

ICON

Published in the UK in 2022 by
Icon Books Ltd, Omnibus Business Centre,
39–41 North Road, London N7 9DP
email: info@iconbooks.com
www.iconbooks.com

Sold in the UK, Europe and Asia by
Faber & Faber Ltd, Bloomsbury House,
74–77 Great Russell Street,
London WC1B 3DA or their agents

Distributed in the UK, Europe and Asia by
Grantham Book Services, Trent Road,
Grantham NG31 7XQ

Distributed in Australia and New Zealand by
Allen & Unwin Pty Ltd, PO Box 8500,
83 Alexander Street, Crows Nest, NSW 2065

Distributed in South Africa by
Jonathan Ball, Office B4, The District,
41 Sir Lowry Road, Woodstock 7925

Distributed in India by
Penguin Books India,
7th Floor, Infinity Tower – C, DLF Cyber City,
Gurgaon 122002, Haryana

ISBN: 978-178578-759-1

Typeset in Freight Text by Marie Doherty

Printed and bound in Great Britain by
Clays Ltd, Elcograf S.p.A.

# CONTENTS

## ABOUT THE AUTHOR

Tony Carr was born in Bow, East London and joined West Ham as a teenager, spending 48 years at the club. He won the FA Youth Cup twice and was made an MBE for his services to football in 2010. He lives in Essex.

# ACKNOWLEDGEMENTS

A heartfelt thanks to Rio Ferdinand, Frank Lampard Jr, Mark Noble, Michael Carrick, Steve Potts and Joe Cole for giving me their time for their interviews.

Thanks also to Ken Dyer and Giuseppe Muro for their help in transcribing the player interviews and particularly to Ken for his stream of advice. To Stuart Prossor for his regular helpful calls from New Zealand, to Steve Blowers, and to my literary agent Jonathan Hayden for his support and enthusiasm in getting the book published. Finally, all the managers, staff and players I have had the privilege of working with throughout my career.

*For my wife Brenda and my children Dean, Neil and Louise*
*in thanks for their constant support throughout my career.*

# LIST OF ILLUSTRATIONS

*Every effort has been made to contact the copyright holders of images used. The publisher will be pleased to credit in future editions any rights holders not mentioned here.*

# 1

# NOTHING LASTS FOREVER

Nothing lasts forever, especially in football where, so they say, a week is a long time – but when the end came, in 2016, it was still a shock.

I had been West Ham's youth academy chief for 43 years, beginning in 1973, but the writing had been on the wall since 2014, when the club's vice chairman Karren Brady called me to a meeting and told me I was going to be replaced by Terry Westley, who had previously worked for West Ham's co-owners, David Gold and David Sullivan, plus Brady herself, at Birmingham City.

At the meeting, Karren told me the club wanted me to stay on as 'academy ambassador' to help Westley settle into the club, to be his sounding board, to offer advice and to help mentor the young coaches at the academy. She said it was a 'new and exciting role' and 'we will call you director of football', but they quickly discovered that the then manager, Sam Allardyce, had it written in his contract that the board could not appoint a director of football so a new title had to be dreamed up. Nevertheless, the board felt I would be the ideal person to fill this 'new and exciting role'.

I gave the offer some thought, talked it over with my family and finally accepted because I felt I could still make a useful contribution. I spoke again with Brady and we agreed a ten-point job description, including mentoring coaches, helping to promote the club within the club's community programme (which I have always been committed to), supporting the new academy director and advising when asked, giving input on player selection and generally supporting staff and players within the academy. I still had fifteen months of my academy director's contract to run, so it was agreed it would continue and the change of role would be implemented when it expired in September 2015 – whereupon I received a new one-year contract and the change of title to academy ambassador.

About nine months into the new contract, one morning in my office I took a call from the club's HR department asking me to attend a meeting later that day. As academy director I had periodically spoken with Karren Brady – usually at monthly meetings – but since my role change, that link had been broken. This time the call was from Andy Mollett, the club's chief financial officer and adviser on HR matters. I later found out that Mollett was the member of staff who was always the bearer of bad news regarding employment issues and redundancy.

At the meeting, which was very cold and to the point, he said the club didn't think the role was viable any more and did not warrant a full-time position. I have no idea why this sudden suggestion the role was no longer viable was offered as the reason for ending my employment; I had more than just performed duties according to the ten-point job description agreed with Brady earlier. He also said that consultations had taken place with various members of staff who were no longer in favour of maintaining the role and the duties I had agreed with Brady. I didn't understand why they should say such a thing as Westley regularly asked me to join meetings and routinely sought my advice on players; and I, in return, went out of my way to be supportive of him. Mollett went on to say that the ambassadorial role would be axed and a new role of 'consultant' was offered for effectively one day a week. The other option on the table was redundancy. It was as cold-hearted as that. I felt in the light of the way things had been laid out that they, the club where I'd spent almost all of my adult life, wanted rid of me – although they couldn't bring themselves to use those words. I was being pushed into a corner with very little room for manoeuvre. I asked Mollett what the redundancy package was, and he told me three months' notice and a minimal payment. That was it.

The timing of the meeting was exactly three months until the end of my contract and because I had technically changed jobs, it proved easy for the club to make this 'new and exciting role' redundant. It ran through my mind how convenient that was! Yet I was more disappointed with the way it was done than anything else. I was upset and, after 43 years of unbroken service, I thought it could have been handled better. It may not have changed the outcome, but it would have shown some respect for a lifetime of dedication to the club. This wasn't the West Ham United way that I thought I knew.

I took advice from the League Managers Association (LMA) who thought they could improve the package for the redundancy, but ultimately the club simply wouldn't budge.

The *Daily Mail* had got wind of what was happening and rang me. They said they'd heard that West Ham were sacking me, so I had to tell them that wasn't quite correct and filled them in with as much detail as I felt prudent. I certainly didn't slag anybody off. I told them HR had handled things when I thought, perhaps naively, a more senior person might have been more appropriate.

A few days later a piece appeared in the paper and my LMA representative, Graham Mackrell, rang to say the club were 'not happy' with the article. I replied, 'I'm not happy either!' The club told Mackrell that they could sue me for breach of contract for talking to the press – it never happened – but they told me to clear my desk there and then and leave immediately.

So that was it after 43 years! It ended on a sad, unnecessarily bitter note. Should I have stayed silent when the newspaper rang me? Should I have said I was happy with the situation? I was told there was a big fans' backlash on social media and subsequently there was a piece in the *Daily Mirror* stating how much I had earned; inaccurate as it was, it was over an eleven-year period and included the proceeds from my testimonial match given to me by the previous Icelandic owners.

The whole thing left a bad taste, as I felt then, and still do, that I had something to offer West Ham with regard to youth development. I wasn't looking for a full-time role; a couple of days a week and a game on the weekend would have been enough. In these times where people say youth development is not what it was, I know, with my experience and knowledge gained over years working with Ron Greenwood, John Lyall and all the subsequent managers, I could have helped with carrying on the West Ham way and traditions. One of the first people to ring me was Tony Whelan, who is an experienced and valued youth developer at Manchester United and has worked with some of United's top players. He said, 'We have just had a staff meeting and your name came up and we are all amazed that West Ham have no use for a man who has 43 years' experience in youth football. We can't believe it!' Well, that call cheered me up.

Leon Britton – a Swansea player, who was very technically gifted and a player with great passing ability – used to be with me at West Ham where I coached him as a youth player; he also rang.

'It can't be right what I've just read in the paper, can it, Tony?'

'Unfortunately, Leon …' I had to tell him, '… yes, it is.'

Steve Heighway, Liverpool's former player and previous academy director, for example, is employed part-time at Anfield, helping out and mentoring young coaches and I believe I could have done something similar at West Ham. With the introduction of the Elite Player Performance Plan (EPPP) by the Premier League, clubs are required to employ more coaching staff; these coaches in the main are young, newly qualified and in need of guidance. This is a role that more experienced coaches like me can help with.

I never had a cross word with my successor Terry Westley. Whether he felt he didn't want me around as a constant reminder of the past, I don't know, but we would only have been working towards the same goal – which was improving West Ham's young players and doing our best to get them into the first team.

I will admit that initially the whole business affected the way I regarded the club. I was angry. Should I have expected more? You could say it's just the way the football industry is, but it's not the way I would do things.

The club let me keep two season tickets for the 2016/17 season and I went back to watch games at the London Stadium with either of my sons Neil or Dean, but the following season they weren't renewed by the club, nor was I given the option to buy them! My son Neil did tell me that when he was in one of the club's new prematch lounges with friends, they had my picture on the wall, but I've yet to see it!

Various clubs such as Tottenham Hotspur, Fulham, Arsenal, Aston Villa, Crystal Palace and Sheffield United all asked me to help out with their coaches – generally advising them and giving them the benefit of my experience of coaching and dealing with young players. I've been back to watch a couple of West Ham youth games at Little Heath and been to a few first-team games. I am also chairman of the London Football Coaches Association, and my work with the Premier League is developing, so I am keeping quite busy.

It's been difficult because, for the first time since leaving school, I have not had a full-time job and a busy day ahead ... and I found it hard – I still do a bit. I've been involved in a small way with the Football Association on their youth coaching awards and have done some work on the FA Pro Licence, presenting to coaches from clubs at the national football centre at St George's Park. After talking on one of the advanced youth award courses, Ugo Ehiogu, who was then coaching at Tottenham, approached me and we had a long discussion on young player development. He was hugely enthusiastic and looking forward to forging a career in coaching. A few months after our conversation, Ugo sadly passed away and although I didn't know him well, it hit me quite badly.

Currently I am in a role with the FA Premier League as a consultant and mentor for their various courses. It is a part-time role and suits me down to the ground, mixing with staff of the Premier and Football League clubs and is something I relish. I hope I offer something of value too, but after 43 years at one club it's hard to let go, even allowing for the interest other clubs have shown in me. But, as they say, in life you must move on.

It's ironic that the reason the club gave for the change in my role away from West Ham's academy director was that there were no players coming through. The day I left, one of my former youth-team players and now a first-team regular, James Tomkins, was sold to Crystal Palace for £11 million plus, while Declan Rice, Grady Diangana and Ben Johnson were already on the academy production line. So, on the whole, with the number of players I helped develop and with the transfer fees they generated, I don't think I did a bad job!

# 2

# AN EAST END EDUCATION

The score is 9-6 to Northleigh House, who are playing Shilling-ford House in the regular game played on the 30 × 15-metre playground on our council estate that was off Devons Road, Bow in London's E3 district. It was usually an eight- or nine-a-side game, very tight with little or no space, but you learnt to cope and to play both as an individual and combining with each other in such a restricted space.

This is where I learnt to play football growing up in the 1950s. Here we were in the East End of London, whose close proximity to the docks had resulted in it being badly bombed during the war. Still the evidence of the Blitz dominated the landscape with bomb sites strewn indiscriminately about. The estate was full of young families, many with young men recovering from the horrors of the Second World War, making the best of post-war austerity. I lived in Northleigh House, and before that in Ranwell Close, on a housing estate which was off Old Ford Road in Bow, opposite Gunmakers Lane which led directly into Victoria Park. We lived here until I was six months old, when my parents moved us to Northleigh House – newly built after all the bomb-damaged streets had been cleared. I grew up with a sense of pride in our new home that we had been given. It had three bedrooms, an indoor toilet and a separate bathroom, which for a young family of the time were unheard-of luxuries! For all its modernity, the only heating was supplied by a coal fire in the 'front room'.

I had a brother, Bernard, and two sisters, Kathleen and Christine, and Mum and Dad – Kathleen (or Kit as she was known to everyone) and Charlie who worked for the London Electricity Board as a joiner, joining electricity cables together underground. On my walk to school, I would often see him down a hole in the road the electricity board had just dug, fixing cables and welding them together with lead from a pot boiling away from a gas bottle. Mum was a typical East End housewife with a part-time job on the side. She used to be up very early, usually before 6 o'clock, and worked in St Andrew's Hospital – long since demolished – right next door to Bromley-by-Bow Underground station, where, incidentally, I was born. She prepared the breakfasts for the doctors and nurses. Dad prepared our breakfast and got us ready for school while Mum would get home at lunchtime.

Family holidays were spent at a caravan site in Burnham-on-Crouch, along with my nan and grandad on my mum's side, Kathleen and Bill, who lived nearby. My father's parents, Bill and Mary, had died when I was a baby. We would all travel down by train from Bow and arrive at Burnham some four hours later. The first stop was always the pub at the bottom of the hill from the station. My brother, sisters and I would sit outside with a bag of blue, red and white-packaged Smiths Salt 'n' Shake crisps ('Look for the little blue salt bag') or an arrowroot biscuit and a glass of lemonade. The caravan site was next to the sea, the River Crouch being an estuary of the English Channel north of the Thames. I would go down to the local butchers with my brother and ask for some scrap meat so we could go crabbing. We would run a line and hook and 'fish' by the water's edge and collect crabs by the dozen. At the end of the day, we would empty the bucket full of crabs and watch them scuttle back into the sea. This was our daily activity and I cannot tell you how much fun we had doing it. The caravan site was also right next door to a scout camp and I can remember quite vividly the trumpeter playing reveille at 6 o'clock and waking everybody up! We went to Burnham for several summers and to this day the happy memories bring a smile to my face. These days Burnham is only about an hour away from my home by car, but back in the late 1950s, the journey seemed like one massive adventure as if we were crossing continents.

A few years later, it would be Nan who would be the first of our immediate family to pass away. I, along with my brother and sisters, had gone round to see them one Christmas morning and we were quickly aware that something was wrong. When we got there the flat was cold and Christmas dinner remained uncooked. Nan and Grandad seemed confused, vacant even. We quickly reported back to Mum, who straight away went over to sort them out. It transpired that this was the first stage of dementia for our nan, who eventually lost control of everything – even of her memory, which was particularly sad to witness. She grew increasingly muddled and confused and would need constant care thereafter. It was not long afterwards that she was hospitalised and died in St Andrew's Hospital – the same hospital I was born in. When she died, I was on holiday with my future wife Brenda and we did not find out that she had passed away – and indeed had been buried – until we got home. I was very upset to have missed the funeral, but you have to remember this was long before the days of mobile phones and instant communication. After a while, Grandad (we called him Grumps) went to live with my mum's sister, Eileen, and her husband John. He lived out the rest of his life quite happily and died peacefully at home. His funeral service was held in a local church in Dagenham, Essex. Having already missed my gran's funeral, this one didn't run too smoothly. The slowly driven hearse left my Aunt Eileen's house at the appointed hour with the rest of the family following behind in cars. When we were about a mile from the church, the hearse broke down and a lengthy line of cars drew up behind it where we all sat waiting for a replacement vehicle. It arrived sometime later and in the middle of the street, to the bemusement of onlookers, the coffin, the wreaths and the flowers were painstakingly transferred to the replacement hearse. Not a great start to Grumps's send-off.

Growing up on our estate brought lots of opportunities for young kids to lark about. Every day the milkman arrived on his horse-drawn cart. He would pull up in front of our flats and start the arduous process of walking up and down the stairs in our four-floor block with bottles in hand. While he was doing this, we used to dare each other to run under the tethered horse; this was great fun until one time the spooked horse moved suddenly and trod on one of the boys' feet. It immediately put paid to that particular adventure and was a very painful lesson learnt by my friend Johnny Hood.

Throughout our East End childhood our playgrounds were the ubiquitous bomb sites around Bow. As kids we spent hours exploring these 'playgrounds' with no thought given to the potential dangers involved.

When Guy Fawkes Night came around we always used to build a 'Guy' and hawk it around the streets asking the timeless, 'A penny for the Guy, mister?' Our nearest bomb site was called the Sand Hills and we would collect wood from bombed pubs or houses, there to build a massive bonfire on which to position our effigy of Guy Fawkes. More often than not, other groups of boys would set fire to our bonfire before the fifth of November, so we had to set a constant watch to ensure this did not happen! As soon as it got dark on the fifth, the bonfire would be lit and cheap fireworks and crackers would be set off. Nobody (including the amused adults) would say it was an organised event – certainly when compared with the safety-conscious organised displays we have today, and it *was* a dangerous spectacle as rival groups of boys would throw fireworks (mostly bangers) at each other.

One such incident was truly frightening and might have had long-lasting damaging consequences. My brother Bernard was temporarily blinded when a banger was thrown into a crowd of boys just as he was bending down to ignite a rocket in a milk bottle. This necessitated a trip to hospital, about which my dad was not best pleased. Fortunately, Bernard made a full recovery. Frankly, we couldn't see the (very real) dangers. It was only as we got older we realised how foolhardy it all was. But I guess most of us are still here to tell the tale.

Every now and then, as a treat, a group of friends would buy a 'Red Rover' – which was an all-day ticket to ride on any red bus in London. We would explore various points of interest, but always ended up at the Tower of London. And in those days, in the late 1950s and early 1960s, you could explore the small beach area at low tide on the River Thames under the shadow of Tower Bridge and mudlark around the water's edges. Unfortunately for safety reasons no one is allowed to do it these days. The steps down to the 'beach' are still there, preserved for history, but the gate is permanently locked.

One of our adventures was a day out at Whipps Cross boating lake. We used to go on the bus or cycle there and it was about a 30-minute journey from Bow. We would mess about on the lake's edge and go out rowing on the lake – many a fine summer day was spent there. On one occasion a circus had arrived in town. We watched agog as the trucks holding a variety of animals came to a halt and brawny-looking men began the lengthy process of setting up the Big Top. For us young 'uns, this was something really exciting and we asked the circus guys if we could help. He told us if we helped clear the animal cages and trucks he would give each of us a ticket for the circus. Well that was all the incentive we needed, so we set about cleaning the cages, getting all the old straw out and filling them with new stuff – and in case you're wondering, there were no animals in the cages at the time (see general lack of health and safety concerns of the era above). There were four of us and we dutifully spent the whole day doing as we'd been asked, at the end of which the guy said, 'Lads, come back in a few days and I will give you the tickets for the show.'

So we came back a few days later and true to his word he gave us a ticket each. My parents were horrified that we had nearly, in their minds, run away to join a circus and to compound matters had ridden on our bikes over five miles of busy London roads back to Whipps Cross to collect our tickets. But it was worth it! A circus didn't come to town that often and we had free tickets. There was a sense of freedom about in those days – a small group of friends exploring the city and surrounding areas – a freedom that is sadly lacking in today's climate. On Sundays it was Sunday school at the nearby Kingsley Hall and most of the kids on the estate attended. It was the usual fare of religious stories from the Bible and a few hymns to sing along to. Kingsley Hall also became our youth club where we could play snooker and table tennis and listen to the popular music of the day, The Beatles being among my personal favourites.

One of the stories associated with Kingsley Hall is that in 1931, Mahatma Gandhi stayed there for twelve weeks while he was visiting London for talks on the future of India. He had refused the offer of a stay in a hotel, preferring to live among the 'working classes'. The visit was a huge success among the local people with whom he freely and joyously mixed. Among his visitors during his stay were Charlie Chaplin, George Bernard Shaw and the politician David Lloyd George. It turns out that Gandhi was a keen football fan and having established three football teams in South Africa, there are reliable reports that during his stay he attended several West Ham United games and even visited the Boleyn pub where he socialised with the West Ham fans while drinking cream soda! He already had a strong connection to West Ham United through his friendship with its founder Arnold Hills (owner of the Thames Iron Works, where West Ham United originated) while he was living in London completing his law studies in 1888/89. During this period Arnold Hills brought the young Gandhi on to the executive committee of the London Vegetarian Society. Today, there is a blue plaque on the wall outside Kingsley Hall commemorating his visit to East London.

# 3

# FOOTBALL: THE START

Every boy on the estate loved football. We would play for hours on the small grassed areas (except when the caretaker would chuck us off!) or, at the weekend, in Victoria Park (Vicky to us). Over at Vicky Park we would normally find another group of boys to play a match with, using trees, bags or jumpers for goalposts (all respect to Paul Whitehouse). This lasted until I left Old Palace primary school at the age of eleven and moved on to secondary school in the early 1960s. Although we played football during games lessons at Old Palace, we never had a team as such. In fact, I would never play in an organised team until I went on to secondary school. Our teacher at Old Palace was a Mr Wilson, whose greatest love was for cricket. In the school he would have us explore the nature and etiquette of the game, explaining the positions, the nature of spin bowling (lost on ten-year-olds) and the intricacies of the rules (soon forgotten). It was a pity he didn't have anything like the same affection for football.

Meanwhile, headmistress Miss Greenaway's passion was for English country dancing! To the school hall we were shepherded where we would have to hold hands with the girls and dance around the hall to 'Greensleeves'. At that age, having to hold hands with the girls was the worst bit! All said, it was a happy time at Old Palace, where I made lots of friends as we all grew up: Tommy Ziepe, Johnny Cook, Kenny Hagger, Johnny Alison, David (Pudding) Hood, Frank (Buster) White, John and Mike Kelly, Alan Parlour, Freddie Hayward, Sammy and Terry Elves and many more. But now it was time to move on: secondary school was beckoning. New friendships would have to be made as the group of boys I'd known for years would all be dispersed to different schools around the East End.

I was sent to St Paul's Way School, a secondary modern which was just off Devons Road, almost opposite the council flats where Harry Redknapp lived with his family. And it was here at secondary school that my football career started to blossom. The school was actually two buildings: for my first and second years (years 7 and 8) it was in Southern Grove just off the Mile End Road – an old Victorian building that had been previously named after the poet Elizabeth Barrett Browning. In my third and fourth years (years 9 and 10) I moved to the site in St Paul's Way itself. I was twelve years old before I played in my first organised game in a team – which happened to be the school team. Along with my new bunch of teammates we played regularly every Saturday morning, mostly over at Hackney Marshes, Meath Gardens (Bethnal Green) or Eton Manor (Stratford).

I vividly remember the very first games lesson at Oakfield sports centre: it lasted all morning after the whole year group had met at Mile End Station for registration and taken the Central Line special to Fairlop and the sports fields that were a short walk away. The PE teacher, Mr George, asked which boys had played for their junior school football teams and, because our school never had a team, I didn't put myself forward. There I was all kitted out in a West Ham replica kit and shiny football boots and he must have noticed me ... He asked why I was not in our school team and I had to explain that we didn't have one. 'Well,' he said, 'you come with us this morning.' Therefore, thanks to my West Ham uniform, I was put immediately into the school team group. Out we went onto the pitches and the first thing that struck me was that the goals had nets. Wow! To shoot at a goal with a net was something really special and was a first for me.

I played centre forward and was always among the goals. Mr George and his colleague Mr Hurley were keen football fans and were very supportive towards an enthusiastic group of kids from the surrounding council estates, encouraging us to play and to enjoy the game.

Soon I was noticed by a local youth football club called Senrab who invited me to play for them. Senrab was a Limehouse, London E14-based team whose name is derived from the local Barnes Street – Senrab is Barnes spelt backwards! Senrab had a great history and many of its players would go on to play professional football including the late Ray Wilkins, John Terry, Jermain Defoe, Bobby Zamora, Mark Falco and many more. A guy named Jimmy Tindall helped run it, but more about Jimmy later.

Senrab's matches were played on Sunday mornings, and we also played in a Tuesday night floodlit league on a red gravel pitch at Glamis Road, Shadwell. In the floodlit league we played with an ordinary brown leather ball that had to be painted white so we could see it; the lights were not that great! Every time you headed the ball, you ended up with a blob of whitewash on your forehead. The balls were also very heavy when wet and heading was no fun. Sometimes it was especially painful when the laces would untie and flap about so when you headed the ball they would flick you in your eye. I won my first ever football medal playing for Senrab and still have it today.

Senrab was a magnet for local professional scouts who, at that time, had a relationship with Tottenham Hotspur. My first contact with a professional club was an invitation to train at Tottenham in the evenings. The club's cohort of schoolboys were invited to sit on small stools around the touchline at White Hart Lane during Spurs first-team games and I did this on more than one occasion. Not long after I also had an invitation to train at West Ham United. It came following a game where I played for East London under-14s, which had just been formed, at Barking Park. I was approached by a scout named Tony, for the life of me I can't remember his surname, and this invitation was simply too good to turn down. West Ham *were my team* so it was an absolute no-brainer.

It was 1964 and I was thirteen. Training at West Ham as a schoolboy, particularly during the winter months, was held on the tarmacked forecourt at Upton Park using plastic footballs and if someone had left a car parked overnight, well, we would just play around it. We also trained under the West Stand and used bread trays as goals; it was all very basic, but it produced players.

Around this time the local district team (East London, now Tower Hamlets) had just started to run an under-14 team and I was picked to play for them. We played all the other London districts on a regular basis, our home ground being either Eton Manor or Victoria Park. I scored lots of goals for East London and this led to being picked to play for London vs Birmingham Boys at Highbury. My team also featured Charlie George and Jimmy Neighbour. I was also promoted to play for East London under-15s in the final of the

Corinthian Shield against Tottenham and Edmonton at White Hart Lane. I remember it was a tough game on a very wet pitch, but we managed to win 2-1. During the first half I turned my ankle and was hobbling around for a few minutes. From the dugout the coach shouted, 'Are you OK?' to which I replied, 'Can I leave it until half-time and see how it goes?' 'No,' he replied, 'the rules state that we can only make one substitution up until half-time and none in the second half.' That concentrated the mind, so I stopped hobbling and fought on and ended up playing the whole game. This was 1965 and substitutes had yet to be introduced into the professional game: the eleven players who started were the eleven that had to finish the match. If you had a bad injury that prevented you from continuing you played on with ten men, which meant at schoolboy level, substitutes had very strict use, but it made me get on with the game and not worry about a twisted ankle!

One day at school I was called to the office of my PE teacher, Mr Hurley, who had recommended me to go for England Schoolboy trials that were being held over five days at Bisham Abbey. One of the coaches staffing at the trials was John Cartwright, who was an ex-West Ham professional and who was coaching on a part-time basis at my school. This was handy as he could give me a lift to Bisham Abbey. Over the years I struck up a good relationship with John, who was a really passionate coach and someone who was highly critical of the tendency to over-coach young players. He was always a champion of the development of players who could run with the ball, dribble and excite the watching public. We had endless debates on the subject and still do.

The day arrived for me to leave for the trial and my dad, Charlie, and I met John outside Bow Church and off we went. I had hardly ever been out of the East End of London until now and I remember thinking we were going for miles and miles, through the City into open countryside and arriving at Bisham Abbey some hours later. It is in a beautiful setting on the banks of the Thames near Marlow in Berkshire. Bisham Abbey is exactly what it says it is – an old monastery built around 1260. Later, apparently, Henry VIII granted the house to Anne of Cleves as part of their divorce settlement but it is now owned by Sport England and was used as the training base for the England football team before St George's Park was opened in 2012. We were roomed in the Old Abbey and for a boy from Bow this was pretty scary stuff. My London Boys teammates Charlie George and Jimmy Neighbour were also there. The trial consisted of a series of skills practices and games. While not intending it as an excuse, I must report that I had back pain all week and was too shy to say anything about it as I didn't want to miss the opportunity. I didn't make the England squad. I had played all week in pain and could not perform to my best. I remember very well our last night at the Abbey. It was a Thursday evening and we were all in the TV lounge watching *Top of the Pops*. Sixties pop group The Animals were performing their latest hit 'We Gotta Get Out Of This Place' and everyone sang the chorus as loud as we could – *We gotta get out of this place, if it's the last thing we ever do*. I think we were all ready to go home after five solid days of intensive training and if my feeling were any guide, suffering from considerable homesickness. Later on in my career as a coach I had a lot of sympathy for boys we recruited who had to leave home, perhaps for the first time, and live in lodgings. I empathised with the lads who felt homesick.

When I reached the age of fourteen, Wally St Pier, who was chief representative for West Ham, asked me to sign as an associated schoolboy. At the time, this form demonstrated a real intent on the part of the club and that they recognised you had the potential to become a professional player. Of course, as a West Ham supporter, I signed unhesitatingly.

As a gang of eleven-year-olds from our council estate we were regular visitors to the North Bank. We would get to the game very early and bunk in (slip in without paying) as the match deliveries were unloading and we would hide in the cage until the gates officially opened. The cage was an elevated area on the north-west corner of the North Bank, surrounded by bar-like fencing, hence the cage. This was quite a regular ruse for a lot of the local youngsters at this time. My playing idols around this time were John Dick, Mike Grice, Phil Woosnam, Lawrie Leslie in goal and a young Bobby Moore.

Around this time, my mum knitted me a claret and blue scarf with all the players' names embroidered in the alternate claret and blue panels. I never took it off and wore it in all weathers. One day – I think I was about ten years old and still in primary school – I went to get my school dinner but the very firm dinner lady wouldn't let me queue for dinner until I took the scarf off. Well this scarf was sacred and I refused, so she made me wait until the very last child had been served before we came to the compromise that if I loosened the scarf and just let it hang around my shoulders I could get served. I was getting hungry, so I agreed, sacred scarf or not!

After I had signed associate schoolboy forms, West Ham reached the final of the European Cup Winners' Cup to be played at Wembley Stadium – the venue where West Ham had won the FA Cup for the very first time, defeating Preston 3-2, twelve months earlier. They were to play TSV 1860 Munich and I queued up on a Sunday morning to get my ticket to the final. We travelled to the game on the London Underground, which was packed tight; it seemed like the whole of East London was going to Wembley. And it was a *great*, fast, entertaining game that West Ham won 2-0 with a terrific performance with free-flowing movement of the players and quick early passing. Manager Ron Greenwood, whom I had just started to get to know, would have hailed this performance as the way the game should be played. It showed the influence he was having as a coach on his new team. The next morning's newspapers were full of praise for what West Ham had achieved. Travelling back, it was a celebration with everybody singing and in a really happy mood. West Ham had never had such success!

The following year, 1966, was momentous. England won the World Cup at Wembley and for the third successive year Bobby Moore, captain of England, was lifting a trophy from the Royal Box. West Ham also reached another final, the Football League Cup final, which was played over two legs, home and away. They played West Bromwich Albion and didn't make it a hat-trick of wins, losing 5-3 on aggregate. This was the last time the League Cup final was played over two legs as the following season it was played as a final at Wembley. My football career really stared to blossom during this period. Playing for East London as an under-15, we were entered into the English Schools Trophy (a bit like the schoolboy FA Cup) in which we could be drawn to play teams from all over England.

I was asked to captain the side after our regular captain, Kevin Smith, broke his leg in an earlier game. Also in the team was Pat Holland, later a first-team regular and FA Cup winner (1975) for West Ham United, Steve Bowtell who later became a professional at Leyton Orient, and Malcolm Jeffrey who later signed for West

Ham, as would John Scanlon. Another St Paul's Way pupil like me was Stephen Moody, who was in my class at school and a good mate, and a good full back. All in all we had a good team.

We had a great run, getting all the way to the final, beating Charlie George's Islington. Charlie, of course, would go on to play for Arsenal, Derby and Southampton and is remembered as a maverick, magician and entertainer who put a smile on the fans' faces. Also playing for Islington Boys was a commanding centre back called Micky Droy who went on to have a good career with Chelsea, playing over 300 league games. We also got drawn away against Ilkeston and Heanor, which is in Derbyshire, and we went up by train on the morning of the match. I had just returned from a school skiing trip to Austria, spending over 24 hours on a train with not much sleep. When we arrived at the Ilkeston and Heanor football ground, it had been raining all day and in other circumstances the game would have been postponed, but play we must as travelling back for a rearranged game would have been financially impossible for an organisation like ours. We came away with a 2-2 draw with me scoring both goals! The replay a week later saw us win 5-2. We played Bristol Boys in the semi-final and won through to the final after a replay. The replay was special for me – it was played at Bristol Rovers' home ground at the time, Eastville, and we managed to win 3-1 with me scoring a hat-trick for the third time for East London. I remember scoring a header, a right-foot volley and a tap-in. My tally of goals during our cup run ended up on twenty from the eleven games we played, which I'm quite proud of.

As a team, we played the ball in behind the opposition a lot, as well as putting in lots of crosses, and I was a willing runner getting in behind the opposition often and putting myself on the end of the many crosses coming into the penalty box. Playing at centre half for Bristol was Geoff Merrick, who went on to have a great career in professional football, playing over 300 times for Bristol City. We played Oxford in the final over two legs, the first leg being at the Manor Ground, Oxford. We won the first leg 3-2 and I scored two goals. The second leg was to be played at Millwall Football Club's home ground, The Den. We had played all our home games here, which I thought was a strange choice as technically it is in South London. I suppose as there was no professional club in the district, Millwall was a logical choice as it was geographically close – just through the Rotherhithe Tunnel. Like the first, the second leg was a tight affair, and we scraped a 2-1 win with me scoring two goals again. So, we won the English Schools Trophy for East London 5-3 on aggregate. It was a great feeling – the first time East London had won the trophy and they haven't won it since! Before the end of that season I was picked to play for Middlesex County, teaming up again with Charlie George.

After my successes with East London, West Ham United offered me an apprenticeship (now called a scholarship); this was a three-year contract until the age of eighteen. My first contract was for £8 a week in the first year, £9 a week in the second year and £10 a week in the third year, but during the summer months of June and July, the club deducted £1 per week, it technically being close season. Talk about petty! Up until this point I had no idea what I wanted to do after I left school, and my teachers were very concerned that I had almost given up on my studies to concentrate on football – not something I would recommend. All I wanted was to be a footballer. With hindsight, if I hadn't been offered an apprenticeship, I prob-ably would have gone into something like being a motor mechanic

–my dad's brother Arthur was service manager at a Jessops Vauxhall dealership in Stratford, East London and mechanics always interested me. I always wanted to know how things worked and were put together. Looking back, I've often wondered why coaching became such a passionate interest of mine: maybe it is this curiosity of what makes things work and how to put things together that made football coaching seem like a real mental challenge. How to analyse problems and try to set about solving them.

Fortunately, the football option was offered, and I began to seriously follow my dream of becoming a professional player. I left school in the summer of 1966 at the age of fifteen to join West Ham full-time. I had made some good friends at St Paul's Way: Keith Lammin, Alan Taylor, Stephen Moody, who played for East London with me, Peter Tanfield, whom I still speak to today, Tony Andrews, Peter Rosengrave, Robert Ashkettle and many more whose names escape me some 50-odd years later. My last day at school was a Friday and I was escorted to the school gate by a member of staff who suspected I might be about to go on some sort of rampage setting off fire alarms and hydrants. It had never entered my head, but it was a strange feeling standing outside the school gates like it was the end of an era and a feeling of finality that school had been such a happy place for me but was now over. I still had a couple of days finishing up my paper round that I had done for the past three years – up at 6am loading up my bag of papers from the local paper shop and delivering around our council estate and up the Bow Road. One such place in Bow Road was a block of flats called Electric House that had a big clock on the wall outside. It was always a scary place to deliver papers, particularly in the winter: small, tight staircase and always very dark – it used to frighten the life out of me and I couldn't get out of there quickly enough! It's still there now and I go past it occasionally when I am driving down the Bow Road and without fail it causes me to involuntarily shiver. With the paper round finished on the Sunday, I started 'work' on the Monday.

# 4

# STARTING WORK

It was my first day's training at West Ham. England had just won the World Cup and as all the players were gathered around Ron Greenwood who was to address them, there I was rubbing shoulders with my heroes – Bobby Moore, Geoff Hurst, Martin Peters, Johnny Byrne and others. I can remember Ron congratulating the World Cup winners but making special mention of Johnny Byrne who, he believed, should have been in the squad after being left out at the final cut by England manager Alf Ramsey. Ron loved Budgie (his club nickname) for his skill and technique and you could understand Ron's strong feelings about Budgie's omission, but you have to remember Ramsey had Jimmy Greaves from Tottenham Hotspur, Liverpool's Roger Hunt, Manchester United's Bobby Charlton and West Ham's own Geoff Hurst – all forwards competing for places. It is the nature of tournament squads that someone like Budgie, for all his talent, might be sacrificed for players with more positional flexibility. During this era club squads weren't as big as they are now, and all the players trained together. So after the summer break and on the first day back in training, seasoned professionals and new apprentices straight out of school were pitched together for cross-country runs through Epping Forest and road running around Lippitts Hill, High Beech, Loughton. It was hard! We travelled there in a coach from the training ground at Chadwell Heath; first stop, Hainault Forest – no warm-up, simply turfed off the coach and instructed to start running. Follow everybody and after nearly a couple of miles, get back on the coach and on to the next stop – Grange Farm, Chigwell. Same routine: off the coach, run, follow and back on the coach. Final stop – High Beech, Loughton. And again: off the coach, run, but this time there were *hills*. Some of them very steep. Without doubt this was the hardest part and for me, a fifteen-year-old schoolboy to all intents and purposes, this was a very tough introduction to the life of professional football. After about three days of this I woke up in the morning and had to use my arms to lift my legs out of bed one by one because they were so stiff. In those days there was no warm-up and rehydration was a word unheard of by coaches. In fact, you weren't allowed a drink of water until the session was over. The influence of sports science was a still a lifetime away.

My first coach was Jim Barrett Jr. Jim's dad was 'big' Jim Barrett who played for West Ham in the 1930s and '40s. After a couple of months Jim moved up to take the 'A' team in the Metropolitan League (this was the third team, under the reserves) and John Lyall became the youth team coach. John had had to finish playing early due to a serious knee injury and worked for the club in the office and coached the schoolboys on Tuesday and Thursday evenings. So we all knew John from our schoolboy days. John was a much more understanding coach than Jim and very much in the mould of the first-team manager Ron Greenwood; both were very technical and tactical in their approach.

Their knowledge of the game, especially Ron's, had us youngsters in awe of him. Ron became John's mentor and they were inseparable, even on social occasions I witnessed where they both drank sherry! Beyond their mutual fondness for fortified wine, their football philosophy was identical: both encouraged skill and technique and rated individualism on the pitch. They rarely worked on the defensive side of the game, although John, when he eventually became manager, was inclined more than Ron to work on defensive principles. In summary, they both wanted a fast, forward-passing, one- and two-touch attacking style. They were like two peas in a pod and a great influence on my later coaching style.

John was always very approachable whereas Ron was more diffident, highly principled and headmaster-like. He was difficult to get to know beyond the professional. One example of him sticking to his core principles arose when, after agreeing with the Kilmarnock manager that he would sign their goalkeeper, Bobby Ferguson, he learnt he had the opportunity to sign the World Cup-winning Leicester goalkeeper Gordon Banks. But Ron had verbally agreed to sign Ferguson, although nothing had actually been committed to paper, so let the opportunity to sign the best goalkeeper in England go. That would not happen today. I got to know Ron better when I moved into coaching, but, in my time as a young player, Ron was the manager – and always maintained his distance.

A training ground incident involving Ron Greenwood has stuck in my mind. During a first-team practice match, Ron noticed, among the young players watching, a young player on the far side smoking. The player in question was goalkeeper Stevie Death and Ron told another young player to go around to tell him to put his cigarette out immediately, which he did, returning a few moments later to tell Mr Greenwood that Stevie Death had said of the manager, if he wants me to put my cigarette out, he can come and ask me him-self. This was typical of Stevie, who was always bucking authority and who had an unusually casual approach to life and his career. Unsurprisingly Ron was not best pleased and not long after Stevie was transferred to Reading – where, admittedly, he had a great career, making 471 appearances and holding the record at one time for keeping clean sheets. He had played only one game for West Ham. Stevie sadly passed away in 2003 aged 54.

During my first few weeks I had turned my ankle and badly sprained it, and the club physiotherapist was Bill Jenkins, whose reputation was formidable. I went in to see him and it gave him great pleasure to inflict even more pain on the injured area by pressing down hard on the bruised area. Yes, you're OK, you can go out and train. I could hardly walk, let alone train. Out I went and tried to join in but to no avail and was sent back in again. Bill this time was a little more gracious and strapped me up and told me to rest it for a couple of days. Maybe Bill was testing me to see if I was properly injured or if I fancied a couple of days off training.

A few days later when I arrived for training there was a very sombre mood about the place. We learnt from Ron Greenwood that Bill Jenkins had suffered a heart attack the previous day and had died. Everybody was devastated and training was cancelled for the day out of respect. A little while later his son Rob took over as his replacement and Rob stayed as physio for over 25 years and has become a good friend. One memory I have of Bill, whom I didn't really get chance to know, was during that first pre-season Bill would bring his dog in and at lunchtimes would play with the dog (a Bull Terrier I think) and would offer it a football which the dog would clamp his teeth on to and Bill would swing it round and round; the dog never let go once, such is the power of their jaw. A small but vivid one and nice memory of Bill.

Training was mainly with a ball, perfecting techniques and practising passing movements. Everything had to be one or two touch. Ron's instructions were always to get a picture in your head of where players were – *before* you got the ball; 'Get a picture! Get a picture!' became a familiar cry during training. It was designed to make you one step ahead of the opposition in knowing where you were going to pass the ball *before you got it at your feet*. Again, all emphasising the fact that the game is played in the head. 'Lively mind, lively body' was one of Ron Greenwood's favourite mantras.

Everything was with a ball. The one movement we practised over and over again was third man running, where, in groups of threes, starting in a triangle about ten metres apart, I would pass to one player who was at the apex of the triangle, who would pass it back to me, and as the ball was on its way back to me, player three, who started at the base of the triangle alongside me, would make a run beyond player one, and I had to find him with a forward pass – and it all had to be performed sharply with one touch. We practised this over and over. Later, when I started coaching I used this drill frequently and it became a West Ham trait – 'up, back and in behind'. The key, apart from developing good technical ability, was to get the player at the apex of the triangle with his back to the target area to stand on the half turn and play the return pass using his back foot – and as this return pass was required to be played with one touch, the initial forward pass needed to be firm but playable with one touch, but not too slowly! Many varieties of third-man movements were practised: players crossing over at the base, two players running forward, setting different distances and variations of final ball techniques – chipping or curling balls into the runner(s).

Many hours were spent by my youth teams practising these movements and it became a common theme on a weekly programme. Many years after leaving West Ham, Rio Ferdinand, who was now playing for Manchester United, and I bumped into each other at a game and the first thing he said to me was, 'Are you still doing third man running?' and started to laugh. I told him we were still doing it. Rio replied, 'It never left me and I still see it as important today.' That meant a lot to me. The other practice was crossing balls into the space at the near post. Long before we had plastic spiked poles to coach with, Ron had wooden poles concreted into large paint pots that were strategically located in wide areas representing defenders so the balls had to bend around them and into the space at the near post. We would repeat these types of drills almost daily.

Tuesdays and Bill Watson came in. Bill was a former Great Britain weightlifter who represented the country in the 1948 Olympic Games. Bill would have us do rope skipping, free weights with dumbbells and abdominal exercises. And it was the abdominal exercises that would really be testing. He created these wooden boards about 1.5m long by 45cm wide with a loop of rope nailed to the top end and we had to lie on the boards, loop our feet in the rope and, after they were inclined, perform various abdominal exercises: 'up for one' and you would perform one sit-up, with your hands behind your head; 'up for two', 'up for three' and so on until it was up for 20! It sounds excruciating now writing about it! We also performed Bill's speciality – leg raises. You lay flat on your back with hands behind your head and then, on command, raised both feet together about 15cm from the floor. Once again it was 'up for one' – lift your legs together and bring them down to 15cm above the floor and now you mustn't touch the floor again until Bill told you to. Rest and repeat – up to twenty repetitions. Bill delighted in prolonging the agony as the session went on, leaving your legs hanging in the air for ages before he would finally say, 'and down' to everyone's vast relief. Paul Heffer, who is still coaching at West Ham on a part-time basis, says it was Bill Watson's exercises that gave him back problems all of his career. I'm not sure he's wrong. Bill's torture sessions apart, training was mostly technically based, and the coaches were always quick to pick you up on poor control, a loose pass or lack of concentration. Everything we did was around technical excellence and creativity. I've taken these philosophies into my coaching and much of what I learnt can be traced back to my early days as a young player at West Ham.

Harry Redknapp was a professional player and offered to give me a lift in to training each day and he also gave a lift to Colin Mackleworth, a goalkeeper at the club who had been a pupil at my school, St Paul's Way. I was grateful and agreed. 'Okay,' said H. 'Meet me at Bow Church at 9am.' What I didn't realise was Harry's unique timekeeping. 9am meant 9.15, which made me late every day, so after a short while Ernie Gregory, the goalkeeping coach, stopped me going with Harry and I had to meet the club minibus, 9am at Upton Park.

As apprentices we had to do various menial jobs around the club – pick up kit, get it dried, get it ready for the next day's training and clean the professional players' boots. On Fridays, when everybody trained at Upton Park, we also had to clean all the dressing rooms and bathrooms, where we would have to cut up large bars of red

Lifebuoy soap into little blocks to use in the large communal bath, clean the players' entrance corridors and polish all the brass on the door handles and push plates. We also took turns washing the club minibus.

At the end of each season, before we could go on our summer break, we had to paint the walls of the corridors sky blue. As you might well imagine, a group of young apprentice footballers with access to paint pots and left largely unsupervised can only lead to skylarking. After liberally loading a brush and applying it to the wall, you would flick the still wet brush at your mate next to you, who would look at you and wonder, 'Did he mean to do that?' Of course it would only be a matter of minutes before he returned the favour and before long the whole corridor was in full paint-flicking battle mode with paint going everywhere but on the walls. I once ended up running onto the pitch with paint pot in hand, chasing the paint flicker to gain revenge! Needless to say, the groundsman, George Isaacs, was not best pleased with his newly sown pitch being covered in sky blue paint. At least it was the club colours!

It was all part of being an apprentice. After training there were always jobs to do and the best part was cleaning the senior players' boots because it developed a sense of pride; while cleaning Geoff Hurst's or Bobby Moore's boots you could imagine them playing in the biggest stadiums around the world for England and West Ham, and you had cleaned them. There was a certain discipline attached to these apprentice routines and duties and you could expect to be put in your place if you got a bit above yourself. You were constantly told you had not made it until you were in the first team and had played fifty games, especially by Jim Barrett Jr, whose favourite saying directed towards apprentices was 'Better to be a has-been than a never was.' Jim was a past master at putting you in your place. Today's apprentices, scholars, with few exceptions, don't have the same interaction with senior players and don't do the same 'jobs' that we used to. I believe it kept us grounded and certainly instilled a discipline that, for me, is sadly lacking, from what I witnessed, in many young players coming through the academy today. The apprentice system I have described lasted right up to the Ferdinand and Lampard years and when I speak to them now, they readily agree that today's scholars have it too easy and discipline is not what it was. They even go on to say how they look back with some affection at their time as apprentices and suggest it did them good in the long run.

During my first season as an apprentice professional, my brother Bernard went on a pre-wedding stag pub crawl around the East End with the groom and a few of his mates. They ended up in a pub on the Isle of Dogs – which now is a very desirable place to live with its riverside apartments, but most certainly wasn't in the sixties when it was a run-down area – and while having a drink an argument broke out which led to a fight. Not so unusual on a Friday night in an East End pub. However, the fight turned out to be with a couple of off-duty policemen. Everybody in my brother's group, including my brother, were rounded up, arrested and charged with affray – a particularly serious offence. My brother pleaded his innocence and swore he was not involved. He had been arrested after he had got home and was told to wear the same clothes he had worn during the evening, except he put on his sheepskin coat as well.

At the time we shared a bedroom and before I went to bed that night, I had moved his sheepskin coat from my bed and hung it up. The significance of this was that part of the police evidence against my brother was that he was identified by the police as seen fighting wearing the sheepskin coat. My mum and dad were beside themselves, worried that Bernard would go to prison if found guilty. The trial lasted five days in Court 4 at the Old Bailey and I was called to give evidence on behalf of my brother to say that it could not have been Bernard wearing the sheepskin coat because I had hung his up before I'd gone to bed while my brother was already out.

Simultaneously, there was another trial at the Old Bailey that was featuring widely in the media. This was the trial of Sri Lankan Emil Savundra whose career as a lifelong fraudster was publicly denounced during an angry television interview by David Frost during which Savundra remained entirely unrepentant and dismissive of his victims – many of whom made up the studio audience. The interview led to a police investigation and an eventual conviction that would see him given an eight-year sentence. We would see him and his family in the canteen during recess. Back in Court 4, I was hopeful that my evidence would create sufficient doubt – which was what transpired and Bernard was found not guilty, to the family's immense relief. Some of the others were found guilty and heavily fined. Being called to give evidence in a criminal trial is not an experience I would want to repeat.

During school holidays, clubs have triallists come and train with the various squads, and on one such occasion we had two fifteen-year-olds come down from Glasgow – Jim Mullen and Kenny Dalglish. I spoke to Jim when he came down to London to say his 'farewell' to the Boleyn Ground and he told me that the week they were down, Kenny had blagged a brand new pair of Puma King football boots for himself and Jim, telling the kit man, Albert Walker, that Ron Greenwood had given them permission to take them. So basically West Ham gave Kenny Dalglish his first proper pair of football boots. But the biggest achievement was getting any kit from Albert, who was notorious for hoarding it. As time went on, I soon learnt this is a characteristic of most kit men even today. Both Jim and Kenny made a good impression on the coaching staff and were offered contracts by Ron Greenwood. Mullen was quick and had a good eye for goal and like a lot of young Scottish players at the time was technically good. Dalglish was quite small at the time but showed great close control and could turn and beat players in one movement. Like Mullen, he was technically very good. Mullen was happy to sign and became an apprentice with the rest of us but Dalglish had his heart set on signing for Glasgow Celtic, which he duly did – and we all know what a great player he became with Celtic and eventually Liverpool.

I made lots of friends during my youth team days: Peter Grotier, with his wife Jackie, we still see today; Pat Holland, Clyde Best, Clive Charles, Steve Knowles, Stevie Death, Roger Cross, Frank Lampard Sr, Trevor Brooking, Joe Durrell, Johnny Ayris, John McDowell, Kevin Lock, Stevie Lay, Bobby Sutton, Micky Glumart and many more. One of the perks of being an apprentice was that on first-team match days a group of about three apprentices would have to clean the away team's dressing room and because they were always in a hurry to get away to catch their train or coach back home, it was one of the better jobs to have, but also a privilege to be among top players.

I remember in the 1966/67 season Manchester United came to Upton Park and had to win the game to win the league. United won 6-1 and they allowed us into the dressing room to clean up before the team had departed. There they all were – Best, Charlton,

Kidd, Stiles, Stepney, Busby drinking champagne and celebrating their achievement. It felt unreal and was a privilege to witness that great team at such close quarters in their moment of triumph. On another occasion West Ham were playing Liverpool during 1966 and the game had finished 1-1 and while we were waiting outside the Liverpool dressing room after the game, Bill Shankly came out and starting chatting to us, asking how we got on that morning in our own youth games and then proceeded to say what a great game we had all just witnessed. 'Two great attacking teams. Skill and flair all over the pitch. Great game, great game!' We youngsters were in awe of the great Shankly and again it was a privilege to have had that brief moment with the great man.

We had great times on club summer tours. The first time I ever flew was on my first youth tour to Augsburg, Germany and during my time we went to Italy, Switzerland and one memorable trip to Zambia and Malawi in 1969. That trip was organised by Tommy Taylor's dad who worked for a mining company in Zambia, who supplied West Ham with the invitation. West Ham tried to get Tommy, who was a Leyton Orient player at the time, to come along with us as a guest player for the tournament. Orient were okay about it but the FA refused – which was a big disappointment for Tommy's dad. Anyhow, sixteen players went, along with a staff of John Lyall, Bill Lansdowne Sr, Albert Walker and Wally St Pier. Looking back, it seems strange that the club failed to bring a physiotherapist with us on such a long trip.

It was such a long way in the late 1960s and we were put in lodgings with families who were mostly European expats. I remember the flight quite vividly: an evening flight to Rome, where we picked up more passengers and refuelled. Then overnight to Nairobi,

Kenya, where we disembarked and had breakfast. We were outside in some sort of garden area where there was this tall sign pointing in all directions with all the cities of the world and the mileage to them. I don't know why, but this fascinated me and I can still see it in my mind's eye as if it was yesterday. Back on the plane – I seem to recall it was a BOAC VC10 – and we arrived in Lusaka, Zambia mid-morning. As we were flying north to south and not east or west there was no jet lag and very little time difference from the UK. The players were all paired up and given to various families around Lusaka, and the staff were put in a hotel in the city. I first paired up with Joey Durrell, Budgie to us, and we were placed with a pilot from Zambia Airways; the problem was he was never there and Joey and I were looked after by their home help – a local Zambian family who cooked breakfast for us and did all our washing. As we moved from town to town around Zambia we swapped room partners and when we got to Livingstone we stayed at Hillcrest Residential School and I roomed up with Pat Holland. My abiding memory of this was one night when we were both in bed we awoke with a start. It was pitch black and we couldn't see a thing but felt that someone was in the room. We jumped out of bed and I shouted, 'I've got him!' Pat shouted something similar and when I turned on the lights, Pat and I were grappling with each other thinking we both had the 'intruder'.

The night skies in Zambia were amazing; with little or no light pollution there were stars everywhere, thousands and thousands, something that has remained fixed in my mind. I'll never forget the trip to see the Victoria Falls, the David Livingstone Museum in Livingstone and the Kariba Dam. On the way back from Kariba the minibus we were travelling in needed fuel so went off road onto unmade dirt roads surrounded by open bush, and we arrived at some faraway outpost to refuel. We all got out of the minibus to stretch our legs. Once refuelled, we all went back to get into the bus, but the driver, a local Zambian, was banging on the ground with a stick next to the minibus and telling us to stay away as there was a poisonous snake under the bus shielding from the sun! For a boy from a council estate in Bow this was something else; you don't get many snakes in Bow. Panic over, the snake slid away and we all got back safely.

On another trip we were all taken by minibuses to the Chobe Game Reserve. As with all these things, there is no guarantee which animals you will or will not see. Apparently, it was just after the rainy season and most of the animals had retreated to the bush. On a full day visit we saw a couple of antelopes and a herd of giraffes; we all expected to see lions, elephants and other big game but it was not to be. Other trips included a boat trip on the Zambezi and a trip to a copper mine in Kitwe. The reason we were in Zambia was to play against local representative sides from Livingstone – Kabwe, Lusaka, Kitwe, Luanshya and Ndola, apparently all along the Zambian Copperbelt. The tour was sponsored by the cigarette company Peter Stuyvesant. We won all of our games bar one and won the Peter Stuyvesant Trophy. Nowadays cigarette sponsorship is frowned upon, but this was Africa in 1969.

Three days after getting home, we were all scheduled to participate in further tournaments in Switzerland and Italy. The Swiss tournament was in Geneva and would be held over three days. We then flew to Milan to play in a town called Casale Monferrato which is in the Piedmont region, roughly halfway between Milan and Turin. I shared a room with Peter Grotier and John McDowell and we were on the top floor of a five- or six-floor building. Next to our room was a door to the roof where all the players came up to sunbathe.

This was Italy in the middle of May and hot. Peter Grotier reminds me of the night I got up in the middle of the night and went over to his bed and shook him and said, 'Where's the queue for the soap and flannel?' I kept saying it which frightened the life out of Pete as I was obviously sleepwalking. I don't know where this came from, maybe all the travelling we had been doing, but Pete just replied, 'Over there,' and I walked away and went back to bed.

The tournament was to be played over a week and we were up against the Italian giants Inter Milan, Juventus, Torino and Fiorentina; obviously a very high standard. I recall the opening ceremony during which each team carried a huge flag and paraded around the narrow streets carrying it by the corners and sides as the local people threw flowers, coins and small mementoes into the flag. We managed to win the tournament and I played a small part, but I do remember playing against Inter Milan and being really impressed with their blue and black striped shirts; they certainly looked the part. I seem to recall we won the game 2-1. It was a very successful trip and after being away for three weeks in Zambia and Malawi we were all very tired. We flew back to Heathrow but the coach didn't turn up to take us back to Upton Park. We all sat on our cases outside the terminal waiting for another coach to be booked – apparently Mrs Moss, the manager's secretary, had forgotten to book it – so the club asked British Airways to supply a coach to take us all home. Two hours later than scheduled we arrived back at Upton Park and when we arrived Ron Greenwood was on the fore-court waiting to greet the team. It was at this time Ron mentioned to me that he had had news from the FA on who had passed their FA Preliminary Coaching Badge and he informed me I had passed, much to my delight.

My very first FA Youth Cup match was West Ham Youth against Spurs at Upton Park under the floodlights. We won 2-1. I didn't score but at the time this was a massive occasion for me, supporting the club as a boy and here I was as a sixteen-year-old playing at Upton Park under the lights and beating Spurs. What could be better? Also in the team that night were Frank Lampard Sr, Roger Cross, Trevor Brooking and Stevie Death. They were all a couple of years older than me and were all to go on and play for West Ham's first team. Sadly, I wouldn't.

The weekly routine was training at Chadwell Heath Monday to Thursday and training at Upton Park every Friday. The apprentices' jobs were mostly putting out and collecting the training kit every day. Every player had a squad number and mine was number 28. The difference back then was the same kit was used every day for a week. We used to dry it in big ovens every day back at Upton Park, and go off to lunch around the corner to Cassettari's café in the Barking Road while the kit was drying. Having lunch in Cassi's was an experience: the club would give us a lunch voucher worth two shillings and sixpence and Phil Cassettari, the owner, would serve us. All his family worked there – mum, brother, sister, wife, a real family affair and typically Italian. Well, Phil was the worst mathematician ever. He would say, 'What did you have today?' Egg, chips, beans, cup of tea and a Coke was the most popular choice and while stroking his chin he would tot up what was owed. 'Egg, um, chips, um, um, tea, beans, Coke, um, three shillings.' Never under the voucher value, always over! Another gem he always used to use was when we were ordering our food. I would say to him I'll have the same as him, pointing to someone who had just ordered. Phil would reply, 'You can't have the same as him, but you can have similar.' We used to get our own back though. Phil used to store the Coke bottles upstairs and when we went up for lunch, we would help ourselves. After lunch we would go back to the stadium to roll the kit up for the following day's training.

By about Wednesday, the kit stank, but it was the same for everybody, World Cup winner or otherwise. Responsibility for doing the jobs and allocating who did what was given to me by Ernie Gregory who made me head apprentice. I had to show Ernie the list of who was doing what on any particular day so he could check the jobs. Ernie was a heavy smoker, as were Ron Boyce and John Lyall, and when we went back to Upton Park in the afternoons, he would often send me or another apprentice over to the local shops saying, 'Go and get me twenty Bachelors and you're on the clock,' pointing to his wristwatch. It became a standing joke amongst the apprentices about who would get the orders from Ernie.

After training one Friday, as I was walking out of Upton Park on my way to the station, a car pulled up and a voice asked where I was going. It was Bobby Moore asking if I wanted a lift. I told him I was going to Bow Church and he told me to jump in as he was going that way. He was on his way to one of the London stations to meet the team for an away game. We spoke a lot of small talk, and I can't remember much of what was said, but he was a player I was still in awe of. We pulled up at Bow Church and I was desperately hoping that someone I knew would see me getting out of Bobby Moore's car. Another time, after I had left West Ham and was playing for Barnet, I was out for a Sunday drive with my girlfriend, later my wife, Brenda, when we pulled up at a set of lights in Wanstead. A Jaguar pulled up alongside us, and it was Bobby. He pressed his button to open his electric window and I was trying to unwind mine by hand (it was a Vauxhall Viva). He asked how I was doing and where I was playing now, then the lights changed and he wished me all the best and sped off as I was still trying to locate first gear. That was Bobby – a gentleman through and through who had time for everybody.

When Bobby played for England at Wembley on a Wednesday night he would often come into the dressing room at Upton Park the next day where I would be doing the kit and ask for Mrs Gregg, the lady who washed all the match kit, and would ask her to wash his England kit from the night before while he went for a run around the pitch. About an hour later Mrs Gregg would hang Bobby's England kit on a dressing room peg. I can still see it now – a white shirt with a red number six, dark blue shorts and white socks all immaculately washed and ironed. Bobby, washed and dressed after his run, would pick up the kit and shout down the corridor, 'Thank you, Mrs Gregg,' and off he would go.

I trained with Bobby on a regular basis, as did all the youth team players, but never played in a match with him, except once many years later. Frank Lampard Sr rang me and asked if I would play in a charity match at Billericay Town. I agreed and turned up on the day and, to my amazement, Bobby Moore was sitting in the dressing room. Also playing were Martin Peters, Ron Boyce, Pat Holland, Kevin Lock, Mick McGiven, Trevor Brooking, Harry Cripps, Trevor Lake, Frank Lampard Sr himself and me. And Bobby Moore – my claim to fame! I have a photo of us all in the dressing room at half-time at home and it is one of my most cherished possessions.

A note appeared on the noticeboard in the dressing room stating that the European Cup final would be played at Wembley in 1968, and if anybody wanted to order tickets, to do so now. The competition was still at the semi-final stage, so the finalists were unknown. A friend of mine from the council estate, Timmy Mooney, was a big Manchester United fan and as United were still in the competition he suggested I order four tickets in the hope United would get to the final. I did that, thinking whoever got to the final, it would still be a match worth going to see. At this time, we were not exposed to a lot of foreign football teams and the chance to watch an overseas team play on our own doorstep at Wembley Stadium was too good an opportunity to turn down. When I ordered the tickets, there were four teams left in the competition – Manchester United, Real Madrid, Juventus and Benfica. So, whoever made it to the final, it was something to look forward to. Manchester United made it to the final and they would face Portugal's Benfica. Me, my brother Bernard, Richie, whose nickname was Happy, and Timmy all dressed up in red Slazenger sweaters – they were the fashion at the time – and took the London Underground to Wembley. It was to our considerable disappointment that while we were all decked out in red, United wore a dark blue kit. Still, it was a great night. All United's legends were playing: George Best, Bobby Charlton, Paddy Crerand, Nobby Stiles, Bill Foulkes and a young Brian Kidd – I believe it was Brian Kidd's nineteenth birthday on the day of the match. Sadly, Denis Law was out injured. Eusebio was the Portugal team's star man but a save from United's goalkeeper Alex Stepney in the last few minutes of normal time, when Eusebio went clean through the United defence and was one v one with Stepney, took the match into extra time. United eventually won 4-1.

I thought he should have scored and won the game for Benfica, but on such incidents games turn. Maybe if he had kept his shot low he may have scored; instead his powerful shot went straight at Stepney and at a good height. Stepney made the save. United became the first English club to win the European Cup. A few years later my brother-in-law, Con, married a Portuguese girl, Sonia, and it transpired that Eusebio was her uncle. I've yet to tell her he should have won the European Cup for Benfica all those years ago.

# 5

# A PROFESSIONAL CONTRACT

So my apprenticeship finished and the club offered me a professional contract for one year on £14 per week. Pat Holland and I
signed our professional forms on the same day, 5 September 1969.
Deep down I knew that breaking into the first team was unlikely to
happen. I'd never recaptured the goalscoring form I'd shown as a
schoolboy for East London. My playing career with West Ham and
Barnet was uneventful – I scored goals but could never manage to
make the big leap into first-team football at West Ham. Maybe I just
had to accept I didn't have what it took to make a career playing
top-tier professional football.

But for anyone who has been involved with a football club,
there are so many memories – good, bad and funny. One such
incident happened at the Chadwell Heath training ground on
a Saturday afternoon while I was playing for the A team in the
Metropolitan League. It was towards the end of the game and John
McDowell got a nasty kick to the head and had to be led off the
pitch as he was becoming delirious. He kept saying, 'What's the
score? Are we winning? Where am I? I can't remember a thing.' At
this point he turned around and started to walk to the goal and
said, 'Oh, I've left my shin pads behind the goal.' Cruel as it now

seems in the era of concussion checks, we have had many a laugh over that one.

It was around this time that I started to get into coaching, Ron Greenwood encouraged all professional players to go into local schools and help coach the kids as he felt it would give us a better understanding of the game and so indirectly help us as players. Lots of the players took up this offer and Peter Grotier and I went into the then Stratford Grammar School, now Stratford School Academy, a couple of afternoons a week. We used to go from the school, which is located in Forest Gate, to Wanstead Flats to assist the head of PE, John Roberts, earning £2 a session. It got me into coaching and I quickly discovered it was something I really enjoyed. At the end of the season my professional contract expired and was not renewed. It did not come as a big surprise.

During my time at the club, the biggest thing that I can say I took from it was that it got me into coaching and led to me passing my FA Preliminary Coaching Award (now the UEFA B Licence). We did the coaching course on the players' day off during the week and the final assessment was held towards the end of the season at Chadwell Heath. Everybody was given a topic to coach and mine was playing off the front men. We were given 24 hours to prepare. I felt comfortable with this topic as I had been coached the previous three seasons on attacking play by Ron and John Lyall. Dario Gradi, who was a former teacher and amateur footballer – and who had become a London regional coach for the FA and later became a coach at Chelsea and Derby County before spending over 30 years at Crewe Alexandra – was chosen by the FA to examine the sessions and many years later during a coaching seminar at St George's Park, I reminded Dario of this and where my coaching career began. He was chuffed that I remembered and said bringing back those memories made his day.

I was called into Ron Greenwood's office and he told me that the club would give me a free transfer. I wasn't shocked but obviously disappointed. He pointed out that I had never given them a day's problem and he would try to help me get fixed up. We shook hands and I left. I spoke to John Lyall who knew I was enjoying coaching in the schools and who had put me through my FA Preliminary Coaching Badge, and he asked if I wanted to go to Lilleshall to take my FA Full Badge (now the UEFA A Licence). I said yes and he told me it would cost £50 – and a month's salary. John got me enrolled on the course at very short notice. When I told my dad about being let go – Mum was never really interested – he was his quite philosophical self. 'Well,' he said, 'you are going to have to find something else to do. What about coaching?' I told him about what John had done and Dad said he would pay for it. So I have to thank Dad for helping to set me on my way for a career in coaching.

After leaving West Ham I had a few offers from abroad and football league teams in the north. I decided to take an offer from Barnet FC in the Southern League, now the National League, whose manager was Tommy Coleman. As this would be part-time, I now had to get a job. Ron Greenwood knew a PE teacher in North London at Holloway School for boys, Alan Wright, and he gave me his number. I rang him and we met at the school where Alan got me involved in their PE department five afternoons a week and also helped me fill the mornings with another school up the road near Finsbury Park, Woodberry Down. The head of PE at Woodberry Down was Dave Thomas and the school was in complete contrast to Holloway. Woodberry Down had a big rugby ethos whereas Holloway was football mad.

Alan Wright was a larger-than-life character who knew everybody in football. During school holidays Alan Wright would put on coaching courses for the local kids at Market Road sports stadium in Islington. I would help staff them. We had Don Revie, the then England manager, come down with his assistant Les Cocker for the day; and on another occasion Alan had got the great Denis Law to come down and coach for a couple of days. As a young coach myself it was fantastic to be in such great company. How Alan managed this was a mystery to us all, but as I said earlier, he knew everybody. The head of the whole PE department, a really nice guy named Clive Grinyer, was really into sailing; the sixth form could choose from a variety of PE activities and Clive made sure sailing was on the agenda, which appealed to quite a few, and they used the local reservoir as their base, which made Clive happy as he really wasn't into football.

Despite this, a number of the pupils during my time there went into professional football: Steve Walford and Chris Ramsey were two. I met up with them both during their football careers, with 'Wally' having a good career at Tottenham Hotspur, Arsenal, where he won the FA Cup in 1979, Norwich and West Ham, where we met up again. John Lyall had been on the lookout for a left back at the time and found out that Walford was available for transfer from Norwich City. Wally has for many years been the assistant manager to Martin O'Neill at the various clubs and countries O'Neill has managed. Chris Ramsey began his career at Bristol City before moving to Brighton and Hove Albion, Swindon Town and Southend United. He started coaching in Malta for the Naxxar Lions as player-coach before taking up a position with the English FA. He also coached at Tottenham Hotspur and is now technical director and head of coaching at Queens Park Rangers. He has recently been awarded the MBE for tackling racism in football. I come across Chris often in my new role at the Premier League and we always speak fondly of our time at Holloway School.

Most of the kids were either Arsenal or Tottenham fans so I didn't make a thing about being a West Ham man. Holloway had always had football players coming in to coach, goalkeeper Bob Wilson being one. During my time, Peter Shreeves, Terry Burton, Terry Murphy and the Morgan twins, Roger and Ian, worked in the PE department. The two Terrys also had coaching jobs at Arsenal. It was now September 1970 and my new club and career were about to begin.

Going to Barnet was a big mistake. They had just sold their centre forward, Billy Meadows, to Hereford and I was brought in to replace him. We couldn't have been more different: he was bigger and stronger than me with lots of non-league experience. I was smaller, relied on a bit of pace and was taught to play a more technical game – it was the wrong fit. No one's fault; we'd both made the wrong choice.

Barnet were good to me though, allowing me time off to attend an FA Full Coaching Licence course. I had attended the same course at Lilleshall Hall National Sports Centre the previous summer. I had travelled up with Bobby Howe, a West Ham first-team player, who was helping to staff the course. I wasn't ready for the intensity of the course and failed it, so getting a second go the following summer was great. I felt I had learnt a lot originally on the course followed by a year coaching every day in the schools, so was much better prepared. This time I passed. The examining member of staff for the FA was Charles Hughes, who had a reputation of being hard to please. Aged just twenty, I was a fully qualified FA coach with very little experience!

I can remember the topic I was asked to coach: 'The covering and defensive responsibilities of full backs'. I had learnt my lesson from the previous year's course when I had to coach 'wing play' and set the practice up, choosing Harry Burrows as the winger to coach. Well, Harry was a great winger, playing for Stoke City, and was so good at everything I asked him to do, I had nothing to coach, which didn't go down too well! This time I asked a centre forward who was on the course to play one of the full backs. I knew he would be uncomfortable in the position and would make errors which in turn would give me lots of mistakes to correct and coach. The session went well and I was really pleased with the way it played out. Almost on the first attack – the set-up was attack vs defence – the ball went wide to the winger and as the full back came in to close the winger down, the winger played the ball inside and ran forward down the line. The full back immediately turned inside and followed the ball as the winger ran past him. 'Stop!' I commanded, and brought the play back to the point where the winger had passed the ball inside and then asked the full back what he should do in this situation. Not being a full back he was a little unsure and I pointed out that in this situation, where your responsibility is to mark the winger, when he plays the ball inside and runs forward your responsibility is to track the run of the winger and not follow the ball. So here is a valuable lesson when you are on a course: don't put the best player in the positions you are going to coach!

After leaving Barnet after one season and not having played particularly well, I knew finding another club wasn't going to be easy. I ended up playing for a friend, Terry Murphy, just to keep fit. Terry was coaching with me at Holloway School and was working part-time for Arsenal, coaching their schoolboys. As fate would have it, playing one Saturday afternoon for Terry's team, I was heavily tackled and broke my right tibia. It put paid to me playing for a while, but little did I know at the time, it would end any ambitions of a professional playing career once and for all. It wasn't the break itself that was the problem, but for some reason the bone would not knit, and I kept having to be put back in plaster. Sometimes fate plays a hidden but significant part in one's life. Looking back now, I can see that breaking my leg sent me in a completely different direction – coaching rather than playing football.

Luckily, I still had employment with the Inner London Education Authority (ILEA) at my two schools, so I started to forge a career as a sports teacher. My football qualifications were sufficient to coach in the autumn and spring terms, September through March. To continue being employed over the summer term I needed to get qualified in a summer sport. I enrolled on an MCC elementary cricket coaching qualification and an LTA elementary tennis qualification just to spread my bets. Fortunately, I passed them both, the LTA award after a retake, so this gave me the qualifications needed to be employed for the full school year. I was so enthusiastic about coaching that over the next couple of years I passed coaching qualifications in volleyball, men's hockey and, most difficult of all, the Bronze Medallion in lifesaving (swimming).

It was now 1973 and the year when Brenda and I got married. I had met Brenda in a pub in Leytonstone called the Plough and Harrow when I was out with a friend of mine, Tommy Ziepe, and I needed a date for the following weekend to come with me to Peter Grotier's engagement party. He was getting engaged to Jackie, whom he had met on a holiday a couple of years earlier. A few of us West Ham players were also there when they had met at Pontins Osmington Bay Holiday Camp in Dorset. Brenda and I spent that evening together in the pub and she agreed to come with me to Pete and Jackie's party. I was eighteen and we have been together ever since. We were married in West Ham Church; Brenda had lived in Plaistow and the church was just around the corner. We held the reception in a hall opposite Northleigh House where I had lived in Bow. After the reception, we didn't go on honeymoon – we couldn't afford it! – but we went to a steak house in Upton Park called 'Dallas Steak House' that was often frequented by West Ham players. When we arrived with Peter Grotier and his wife Jackie, we sat with Clive Charles and John McDowell, both West Ham first-team players at the time. During the meal a bottle of red wine was knocked over John's suit and he was frantically trying to clean up while angrily bemoaning that he hadn't paid for the suit yet! Of course all we could do was crease up. After the meal Brenda and I went back to the flat we had rented in Forest Gate. It was back to work on the Monday! Brenda reminds me that she also had the wedding cake on her lap as we drove back home!

After recovering from my broken leg and thinking about playing again, I got a phone call completely out of the blue from John Lyall, who was now the assistant manager to Ron Greenwood at West Ham. He asked me if I was interested in coming back to West Ham as a part-time schoolboy coach; there was a vacancy because the existing coach had resigned. The coach in question was John Dick, former West Ham first-team player and Scottish international, who, by coincidence, I knew from my daily visits to Fairlop Sports Centre with Woodberry Down School. John was the resident coach at Fairlop, assisting all the visiting schools. A further coincidence was that I used to go with my school, St Paul's Way, for our sports lessons at Fairlop Sports Centre. John Lyall said he had heard I was recovering from a broken leg and indicated that if I was not ready yet to give up playing then at least the coaching would keep me fit until I found a club. I'm sure it was John Dick who had mentioned to John Lyall that I was looking to get on in coaching and that I was suitable for the role he was now offering me. Lyall asked me to come for an interview with the manager Ron Greenwood, which was quite informal, and he offered me £10 per week and told me to coach the way I had been coached when I was there as a player. That was it! The salary was never an issue as I was just pleased to be given the opportunity to coach at a top level. This was the summer of 1973 and was the start of something I could have only dreamed of! I was now coaching at Holloway and Woodberry Down schools during the day and coaching at West Ham on Tuesday and Thursday evenings, plus running junior teams on Saturday and Sunday mornings. I was used to coaching in the evenings as for a couple of years I had been coaching in evening institutes in South London – one was in Brixton and the other in Clapham. They were tough neighbourhoods and the kids certainly kept you on your toes, very demanding but good kids. They just wanted to play football.

Looking back now, these sorts of areas in South London were a hotbed of football talent and reminded me that this is where Rio and Anton Ferdinand were brought up, in Peckham. I spoke to Rio and asked him about his football development and growing up in Peckham.

**TONY:** When was the first time you remember playing football?

**RIO:** Probably when I was five or six years old. I remember I had the 1982 England kit, the red one, complete with headband! My uncle had a team called Bloomfield's who played in Kennington Park, South London and he asked me to come and play for them. I was about eleven then, quite old I suppose. I had played with mates on the estate in Peckham before that, but that was the first organised team. My cousin also played for them. We would train on Saturday and play on a Sunday. I also played for my school team and in the playground and over the adventure playground but before I joined Bloomfield's I hadn't known where to go and play for a team. My mum wasn't pushing me into football so it wasn't until my uncle, who knew I was fast, said, 'Why don't you come and play for my team?' For my first year in organised football, I played as a centre back before I went into midfield.

**TONY:** When did you first realise, *I'm not bad at this; in fact I'm better than some of these?*

**RIO:** I knew I was quite good when I played on my estate because I was the youngest and the others were a few years older than me. When I went into my school playground, I was one of the best, if not the best. The Met Police used to organise a five-a-side tournament for the whole of London, and I used to think, I'm the best player here! And that was the first time I thought *I want to be a footballer*. The first time, though, that I thought I could be a footballer and make a living was for West Ham Youth against Chelsea Youth in the South East Counties League Cup final at Stamford Bridge. I was still at school and a lot of the youth team had been chosen to go to Australia with the first team on a club centenary tour. I remember Frank Lampard also played in the game. I scored a goal and then another one in the penalty shoot-out. I left that game thinking, for the first time: *I feel comfortable at this level.*

TONY: I thought the same. I looked at you as an individual and thought, *This kid can really play.* You played midfield that night. This was the first time the youth team had won something for many years. What was the first professional club you went to?

RIO: QPR (Queens Park Rangers). I was playing for Bloomfield's around eleven or twelve and a scout named Sandy pulled me out of the game, along with two or three others, and took us along to QPR. I trained there Tuesday and Thursday evenings and played the odd game. Then I was scouted by Middlesbrough. I also trained at Charlton, Chelsea, Norwich and West Ham. I never looked back after that.

TONY: I bumped into Dave Goodwin not long ago and he told me the story about meeting you for the first time. He had been sent by Middlesbrough to QPR to scout on Nigel Quashie in a game and thought you were him. He said, 'Hello Nigel,' and you replied, 'My name's Rio!'

RIO: I don't remember that, but he was the first coach who took an interest in me. He used to take me to matches and make me watch teams. He used to ask me to write down formations, what they do at set pieces, write down where they are in the box. He made me feel a million dollars. He would say, 'You're like Pelé.' Rio/Pelé, it goes!

**TONY:** So you chose West Ham. I think Frank Lampard Sr played a massive part in that?

**RIO:** Yes, he would come and watch me. He would say, 'Come down to West Ham,' and I went there for a trial one time. It was quite a way from South London – it took me two and a half hours to get there. I got there late and turned up in a QPR kit, which didn't go down too well. Paul Heffer, I think, took the session. A few of the lads looked at me and you could see them thinking, *Who's this?* I was embarrassed because I was late and I thought to myself, *I don't really like it here.* I trained a couple of times and thought, *I don't want to go back*, but Frank said, 'You've got to come back.' A period of time passed where I had to make a decision to sign schoolboy forms somewhere and I was sitting there thinking I'll maybe sign for Norwich or Middlesbrough, because they gave me loads of boots, or perhaps Millwall because it's just around the corner and I can stay at home. But Frank, Jimmy Hampson and Jimmy Neighbour were talking about giving the kids a chance, bringing back the days when the academy was so good. They made that a big sell and that was the only reason why I signed for West Ham, no other. They sold me a dream. They already had Lee Hodges, one of the best young players around at the time, and Manny Omoyinmi. So I thought, *If they've already got those two and they are really going to push others, then it's a good reason to go there.*

**TONY:** I got to know you better when you were a bit older.

**RIO:** Yes, it was intimidating when you came to watch. I thought, *Shit, Tony Carr's coming over; I've got to play well.*

**TONY:** When anyone asks me, who is the best player I have ever worked with, I never ever say one player but I always used to reply by saying, 'While Frank Lampard had to work really hard to get to that top level, a lot of Rio's talent was natural.'

**RIO:** Yes, I think I was born with athleticism, but I always had a ball. When I came out of my house, I asked, 'Who's got the ball?' We used to knock for a Turkish kid early because he had a ball! Me and my mate Gavin used to go everywhere with a ball. He manages Dulwich Hamlet now. He used to say, 'Rio, let's do these drills.' I was always working with the ball on my touch. Even at West Ham, Frank and I used to stay out there for ages, knocking balls to each other. My touch used to become second nature and I could bring a ball down better than some number nines probably because I had worked for all those hours.

**TONY:** You didn't start playing in a team until you were eleven but academies have developed since you started. Do you think now that young kids are sometimes over-coached and that natural instinct is frowned upon?

**RIO:** My boys are in the system now and you see a lot of robots. They're all programmed to play a particular way. I saw a kid at QPR recently who was brilliant because he was doing stuff differently; you don't see that often now. When I was young you saw players taking people on all day long. You had to tell them to stop doing it sometimes. Now the coaches are asking, 'Please take someone on.' The difference is that, when I was a kid, you got to fourteen and you still had a chance of making it, while now if you miss the boat at seven, eight or nine and you try to come in at fourteen, the gap is so much bigger now because they are so far ahead. It's almost impossible now to get in at fourteen unless you are a ridiculous talent. They can be over-coached, and I've made a conscious decision with my boy, who is eleven, not to go into the system yet. One reason is because of his personality – I think he would get a bit big-time – and secondly, I want him to keep that rough edge. If you're too polished, you almost have to be perfect to make it.

TONY: I feel some of that. I watch youth games now and everyone is the same. I feel something isn't quite right, but I can't put my finger on it because I'm not in the system any more. You developed your own game until you were thirteen or fourteen and then got indoctrinated into a football club.

RIO: When I was growing up my mum threw me out after breakfast and told me not to come back until 5.30. I was on a council estate socialising and playing football with and against people of different ages. If you play against the same age group all the time you don't have that variation, and you don't have to work things out.

TONY: When you first came into the youth team programme (under-18s), we would play Tottenham, Chelsea and Arsenal but also Gillingham, Cambridge and Millwall, sometimes on poor pitches.

RIO: We were thrown in and around the men, so you had to sink or swim. You had to clean their boots for an example and that was such a big thing because you got grounded straight away. I used to go into the dressing room, a South London kid, a bit chirpy, and the senior pro would say, 'Where are my boots?' Also, 'Where is my kit?' I used to reply, 'I'm not supposed to get your kit,' and he would say, 'You're my boot boy so go and get my kit for me.' There was a hierarchy. Now the top boy in the youth team thinks he owns the place because there is no one looking down on him, keeping him in check.

TONY: And he drives a Range Rover!

RIO: Exactly, it's mental.

TONY: When you were injured, and I remember you had some trouble with your back when you were growing, did you still watch the game?

RIO: Yes, because I was obsessed with football. I want to see that in my kids because if you want to get to the top level, you have to be obsessed. I was obsessed with all football; I could tell you the women players' names when it was on Channel 4.

TONY: What your first-team debut for West Ham?

RIO: Sheffield Wednesday at home. I came on for ten minutes on the final day of the season. The following season I did the pre-season and then had possibly two of the worst games of my entire career, both against Luton, home and away for the reserves.

TONY: What did that tell you?

RIO: I wasn't sure if I was going to make it. I was questioning myself. The Luton home game was at Chadwell Heath and although I was terrible, Mel Machin – manager of Bournemouth at the time – asked to take me on loan at Bournemouth. Then we played Luton at Kenilworth Road and I was shit again. Harry called me afterwards and said they still want to take me on loan. I remember it was my eighteenth birthday and I said no because I had a birthday party planned. Harry said, 'You've got to go. It will be good for your career.' I went and that new environment really made me kick on.

**TONY:** I remember when you came back from Bournemouth, I spoke to Mel and he said, 'Rio is a good player; he can play either side.'

**RIO:** He used to call me class. He said, 'I'm not going to call you Rio any more. Lads, call him class.' That was so good for me and Dave Goodwin had done the same thing. You need the blend though. You were harder to please. The lads used to say, 'We don't know if he approves or not.' I needed that, though, in case I got too big for my boots.

**TONY:** I remember Mel Machin also saying, 'The one thing he has to work on is his heading.'

**RIO:** That's where Frank Burrows came in. He would stand out there in any weather and get Jerome John – the youth team goalkeeper – to kick 20 to 50 balls and say, 'Jump through me.' I became a decent header of the ball after that.

**TONY:** You're in the first team at West Ham. Then you go to Leeds and on to Manchester United. When you cross the white line, do you hear the crowd? Do you appreciate the passion of the fans?

**RIO:** Not when you're playing, really. For the first part of my career, I used to think, *Who is in the stadium today? Who did I give my tickets to? I'm going to impress this or that person today.* I'd play for the crowd a little bit. Then, in the 2002 World Cup in Japan, I played in the game against Brazil and when we went out and they played the national anthems, I stood there in line and I could hear my mum screaming and shouting. I started to get all emotional and I was welling up. The game started and it was a light-bulb moment because the game passed me by. That was the moment when I thought I would never ever let the emotion get to me again. After that, I could count on one hand when I heard the crowd.

**TONY:** When you came to West Ham as a youth team player, you were a central midfield player. My memory tells me I went on a youth programme to Lilleshall for a couple of days and I watched Andy Roxburgh, who was the UEFA technical director. He said the Germans had devised three at the back, wing backs pushed higher up the pitch but with their best midfield player at the centre of the three to break into midfield when the situation was right and start attacks that way. I remember the conversation with you, and you weren't sure. You weren't keen at first but when I said you could break into midfield to create overload, you said you would give it a go.

**RIO:** I was reluctant at first. I thought at first that someone hadn't turned up and that's why you were going to play me at the back. I remember thinking, *I'm not going to score goals from there.* I played there and straight away I felt a new-found respect for me from the coaching staff. I fed off that.

**TONY:** I can remember going to Harry (Redknapp) and asking him if I could change the formation because everybody was playing 4-4-2. He said, 'No problem,' and I know we felt you had the biggest influence from the back and often, you would end up beyond the midfield.

**RIO:** I think my first five games for the first team were in midfield, playing off the front men.

[**Tony aside:** This showed the talent and versatility of Rio.]

**TONY:** What has been your greatest moment on the pitch?

**RIO:** Winning the Champions League for Manchester United against Chelsea because it's the place you never really believe you will reach. I had got to the semis with Leeds and the quarters with United, but I felt it was going to be impossible. Then you get there and you do it! You can go anywhere in the world and there will be people who have won leagues but not many have won the Champions League. It's the hardest to win.

**TONY:** What was your worst moment?

**RIO:** There are too many! I could talk about cup finals but not one game stands out as worse than the rest.

**TONY:** Were you ever captain at West Ham?

**RIO:** No, but I was captain at Leeds two months after signing and then at United at various times. I took it in my stride. David O'Leary gave me the captaincy at Leeds and he said, 'Don't change anything, be the same, that's why you are captain.' That was the best bit of advice, just carry on as you are, and you will develop as captain. When I was captain at United or England, I wasn't any different. If someone needed telling in the changing room, I would tell them. I was vocal and that developed because, although I was brash off the pitch, I was quiet on it because I didn't understand the game enough. It was probably the season before the 2002 World Cup when it came together mentally for me. I was screaming at Nicky Butt in front of me, screaming at Danny Mills, Sol Campbell. Left, right, up, back. To protect the team. After that I felt I could say something I believed in. Before that, I didn't know completely what I was talking about.

**TONY:** What players have influenced you?

**RIO:** I never wanted to replicate anyone, but I loved Paul Ince, Gazza, John Barnes; but I never looked at any player and thought I want to be like him – apart from Frank Rijkaard maybe. Roy Keane, when I went to United, was the first player about whom I said, 'Wow!' He has that high standard every day. He might not play particularly well every day but he demanded high standards from everyone every day. At West Ham, I found a lot of the players wanted to be mates with everyone, apart from Julian Dicks who didn't want to be mates with anyone. It was the same at Leeds – a young squad, all mates. At United the mentality all week was geared to playing on Saturday, to win. If your standards are shit on Thursday or Friday, you can't expect to play at a high level on the Saturday. That was United but at West Ham there were always loads of people messing about and having a laugh. It was almost a place that was showing you how not to be. You had to be a strong character and try not to get carried away. Players like Bertie Brayley, who had his foot on the first step of the ladder to maybe getting there but his mentality wasn't strong enough.

**TONY:** Michael Carrick said the training at United on a Friday was sometimes harder than the game on the Saturday.

**RIO:** The speed and intensity of the training was unbelievable. Walter Smith came and trained with us for about eight months. I was banned at the time, but I trained every day. I remember him saying, 'I can't believe this training. Everyone's smashing each other, screaming and shouting.' It was just the way it was, and the manager liked it. That was the culture of the club. The manager never came into the changing room. He had people in there: me, Roy Keane, Gary Neville, Ryan Giggs, Vidić – we would control that dressing room in terms of timekeeping, application, etc.

**TONY:** Is the Premier League the greatest league in the world?

**RIO:** I think it is. It's the most entertaining, definitely. You could argue that the Spanish League is technically superior, and I would probably think it is, but as a spectacle, the Premier League stands out, and the standard is going up.

**TONY:** You've already talked about the culture of clubs, where one is all about winning and another is about perhaps finishing halfway down and how that's okay.

**RIO:** It's about the individual as well. It would be interesting to hear what you thought about me. I thought of myself as someone who trained hard.

**TONY:** I was talking to Frank Lampard Jr and you were good mates, weren't you? He said that he felt you and he had something in common. I said that what I thought about the pair of you was that you were impatient; you weren't content to be in the youth team, you wanted to be in the reserves and then when you were there you were almost touching the first team – you wanted constantly to be challenged. I remember the last game you played for West Ham's youth team. It was at Chadwell Heath against Norwich and I said to you, 'That's the last time you'll be playing for the youth team.' You'd got sloppy. It wasn't a challenge to you any more. It's wasn't right for you any more.

**RIO:** Now you've said that, I remember. I thought I'd let you down.

**TONY:** What distinguishes good players from great ones?

**RIO:** Desire. If you look at Messi and Ronaldo, what sets them apart is their desire. Each year they maintain and improve standards. That comes from making sacrifices and the rewards will come. There aren't days off. I was an obsessive trainer and a bad loser at Leeds and Manchester United. You have to have that in you.

**TONY:** Have you a desire to go into coaching or management?

**RIO:** Not now. I did want to be a coach and manager, but my circumstances have changed, with the children and my new missus. You have to be 'all in' as a manager and I can't do that.

**TONY:** The final question: what are your thoughts about the owners of Premier League clubs, their motivation?

RIO: As a player, you don't feel it. Now I'm out, I can see for example the American influence on United. When I was at the club there were a handful of sponsors. Now there are a hundred or more. Twice a month now the training ground becomes a commercial compound where all the sponsors come and the players have to go through pods and all the commercial stuff. That's the way it is. It's not just football now. When you are getting paid that sort of money, your contract says you have to do so many hours a week commercially. I have to be honest, the Glazers have spent money when the managers have asked it of them. Mourinho spent over a quarter of a billion pounds! I don't mind an owner coming in and employing the right people who stipulate to the manager, 'I want young players in the first team and give them time.' That should be a stipulation and that means the fans still feel part of the club. That's why, wherever I go, West Ham fans talk about the players that came through: Joe Cole, Michael Carrick, Frank Lampard, etc. – they feel an identity with the club. That's why you have to respect Pochettino. While he was in this country, he had more youngsters in his first team than anyone.

TONY: That's right. I had a conversation with the former Tottenham academy director, John McDermott, and he said he had a fantastic relationship with the manager Pochettino. In contrast, at some clubs up and down the country the managers don't even know who runs their youth departments.

RIO: That's what I'm saying. When I was at West Ham, Frank Lampard Sr would be at a youth game, so would Harry or Roger Cross. It makes you think there is a pathway and gives kids a belief. Owners should make sure that when a manager comes in, they say to him, 'Part of our DNA is to bring kids through.' Pellegrini? Who did he bring through? That's why I would love to go back to West Ham, maybe in a consultancy role. I spoke to the owners and said, 'I would love to come in and help you a couple of days a week.' Jimmy Frith – an assistant schoolboy coach at West Ham – has been there for years and years. They should be celebrating him. The kids who come in should know he's been at the club for 40 years. You should be an ambassador. At Manchester United, the former kit man is an ambassador. His name is Albert Morgan and he goes around the boxes and talks to people on match days. He is part of the fabric of the club. West Ham needs to cling on to the 1 per centers who will help the club maintain its integrity. The new history is not sustainable without the past. Why did I sign for West Ham? Only one reason: because I thought it was a pathway to the first team. They need to get back to that. I don't understand it. The catchment area is unbelievable.

At West Ham, the first group I got involved with was the under-16s, who played on Sunday mornings as Poplar Boys Club and I worked with them on behalf of West Ham. At this time professional clubs were not allowed to run their own schoolboy teams so a way round this was to enrol your squad with a local Sunday club and play under their name. The two big players were Alan Curbishley and Paul Brush, two local boys who went on to have great careers as players with West Ham and beyond. They both eventually went into coaching and managing and very successfully too! Alan eventually became manager of West Ham with Mervyn Day, another former

Hammer, as his assistant. They had been together for many years in similar roles as manager and assistant at Charlton Athletic.

The full-time youth coach at the time was Ron Boyce, who had not long retired from playing, after which John Lyall had given him the job. I assisted Ron when I could during school holidays, youth tours and FA Youth Cup runs. The first youth tour I was asked to go on was to Stuttgart, Germany. When we arrived, all the teams were greeted at the clubhouse of the hosting team. All the other teams were in their club tracksuits and we were still dressed just in the clothes we had travelled in and looked right out of place. At that time at West Ham we were not supplied with tracksuits for the players – I don't think there *was* an official club tracksuit – and were used to turning up at games in a collar and tie. On this tour, with games being played over a three-day period and on some days having two games, wearing a collar and tie was not exactly practical, so the local team loaned our squad a set of tracksuits to wear for the duration of the tournament. I have to say Ron Boyce and I were somewhat embarrassed by our lack of preparation and having to borrow kit from our German hosts.

Over time Ron and I developed a good relationship and worked for many years together. Ron had coached the team to the FA Youth Cup final of 1975 – the same year the first team had won the FA Cup vs Fulham – and had a promising group of youngsters who went on to play for the first-team, players such as Geoff Pike, Alvin Martin, Alan Curbishley, Paul Brush and Terry Hurlock. We lost the final over two legs to Ipswich Town who themselves had a very good team. It is obvious that success at youth level is all about producing players who eventually play in the first team, so although we lost the Youth Cup final, we produced four or five players who went on to play for the first team, so for that year it was job done. Ronnie Boyce was a dyed-in-the-wool West Ham man. He had been at the club all his working career, playing over 300 games for the first team and going into coaching straight from finishing playing. He had to learn to coach on the job and I helped him in a small way with organising groups and setting up practices. Ron knew the game inside out but needed a little help at times with the basics of coaching. We bounced a lot of ideas off each other and developed a good working relationship, especially when I came in during the evening coaching sessions.

It was while working for the club part-time and coaching in the schools that I was approached by the head of youth football at Charlton Athletic and asked if I wanted to become their full-time under-18 youth team coach. I was surprised by this approach and went to speak to them. I told John Lyall and he said it was up to me if that's what I wanted to do. Charlton offered me a two-year contract and a decent salary, which I initially accepted, but had second thoughts later in the day and rang them to tell them I was staying at West Ham. I rang John and told him of my decision and he just said, 'I'm glad to hear you're staying.'

My career might have panned out very differently if I had I left the club at that point. My decision to stay at West Ham was based on the fact that I felt West Ham was 'my club' and they had given me an opportunity to further my coaching career. It could never have been based on any financial gain that I may have secured if I had gone to Charlton. Basically, I was happy with this set-up – of working for the Inner London Education Authority and part-time for West Ham. After my experience with Barnet, I never really missed playing that much. In truth I had become somewhat disillusioned. Playing had become a struggle to enjoy it. I had got married to Brenda in 1973, our first child, Dean, was born in 1977, and two more were to follow – Neil in 1982 and Louise in 1985 – so the most important thing for me at the time was stability. Coaching in the schools and working part-time for West Ham was an ideal scenario.

In the summer of 1980, it all changed again. West Ham had just won the FA Cup, beating Arsenal 1-0, and *finally* I could gloat to all the kids at school about West Ham. John had got his tactics spot on during this match. Arsenal were the odds-on favourites and he thought about a way of giving Arsenal something tactically to think about. He felt their centre backs, David O'Leary and Willie Young, would feel uncomfortable not having two strikers to mark, as most teams at the time always played with two strikers. So he played Stuart Pearson in a deeper-lying role off David Cross, West Ham's traditional striker. This tactic worked well, with Pearson linking with midfield players regularly and sitting in the area just behind their midfield and in the spaces in front of the back four of Arsenal. This deeper-lying role gave Arsenal the problem of who should mark Pearson. Should it be one of the centre backs, who would have to come out of the back line to push on to Pearson? Or should it be a central midfield player to drop off deeper to mark him? Either way, it presented Arsenal with a tactical problem and went a long way to West Ham – who we should remember were in the second tier of football at the time, the old Second Division – winning the FA Cup.

Schools broke up for summer and I went on a driving holiday to Austria. I came home and thought I would pop into the Chadwell Heath training ground to discuss the summer schoolboy programme with Ron Boyce. As we sat drinking tea, John Lyall – who was by now the manager in his own right after Ron Greenwood had left the club to become the England manager (replacing Don Revie who in turn had left the FA for a more financially lucrative offer to manage the United Arab Emirates) – asked me to come to the office. I wondered what he could possibly want. We sat down and John asked if I would like to become the full-time youth coach. Ron Boyce, with Mick McGiven, would move up to the first team and I would replace Ron as youth coach. As it turned out, Mick and Ron would share first-team duties. It was a bit of an unusual set-up: they trained together as a group with the reserve team and for two weeks each one took the reserve-team fixture on the Saturday while the other went to first-team games with John. I found this all a bit strange. It was as if John didn't want to have to choose between Ron and Mick as to who was first-team coach – so they had a compromise and shared it. But it seemed to work well enough and there was a good deal of trust among us and we simply got on with it.

After a short discussion about having to give notice to the schools and about my salary, I accepted and started work the following Monday on a salary of £150 per week. I hadn't even discussed it with my wife Brenda; it was something I wanted to do, so I accepted on the spot. So much for stability! But I felt this was the right decision. I trusted John and he had said I would be there as long as he was manager, and even in the uncertain world of football management, it felt the right decision.

One of the other reasons that a position had become available was that previously, during my time as a part-time coach, Bill Lansdowne Sr had been reserve-team coach. Bill was an ex-first-team player and was in the promotion-winning side of the late 1950s. He was also father of Bill Lansdowne Jr who played nine games for the first team in the early 1980s. I was told that Bill Sr had had an argument with the club secretary, Eddie Chapman, over bonuses he felt he should have been paid. The club were due to play a cup game and Bill felt a bonus should be paid if they won. Eddie disagreed and so Bill stormed out of the office, allegedly saying, 'I hope they lose then!' Eddie Chapman reported the conversation to the board and the manager – and Bill left the club shortly after.

Eddie Baily, who was previously assistant manager to Bill Nicholson at Tottenham Hotspur and a former England international, had taken over from Wally St Pier as chief representative, and he tried to talk me out of taking the job, telling me all the pitfalls of professional football and was I sure about leaving the relative security of teaching? I don't know if Eddie had someone else lined up if I didn't take the job. I had not been a success as a player at West Ham but was determined to make my mark as a coach.

When I got home later that day and told Brenda what had happened, she was entirely supportive. 'You have to do what makes you happy,' she said, and I was certainly very happy. As part of the package, John had told me I would also be included in the Football League pension scheme that players and staff were part of. I was leaving the teaching job with the Inner London Education Authority and had been in the teachers' pension scheme for ten years, so to join the Football League pension scheme and to carry on paying into a pension seemed the sensible and logical thing to do – but unfortunately nobody told the club secretary and so a year-long battle to get myself enrolled in the scheme commenced. After about thirteen months of haggling, the club eventually enrolled me into the scheme and after staying with the club a further 35 years or so, it was certainly worth haggling over!

# 6

## COACHING FULL-TIME

My first day as the full-time youth coach was pre-season before the 1980/81 season. I was living in Chadwell Heath at the time, so getting to work was nothing more arduous than a ten-minute walk. I remember the occasion well for one particular incident: the normal routine was that John Lyall would take the first-team squad for a warm-up routine and Ron Boyce and Mick McGiven would assist. As it was my first day, and with no notice, John turned to me and said, 'Tony, warm the players up.' I was taken aback and very nervous about the players' reaction to me. I needn't have worried; the players were very professional and performed every instruction I gave them. After about twenty minutes of me putting the players through their paces: jogging in pairs, jumping, turning, side skipping, touching the ground, opening up the groins, all the while jogging up and down the pitch, and, at the end, a few minutes of doing some stretches – basic stuff really, but nerve-wracking on my first day – I handed the players back to John, Ron and Mick, and I went off with my youth squad who had also been part of the warm-up. As I walked away, I said to myself, 'I have just put the FA Cup holders through a warm-up routine and they couldn't have been more professional about it.' It gave me a lot of confidence.

My first group of players that season were a great bunch: John Vaughan in goal; Adrian Keith and Everald La Ronde as full backs; Keith McPherson, Chris Ampofo and Robert Wall as centre backs; midfielders Bobby Barnes, Mark Schiavi, Wayne Reader, Glenn Burvill, Alan Dickens – who was still at school; and Steve Milton and a young Tony Cottee up front. Paul Allen was still eligible to play but was already in the first team and had picked up an FA Cup winner's medal the previous May. The team had a great season, reaching three cup finals: the Southern Junior Floodlit Cup, the South East Counties League Cup and the ultimate youth competition, the FA Youth Cup. We won the League Cup and the FA Youth Cup but lost in the Southern Junior Floodlit Cup final to Aston Villa.

After the defeat against Villa, John Lyall said we should go up to his office to discuss the game, so Ron Boyce and I went up to John's office to talk about the players' performances. Well, this went on well into the night. Had we prepared right for the game? Had we played with the right commitment or tempo? Had we had the right tactics and were the players playing in their right positions? This was typical of John – dissecting every detail of a game, even the smallest aspect; questioning the coach's role; could we have done more? Questioning the players' roles and individual performances. Were they going to be good enough to play first-team football? Whenever I gave an opinion on a point or a player's performance or future, John would immediately ask me to expand on and develop my thinking and we would then analyse each other's comments. We did not always agree. This process was going to be insightful, telling me what and where I had to improve if I was going to go on to become a top coach. I had so much still to learn. I got home at about 2.30am and Brenda found it hard to believe we could talk football for so long; she was convinced I had been out after the game ... boozing. Truth was, she didn't know John Lyall.

These discussions before and after games and before training became a regular thing. We, the coaches and John, would get to the Chadwell Heath training ground around 8.45am every day and over a cup of tea discuss the day(s) ahead. It was like our own 'boot room' where we could discuss every detail of the day's training – who would do what, which players were available, whether the youth team players were needed or if I would take them away as a separate group. We would also do the same after the players had gone home – discussing how the day had gone and thinking ahead to the weekend matches for all of the teams. These occasions, which lasted about 45 minutes, could only shape you as a person and a coach. The exchange of experience and knowledge drip by drip proved invaluable as a developmental tool.

One day we were talking about employing new staff. At the time at West Ham we were a very small, closely knit group that had complete trust in each other. Our being together every day made it relatively easy for John to manage his team. Everybody knew and understood their role and there were never any arguments about who was doing what with whom. Nowadays, in the light of the Premier League and the new academy set-ups with the much-heralded Elite Player Performance Plan (EPPP) – more about this later – and with staffing levels at an all-time high, the task of managing the coaching hierarchy is very much more difficult. Remember that during the eighties and nineties I was the only full-time member of the youth coaching staff. John Lyall's advice was always when you appoint new staff make sure you don't appoint anybody who could be a threat to what you have already created or have their own agenda. This was something I always bore in mind when staffing levels started to increase. I didn't always get that right but for the most part I did.

The run to the FA Youth Cup final of 1980/81 was marred by our experience at the Vetch Field, Swansea. We won the game 3-0, but our winger David Oswald 'Bobby' Barnes was subjected to terrible racist abuse from the small crowd, something which took all the joy out of winning the game. Bobby, needless to say, stood up to the abuse and produced a fine performance. Bobby would go on to have a fine career as a professional player making 43 appearances for West Ham before moving to Scunthorpe, Swindon and Bournemouth. After his playing career finished, he became an executive at the Professional Footballers' Association (PFA) where today he is deputy chief executive. But this was 40 years ago when this sort of pathetic abuse went unrecorded or investigated. The situation now is very different with the vibrant and universal 'Let's Kick Racism Out of Football' organisation, inaugurated in 1993 and now simply known as 'Kick It Out'. And very recently the Black Lives Matter movement bringing racism into everybody's thinking. Today there are procedures in place to stamp out this sort of unacceptable behaviour, but back then there was little anyone could do and this was a youth team game with impressionable kids on the pitch for goodness' sake! How low can you get?

We still can't be complacent. Racism will rear its ugly head after all of society's efforts to eradicate it and despite the good work from the Kick It Out campaign. Lately there have been England international matches where we've witnessed racist chanting, causing players to threaten to walk off the pitch. There is still work to be done. Bobby has always been a staunch campaigner for racial equality and in 2020 was appointed as the first black member of UEFA's control, ethics and disciplinary body, and I know Bobby is very proud of his appointment and sees it as one step in the right direction.

We went all the way that season and played Spurs in a two-legged final with the first at Upton Park. We won 2-0 with Bobby Barnes and Wayne Reader scoring. We played well and dominated most of the game, missing some good chances to increase the first-leg lead, but at 2-0 we were confident we could win the tie overall. The second leg, played a week later, was at White Hart Lane, which had its main stand undergoing redevelopment so the teams had to change in Portakabins. The game was a bit of a stalemate with Glenn Burvill missing a glorious chance to make it 3-0 after a great run down the right by the full back Adrian Keith. A photographer got a great photo of Glenn with his head in his hands. I'm sure he still thinks to this day, *How did I miss that one!?* Spurs scored late on but we held on to win 2-1 on aggregate.

Paul Allen was allowed to play in our FA Youth Cup run and played his part in the win, so Paul has the rare distinction of winning an FA Cup winner's medal *before* winning an FA Youth Cup winner's medal. A good pub quiz question, that one. My one regret from that night concerned midfield player and goalscorer from the first leg, Wayne Reader. I had decided to play Alan Dickens in his place for the second leg; we were 2-0 up and did not need to chase the game and I thought that Alan would use the ball better on the counter-attack. All this was fine and Wayne took the decision very well, but to my eternal regret he was not given a winner's medal as the FA only supplied twelve and Wayne missed out. I should have ordered an extra one from the FA after the final but I did not think of it and I regret that lapse to this day.

The Spurs team for the final included goalkeeper Tony Parks, defenders Simon Webster and Mark Bowen, midfielder Ian Crook and forward Terry Gibson. All went on to have very good football careers. For us, Paul Allen was already in the first team but not long after Everald La Ronde, Bobby Barnes, Keith McPherson, Tony Cottee and Alan Dickens would follow with first-team debuts. After the youth team played on Saturday, I would ask them to write a short summary of their performances, reflect on the game and give it to me on Monday morning. Most players obliged, but some didn't, although I didn't chase them. If they were not interested in self-inspection in order to help them improve, I was not going to bully them into it. Tony Cottee was always very descriptive; he would write, *I scored two goals today and I thought I played well. However, I missed a couple of easy chances so I went to the park with my dad (Clive) and practised those situations again and again. Now feel I am better placed to score those chances should they come along again.* This was typical of Tony – very focused and single-minded, and always looking to improve and score more goals. It was a useful exercise and gave you as their coach an insight into the way these young players saw themselves and how they assessed their performances.

Many coaches ask me what the best way is to develop young players. It is a process and important that as a coach you have a philosophy of how you want to see your players and team play. At West Ham my biggest influences were, and remain, Ron Greenwood and John Lyall. It was instilled into me that good technique is vital, along with good positional understanding and an understanding of your role in the team. Physicality was never really discussed at the development phase: speed of thought was as important as speed across the ground. Player dedication and hard work were considered equally important. The other big factor is being at a club where there is a genuine opportunity to break through into the first team, the corollary of which is a first team that has a manager who is not afraid to give young players their chance. Sure they have to be good enough, but opportunity is key. Sadly this is lacking in today's game, although it is getting better with the present England team showing a group of young talent who were given their first-team opportunities early in their careers. At West Ham it is something we have always done.

It was during this first season that John Lyall put on a coaching night for the London Coaches Association – held at the training ground in Chadwell Heath. John was always very keen to help other coaches and to stimulate new ideas. I, along with Ron Boyce and Mick McGiven, were given topics to put on for the coaches to watch while John would give a running commentary on the points we were trying to achieve. As we were FA Cup holders, he thought it would be a good idea to bring the FA Cup to the coaching evening. I loaded it into a kit bag and brought it from Upton Park. After the coaching session finished, John held a question and answer session with the London coaches, which went on until quite late as I recall, around 11pm.

We still had the FA Cup and there was no way we could get it back to Upton Park so I put it back in the kit bag and took it home for safekeeping. I ended up sleeping with it on my bedside table. Unsurprisingly, the phone at Chadwell Heath was ringing off the hook as the club secretary frantically sought the location of the Cup. I returned it safely that afternoon, but couldn't help laughing at the surreal situation I had somehow got into.

The first team had reached another cup final – the League Cup final vs Liverpool at Wembley. It was notable for an incident at the end of the game. The final ended 1-1 with Ray Stewart converting a last-minute penalty to equalise a controversial Terry McDermott goal for Liverpool. It was felt that Liverpool player Sammy Lee was in an offside position in front of our goalkeeper, Phil Parkes, as McDermott shot. At the end of the game as we stepped on to the Wembley turf to head back to the dressing rooms – they were behind the goal at the old Wembley – I walked behind John Lyall who I watched approach match referee Clive Thomas. John said, 'Clive, we feel we have been cheated, the Liverpool goal was offside.' Clive Thomas replied, 'I don't agree and will report you to the FA.' At this point we had to usher John away to the dressing room. He was beyond incensed.

After the game, the club held a reception at the Grosvenor House Hotel in Park Lane. During the dinner John came over to our table and said the FA were charging him with calling the referee, Clive Thomas, a cheat. I immediately said, 'John, you didn't call him a cheat, you said we feel we have been cheated, I heard you say it.' The following week John was duly charged and I ended up at John's hearing at FA headquarters in Lancaster Gate as a witness of what was actually said. The hearing was quite formal – Clive Thomas gave his version and said that John had called him a cheat. John said he did not call him a cheat but had said we, as a team, felt cheated. Evidence to back up John's version included a newspaper picture of the game that showed me next to John as he remonstrated with the referee, to prove I *had* heard the conversation. John was found innocent of the charges but was warned about his future conduct. After the hearing the three of us, John, Clive Thomas and me, went around the corner to a local pub for lunch just to show there were no hard feelings. I remember John making a call to his secretary to tell her the good news and to let the chairman know. He was clearly relieved at the verdict.

After Wally St Pier had retired, following our FA Cup final win over Fulham in 1975, John appointed Eddie Baily as his replacement. Eddie, whom I mentioned earlier, was a former England international so he had lots of experience. My role as youth coach brought me directly into contact with Eddie regarding the recruitment of schoolboy players and our success in the 1980 FA Youth Cup win over Spurs was a direct result of Eddie's recruitment. He overhauled the scouting and made us more competitive. Following in the footsteps of Wally St Pier was never going to be an easy task as his success in the late 1950s and 1960s was unbelievable – Bobby Moore, Geoff Hurst, Martin Peters, Ron Boyce, Eddie Bovington, Ken Brown, John Bond, John Sissons, Harry Redknapp, Brian Dear, Jack Burkett, Alan Curbishley, Paul Brush to name just a few.

Wally was a jolly, smiling man who always greeted you with a 'Hello mate.' He lived in Harold Hill, Essex and legend has it he would walk to Upton Park most days as he didn't drive. A chief scout who didn't drive would be unheard of today; he must have had good shoes! Wally retired in 1975 and the club awarded him a testimonial for his 47 years' service. It was to be played on the Monday after West Ham played Fulham in the FA Cup final at Wembley, with Bobby Moore playing for Fulham! I mentioned to Wally that the timing of his testimonial was perfect. If West Ham won the cup, he would get a full house. 'Yes,' Wally replied, 'but what I'm worried about is if we DON'T win the cup!' Wally needn't have worried as West Ham beat Fulham 2-0 and Wally was rewarded with a bumper crowd of over 25,000 supporters; a fully deserved reward for his brilliant service to the club.

By now much younger players were being signed by clubs so you needed to employ more scouts to find the hidden gems of talent. The problem was that all the clubs in the catchment area – essentially all of London – were doing the same. Finding *scouts* good enough to find the talent and at the same time ward off the competition was a challenge in itself. The so-called big clubs of London would spend hugely on recruitment so West Ham, who had always been careful on expenditure, were finding it harder to compete with the likes of Tottenham, Arsenal and Chelsea. Eddie Baily would have a big job on his hands.

Eddie Baily wasn't an easy character to get to know; he didn't mince his words, was sometimes loud, aggressive and often confrontational. He didn't suffer fools lightly and was by no means everyone's cup of tea, but he set about the job and hired good scouts. At one point Harry Redknapp brought his son Jamie down to Chadwell Heath to play in a friendly game. Jamie was about fifteen and Harry was manager of Bournemouth at the time. Jamie played in the game but chose not to sign for us and signed for Tottenham as a youth player, but eventually went back to Bournemouth with his dad, making his debut for Bournemouth as a sixteen-year-old. Eddie had invited Harry and Jamie to the match and was dealing with them as I was involved in the game. Sometime later Harry told me that one of the reasons Jamie didn't sign for West Ham was that he didn't like Eddie Baily's aggressive and blunt approach and felt he wouldn't enjoy playing for the club.

Later down the line Eddie's role involved him with more and more senior player recruitment, and I asked for a meeting with John and Eddie because I felt schoolboy recruitment was suffering and lagging behind our competitors. What I felt was needed was a dedicated member of staff solely responsible for schoolboy recruitment – this is commonplace nowadays – leaving Eddie to concentrate on senior scouting. During the meeting Eddie was his usual 'we don't need change' attitude. John listened and agreed with me and, to appease Eddie, appointed Len Hurford, one of Eddie's part-time scouts. Len worked for the gas board by trade and as a trusted scout had been responsible for bringing Paul Allen to the club some years earlier. He knew what he was doing. My only concern was, as he was so close to Eddie, Eddie would control him from above. So it became a compromise – but was better than the situation before. Len came on board and was the clubs first youth development officer or YDO as it became known.

The early 1980s were still a good period for producing young players. Paul Allen was an early debutant, followed by Dale Banton, Bobby Barnes, Everald La Ronde, Tony Cottee, Alan Dickens, Kevin Keen, Steve Potts, George Parris, Greg Campbell, Paul Ince, Eamonn Dolan and Stuart Slater. One debutant I haven't mentioned is Ray Houghton, who after only one first-team game (against Arsenal) was released by John Lyall and given a free transfer. Looking back with the benefit of hindsight, it was a big mistake. Ray went on to great things as a player at Fulham, Oxford, Liverpool, Aston Villa and Crystal Palace. He also became a Republic of Ireland international, playing in the 1994 World Cup in the USA. His international appearances for Ireland seemed a bit strange to me as he was born in Glasgow and we at West Ham knew him as Scotty because of his strong Scottish accent ... I wasn't involved in the decision to release Ray but Ernie Gregory, the goalkeeping coach at the time, told me later that he had a big discussion with John, telling him not to release him, but to no avail. I believe John let him go because he had an abundance of quality midfield players – Brooking, Devonshire, Pike and Dickens coming through – and he felt Ray wouldn't get games, so to give him a chance of a career he let him go. This is probably the biggest mistake the club has ever made with regard to releasing a young player!

Most of the youth players at this time were local or London boys with the exception of Stuart Slater, who came from Suffolk. He was also being chased by Ipswich Town, his local club, for his signature. He used to come to training with another Suffolk boy, Jason Dozzell, whom we also tried to sign. Ron Gale was the scout that did a lot of the work back and forth to Suffolk trying to get both of these boys to sign. They were both very good players and Ron did all he could to get them to commit to West Ham. Stuart did eventually sign for West Ham, but Jason decided to stay local and signed for Ipswich Town. They both had great careers and Jason was one of many that got away.

Tony Cottee and Alan Dickens were local boys and didn't take much persuading to sign. The same scout that worked so hard to get Slater and Dozzell to sign, Ron Gale, was very instrumental in getting Tony Cottee to come to the club in the first place. Tony was always a prolific goalscorer and as long as he was scoring, he was happy. He rarely needed more than two touches to score and more often than not one touch was enough. Like Paul Allen and Paul Ince to follow, Tony was sold for a large fee. It was to become a familiar event: the youth department unearthing a great talent while the club, under constant financial pressure and a need to balance the books, would sell its only assets – players.

I remember Tony's debut vs Tottenham Hotspur at Upton Park. It was New Year's Day, 1983 and he didn't know he was playing until about an hour before the kick-off. In the dressing room before the game, Alan Devonshire spoke to me about Tony and said, 'If I cut inside and play into his feet, is he good enough to hold it or get it back to me?' I assured him he was. Tony scored his first senior goal for the club that day and went on to become a prolific goalscorer throughout his career.

Tony was sold to Everton for a club record fee at the time of £2.2 million. John asked the board to give a bonus to the youth department for their efforts in producing Tony. As I remember it, the board gave £25,000 to share out, which worked out to around £500 each for coaches, scouts and other staff. We all felt at the time this was a generous gesture, typical of John Angus Lyall, who was always thinking of others.

Alan Dickens was a much more understated player with a very quiet nature but technically a very gifted player. As noted previously, Alan's presence at the club was one of the reasons John let Ray Houghton go. In the mid-eighties Paul Ince arrived on the scene with two great goals in a famous 4-1 League Cup victory against the all-conquering Liverpool at Upton Park. The game that night highlighted Paul's talents: aggressive in the tackle, unafraid, great passing ability and a goalscorer. Paul's big mentor/father figure was the manager John Lyall, who guided Paul through some troubled times as a youngster. Paul's best friend at the club was another youth-team product and future West Ham captain, Steve Potts. They were never far away from each other.

During the 1988 season both were in the first-team squad to play QPR away, on QPR's plastic pitch at Loftus Road. John had arranged for the team to train on a plastic pitch at Gloucester Park, Basildon on the previous Thursday before the Saturday match and this meant the players had to drive the fifteen miles from the Chadwell Heath training ground to Basildon. Pottsy and Incey drove together, with Incey driving. The route is along a long, straight road from Romford to Southend-on-Sea (the A127) with Basildon located part way en route. There was a big convoy of cars of staff and players and Paul decided to liven things up with a bit of overtaking and undertaking, making faces as they passed teammates. As they overtook coach Ernie Gregory, Steve and Paul's fooling around got the better of them. They failed to see the car in front of them braking and promptly rammed into the back of it. It resulted in both Paul and Steve suffering cracked ribs and much bruised egos. Not only did it stop them from training but it put them out of Saturday's game at QPR. You can imagine how displeased the manager was. I ended up at the hospital with the pair as we waited for them to be X-rayed and examined. We were joined by the players' worried girlfriends, Claire (Paul) and Joanne (Steve). They would eventually marry the girls and the foursome are still good friends to this day. Recently I was invited to the National Football Museum in Manchester as a surprise guest for the inauguration of Paul Ince into the 'Hall of Fame'. I was pleased to go and Paul was very surprised to see me and that I had made the effort to travel to Manchester for the event. I hadn't seen Paul and his wife Claire since John Lyall's funeral and it was great to catch up and talk about old times and the successful career he had. I have spoken to Steve Potts recently about this period of his career and the interview is below.

TONY: When did you first start playing football?

**STEVE:** I started playing football in an under-9s team called Dagenham United. Someone told me about trials that were going on and I went along and as I look back on it now, think it was a really lucky break. The manager of the team doing the trials was Tony Adams' dad, Alex. I didn't know him, but because it was Alex Adams then obviously Tony was going to be there. I got into the team, and from the under-9s through to about the under-15s, over six years or so, I played for Dagenham United under manager Alex while playing alongside Tony. And, of course, everyone knows what Tony has done in the game – Arsenal captain and I don't know how many England caps. Yet it was pure coincidence that we ended up playing together. He went on to Arsenal and I came to West Ham. He could have come to West Ham, but Tony picked Arsenal and I picked West Ham and, as it turned out, we both had really good, long careers at our respective clubs. I had a real fantastic grounding with Alex. You know he's really knowledgeable and we had a really good team with some good players who didn't all make the grade for whatever reason, but it was a real competitive Sunday league. I think that it really helped me. I can remember that there were some real edgy games, even as an under-12 we played Senrab and it got really competitive.

**TONY:** So, when did you first realise that you were not bad at this game, that you were quite good, you know?

**STEVE:** I was okay, but it was a good team. I wasn't the best player in that team by a long way. I stayed there and I was good enough to be in that team and then as the years went on, you battle away to get into your school team, you battle to get into your district side, represent London, your county side, and then eventually try to get into England teams. I think that side of it really makes you harden up as a kid, you're striving all the time to get in these teams and then stay there. So, I look back and think I had a really good grounding as a schoolboy.

**TONY:** When did West Ham approach you? Were they the first club?

**STEVE:** Yeah, yeah. Ronnie Gale got me over to West Ham one evening for the under-15s. In those days that's when you went to a pro club, fifteen. Fourteen or fifteen. For evening training. It was the same sort of thing – you're striving to get in the West Ham team or to get noticed, and for them to like you, but I'd had plenty of that up to then. I look back and I think I was ready for it. And that's how it worked out: West Ham offered me schoolboy forms and eventually gave me an apprenticeship.

**TONY:** In those days you played with Tony in the Barking team as well, didn't you? The district team. Back then, was he a leader? Even at that young age?

**STEVE:** He's the best I've seen. What you saw with Tony in an Arsenal shirt was what he was like as a kid. It was ridiculous the leadership quality he showed at a young age. A lot of that I think was instilled by his dad, and what he was all about, but Tony was fantastic from that point of view. It was like he always wanted the team to perform and if it wasn't right, well, he'd tell you. Nowadays, I look at a lot of kids at West Ham. I get to see the younger groups because it goes down all the way to the under-9s, and there's a different sort of culture.

**TONY:** This is when you're, like, ten and twelve years of age ...

**STEVE:** Ten or twelve years of age. You don't quite see the hunger, that competitiveness as much now.

**TONY:** I think my own experience is these days with youth teams that the competitive edge seems to have gone out of the game. All right, you don't want to win at all costs, but certainly you need a competitive edge.

**STEVE:** With coaching now, we're the first to be critical of the boys if they're not showing enough effort, not showing enough passion to win a game of football, so you've got to have that, but it isn't win at all costs, far from it. But you've got to have it, because we see plenty of players, good players, who haven't got that real desire to make it to the top because of that. So, you want them developing, but they've got to want to win as well.

**TONY:** I think it's important and it's a debate that's going to rumble on, but what do you remember about your youth days – and I say that with a smile on my face because I was a youth coach.

**STEVE:** I can honestly say that I loved it. I loved the schoolboy years but when I became an apprentice, and recall my days in the youth team, I can say I really did enjoy it, I really did. We had a good team, we were competitive, but, you know, we had some good characters around. I was good friends with Paul Ince.

**TONY:** We'll come to that a bit later.

STEVE: I had a real good time, really enjoyable, but you knew you were there to work and it was all down to you. We knew we had to perform and if you weren't performing you knew about it, from yourself, Eddie Baily, John Lyall; there was a real focus on you all the time. When we played the youth team games at Chadwell Heath and John Lyall, the manager, was watching the first half – he had to disappear to go and do the first team, but to have that and be under the spotlight like that, well it was sink or swim. And I think you put pressure on the boys in the right way, questioning whether they've got what it takes to be a footballer. You're being tested. It always felt like a test, day in, day out.

TONY: I remember watching you play at Fulham one day for England. And what age did you make your debut for the first team?

STEVE: Seventeen.

TONY: Seventeen. And who was that against, can you remember?

STEVE: Queens Park Rangers on New Year's Day.

TONY: Did you win?

STEVE: We got beat 3-1. John Lyall just called me in an hour before the game and said, 'Are you ready to play?' I went, 'Yeah.' He said, 'Right, you're playing.' And it was as simple as that. We were 1-0 up and then Paul Brush scored a goal that was disallowed, but you can look at the footage today and see there was nothing wrong with it. So, we were close to going 2-0 up when the game turned.

**TONY:** And how did that feel when you were told you were going to play? Can you remember how it felt?

**STEVE:** Yeah, it was like woah ... here we go, but you got straight back in the dressing room (because John had called me in the office) and all the other players know that I've been called out and he's saying, right you're playing, and you had characters in there like Tony Gale and all the others, they're on you straight away but everyone took the edge off it.

**TONY:** How much of an influence at that time was John?

**STEVE:** A massive influence. He took a real interest in the boys and everyone at the club. He knew everybody's name. He knew you from the first day of pre-season when they started looking at you. You turn up and you'd be running with the first team, as one big group, but I always felt with John, he was like a father figure who looked after you on and off the pitch, and I think if you didn't perform as well, you felt like you were letting him down. It was that sort of relationship. If I didn't perform it mattered personally. And you'd know about it. He'd give you a well done but if things weren't right ... well, I can remember the team talks. They used to go on and on, an hour long. If he got a bad result on a Saturday, you'd certainly know about it on the Monday and it would be really tough training that day.

**TONY:** A bit different now!

**STEVE:** Different now for sure. A lot really has changed now from that point of view, but again it hardened you up, it really did. Yeah, mentally it really did.

**TONY:** It's a tough industry really, it is. You mentioned Paul Ince earlier. You were good mates with Paul Ince – still are, I believe – you were his calming influence I think, because always Incey was a bit feisty, a bit fiery is the word I'm looking for. How did that relationship develop? You were best man at each other's weddings, weren't you?

**STEVE:** He was in the year below me and we came from a similar area so we ended up travelling in together each day and our wives – girlfriends at the time – became good friends as well. We used to socialise together as a four, and we just really clicked. Yet we were totally different characters.

**TONY:** That's the point I'm trying to make: you were calm and Incey a bit fiery ...

**STEVE:** I was calm while Incey wouldn't care about anything – I can remember him as a seventeen-year-old really laying into first-team players, and you're watching and thinking, Incey, you can't do that, mate. But in fairness, it's what made him; he believed in himself, he believed in his ability, he was a great player but another one who showed great leadership qualities in the youth team. If you weren't doing it, he'd tell you, even at that age, and I think he carried that on throughout the rest of his career.

**TONY:** The story goes he walked into the dressing room at Manchester United, when he first arrived, threw his boots on the floor and said, 'I'm the guvnor now.'

**STEVE:** That wouldn't surprise me.

**TONY:** It's only hearsay, but it wouldn't surprise me either because that's Incey all over, isn't it? And that's what made him and his career.

**STEVE:** Yes. He totally believed in his ability, and he could look after himself. He looked after himself as a kid, he had a tough upbringing, but he looked after himself on the football pitch as well.

And the other player I always look back on and think, you'd want him in your team was Tony Adams, of course. You would always want him in the team. Paul Ince, you'd want him in the team. Those sort of real, hardened characters who combined it with great ability.

**TONY:** Do you want to talk about the car accident? What do you remember about that? It's funny now but it certainly wasn't funny at the time.

**STEVE:** We were due to play Queens Park Rangers away on the Saturday, and in those days QPR had an AstroTurf pitch, so John got us training at Basildon on an AstroTurf pitch, to get used to the surface. I am in the car with Incey who's driving as we head up the A127 towards Basildon from where we lived, but on the way we've seen goalkeeping coach Ernie Gregory in front of us and Incey, being classic Incey, has gone up on the inside of Ernie's car while we're driving at about 40 miles an hour. He winds down the window and is giving Ernie a bit of stick, saying 'Ernie you f******' whatever. I'm in the passenger seat thinking, *Incey, the traffic in front has come to a standstill*, but he's still hanging out the window abusing Ernie and then he's seen the stationary traffic ahead, but it's too late and we've gone into the back of it. I've ended up cracking my ribs while Incey comes out of it unscathed. This was on the Friday and I was in real pain. I saw the doctor but he thought I was perfectly okay. By that evening let's just say I've never been in a bath that I could not get out of until then ... because the pain was so bad. In the end I had an X-ray and they said I had cracked ribs. Incey was still able to play the game, but that's Incey for you.

TONY: A story that typifies Paul, doesn't it? Carefree ...

STEVE: Carefree, and someone who thinks he's invincible.

TONY: I've been looking up your appearances. As we all know, you were a one-club man, who started in 1985 and finished in 2002, with over 500 appearances. When you were approaching the end of your career and you started thinking, well, I haven't got long left, did you consider taking up coaching and getting your badges?

STEVE: No, I didn't, I didn't at all, really. I had in my mind I'd play and then I'd go and do something different. Towards the end of my career, I didn't really play that many games, and I don't know if I was getting frustrated with it or not, but I just thought right, I just want a bit of a change in my life. But by then my eldest boy was at the club then, Dan, in the academy system ...

TONY: Dan's now at Luton, isn't he?

STEVE: He's at Luton. So, I left at 35, but didn't really leave the club as such, because I was still coming back and watching

Dan train three nights a week and play on Sunday, so I was still over at West Ham four times a week, even though I'd technically left the club. All the time there's me thinking, oh, I'll go and do something different, but I never got away from it. And it was only when Freddie, the youngest, came over to the club – Jimmy Hampshire, foundational coach, said, get him over on a Friday. I said, Jim, he's only *five*. He said, no, no, we've got kids a bit younger than that. So I said to my wife, I'm not sure. If he does go through the system, can we go another ten years of just standing and watching? And that's when I've had a chat with you. You were good enough to say, yeah, we'll get you involved and then you rang me up and said you wanted me to do the under-15s. I thought maybe you'd say, right, you can take the under-10s or whatever, but you put me straight in at quite a high age group, and before I knew it I was doing the 16s and quickly moved to the 18s, because Nick Haycock moved to the 23 group and then it just went on from there really.

**TONY:** So, you slowly got into it but it wasn't a plan as such?

**STEVE:** No, it wasn't a plan, but I'd got an open mind about everything; but then it really did grow on me, and I got involved and really enjoyed it.

**TONY:** Less pressure than playing but still involved in the game?

**STEVE:** Yeah, still involved. But as I say, I've really enjoyed my time coaching at West Ham, seeing the players come through.

**TONY:** So the turning point to take up coaching was essentially your two boys getting heavily involved at West Ham and with aspirations of being apprentices and possibly professionals.

**STEVE:** It was while watching the oldest one train and seeing the coaches putting sessions on and it took me back to my own playing days. I just fancied getting involved rather than standing on the touchline. I thought maybe I've got something to offer, but I don't know. Other people would know whether I had.

**TONY:** You're constantly learning, that's for sure. How long did the transition from playing to coaching take?

**STEVE:** I think maybe about six years?

**TONY:** Oh, right. It was as long as that? I didn't realise.

**STEVE:** Well, I'm thinking I'm 53 now ... yeah, about a six-year gap in between.

**TONY:** And how did you find the transition? All of a sudden you're not a parent any more, looking on, you're now the lead coach. How was your first session?

**STEVE:** Oh, the first session was a disaster ...

**TONY:** I bet you were a nervous wreck, weren't you?

**STEVE:** I think probably people on the outside would think, he's played a load of games and this will all come easy, but it certainly doesn't.

**TONY:** That's interesting to make that point.

COACHING FULL-TIME • 101

STEVE: Yeah, and I think ... any ex-player, if I had to speak to them, I would say, to start with, go and learn the ropes a bit before you take a job, because it is totally different. It looks simple from the outside, but it's not. I'd recommend getting involved with the academy, you know, whatever, even if it's a top player, go and take an academy group for a few years.

TONY: While you're still playing?

STEVE: While you're still playing, to gain the experience of doing sessions. What works and what doesn't.

TONY: Watching what goes on ...

STEVE: Yeah, because I do think as a player you just take it all for granted in the end.

TONY: You think, *I know the game* ...

STEVE: Yeah. Maybe you think you know it all, but ...

TONY: ... there's more to it.

STEVE: You've got to try to fathom out what works and what doesn't work, and that certainly is the case with some sessions you put on – you think, that worked well today, and others, no, no, I wouldn't do that again, or I'd tweak or change it or something.

TONY: I've had many a day like that ... And what's your goal for the future? Do you have one? Do you want to manage one day?

STEVE: Hmmm ... real open mind about that, Tony. I've never had real ambitions to manage, but by the same token, I probably wouldn't say no to it either. It's similar to when I got into coaching: I didn't have real ambitions to be a coach, but I like coaching and I used to say, if there *was* a chance, would I like managing? I don't know. Am I saying here, yeah, I want to manage? No, I'm not, but if the opportunity arose, I probably would give it a go. I'm not really putting myself out there, but if something came my way, then I would probably consider it, but I'm not looking around thinking, oh yeah, I'm going to go for that job or whatever.

TONY: In other words, it's something you'd consider if the opportunity arose.

STEVE: Yeah, if it came my way, a senior level coach, or whatever, yeah, you'd look at it, but I'm not openly looking for something like that, no.

TONY: Interesting. So, going back to what you just said about someone coming into coaching, at academy level say, in any division, what would your advice be?

STEVE: I think I'd change my ways ... I think with the young players I was a bit standoffish but now I think I've changed a bit and I'm working with them more. Maybe more encouraging, but in a serious way.

TONY: Getting to know them a bit better ...

STEVE: Yeah, but not light-heartedly. I think that works. I've noticed that works better for me. Again, I think it all comes down to experience, the more you can do, the more sessions you can put on, what game situations, like things that happen during games, what works, team talks, it all changes ...

TONY: Can you stand up in front of a group and deliver something?

STEVE: Yeah, sometimes it might be a real firm team talk, or you think I want a reaction from them; you've got to try to judge the situation, the mood of the boys. It's a real test of everything and something you'd know better than anyone. Sometimes you might go hard on a player just to get that bit of a reaction from them, or it might be to get a reaction from the team; it might be that things have not gone well, so do you go down the route of *not* going down that route and thinking, well, I'll encourage them and try and turn it round? I don't know ... there's no right or wrong, you've got to judge every situation on its merits ... and I think that's the beauty of it.

TONY: Yeah. I think by the way you've explained that – and it's difficult to put into words sometimes – is that it's not just about going out, delivering a session, coming in and finishing.

STEVE: No, not at all.

TONY: You know, you've got to analyse how it went ... and obviously today with those individual plans for players, as you say, you're getting to know each player.

STEVE: Yeah. And I think everything is covered now in this EPPP academy system: you know, they're getting the coaching obviously, they're getting the sports science, they're getting great medical treatment, they're getting psychology, everything's covered. But I think we've got to be careful that it's not covered so much that the boys are not thinking for themselves any more. Yeah, we'll use the great resources we've got, but ultimately it's got to come from the player and what they're all about. It can't be driven by all these other people, and then the players ...

TONY: They just get told what to do ...

STEVE: Yeah, told what to do, or there's nothing about them. I think it's a real balance with that, and I feel there's a real balance with how it used to be when there was nothing really, apart from the coach and a physio ...

TONY: And when you first started, we had to share the physio, because Rob Jenkins was the physio for everybody.

STEVE: Exactly. And you know, now, all the teams have got a physio. So there's so many resources available, but there's a balance where it could be too much, I think, and the players getting pampered to a certain degree.

TONY: So many ex-players have said that to me.

STEVE: Yeah, and I do think there's a, you know, it may be a society in general thing where there are different types of players; where I talk about Tony Adams or Paul Ince, you don't see many of them. That might be society in general, but from a football point of view, I think we've got to be careful of that, we really have.

**TONY:** Yeah, it's a very good point, because it's that balance between, where's the passion, where's *your* passion as an individual, where's *your* desire, how much do you want to be a pro, rather than having to rely on every other department to give you the answers.

**STEVE:** Yeah, yeah, exactly.

**TONY:** All you can do is show them the way and it's up to them, then.

**STEVE:** They can analyse all their games, they can analyse any football match, it's all there for them, but it's only as good if the boy or girl really wants to use it for themselves and really push themselves on to the next level, I think, rather than, 'here you are, watch this' and you know they're not really taking it in. If it comes from within ... You've just got to be wary of that, I think, and on top of that, as well, I think, the boys being in the system for so long, do they just become part of the furniture? The contrast is with what I described earlier – where you're striving to get in the district team, the London team, and every other opportunity to play. Now you're not striving really as such, you're in your age group, you're getting a certain amount of minutes every week, whether you're playing well or not. If you're under contract in the academy system, you'll get in X amount of minutes, and that's it. It is not how it was years ago where if you were not performing ...

**TONY:** You don't play.

**STEVE:** You simply don't play, even as a twelve-year-old, you're not in the team, you're a sub.

**TONY:** I think that balance has to be right in the sense that you do as much as you can for the individual but still you want that from them as well. What are *they* giving, what are *they* bringing to the party, really?

**STEVE:** Yeah, that's the real hard bit.

**TONY:** That's the tough bit.

**STEVE:** Rather than finding yourself having to drive the boys – you've got to do this, got to do that ... I mean we can all see what needs to be done, but, unless it comes from within – and there's no coincidence, I think we've just got to look at West Ham; the ones who have come through lately are the ones who've got that, you know ... Josh Cullen and Declan Rice are great examples. Ben Johnson is doing it ... they're at it every day, every single day.

**TONY:** Mark Noble, constantly, who's still here, in the twilight of his career. But what an inspiration ...

**STEVE:** The young boys don't have to look any further than the examples we've got at West Ham.

**TONY:** Exactly.

**STEVE:** The names we've mentioned.

**TONY:** OK, Steve, well, thank you very much.

**STEVE:** OK, Tone. It was good!

*

I was still walking to work along Chadwell Heath High Road and one day I noticed a man I thought I recognised sitting on a bench. He looked like a down-and-out, dishevelled, unshaven with a very dirty white raincoat tied at the waist. It came to me suddenly. This was Dick Walker – a former West Ham player who had played almost 300 games for the club and who later had become a scout for Tottenham Hotspur. I spoke to Ernie Gregory who had played with Walker in the 1940s and '50s. Ernie was very concerned and reeled off stories of how Walker was a very smart man and always immaculately dressed. This couldn't be the Dick Walker I know, thought Ernie. Unfortunately, it was. We discovered he had recently lost his wife and was suffering from memory loss and consequently had stopped looking after himself. Ernie alerted social services and help was given to Dick to help him cope with his problems. But it was so sad to see a top footballer, and in Ernie's words an always immaculately dressed and smart man, looking so utterly lost.

It was the early 1980s and over a cup of tea one day at the end of training we somehow got on to the subject of holidays. John Lyall said he was going to some foreign beach in the Mediterranean and asked where I was going. Well, I said, we planned to drive to Austria and stay in a small village just outside Innsbruck. A friend of mine had been and said it was a beautiful place, especially in the summer. As neither Brenda nor I were really sun worshippers, it really appealed to us. We had two young children and felt it would be good for them too: the mountains, the fresh alpine air and plenty of scenic walks. The problem, I told John, was that my car had recently been giving me a lot of trouble and I couldn't trust it on such a long journey. It was absolutely typical of John that he immediately said, 'If you go the same two weeks as me, you can borrow my car.' It was his club car – a Ford Granada automatic. I couldn't believe it, the manager of a top-flight football club loaning me his car for two weeks. That was John though. If he could help someone he would. I took him up on his offer and drove to Austria in style.

John liked to involve the coaching staff in all aspects of the club. He would send us home some days asking for us to think up a different warm-up for the following day's training or to design a new shirt for next season as we were changing kit suppliers! I used to sit on the first-team bench for home games, listening to the manager's instructions. I'd be in the dressing room at half-time and again at the end of games hearing John's summations – the good, the bad and the ugly. John was a generous, thoughtful guy, always thinking of others, but was a passionate manager and could get annoyed with his team when they under-performed. He would often remind his players not to mistake his innate kindness for weakness. He certainly had a tough side all right – and would let the players 'have it' if he felt it necessary. Regularly, after a poor performance, John would talk to the players for more than an hour. Why did we do this? Why didn't we do that? Or, we were not competitive enough today ... He would rarely highlight an individual's performance and held true to the 'We win together, we lose together' attitude. He used to say to the coaches, 'During press conferences, when we win I praise the team, but when we lose I take the criticism.' He always protected the players and this philosophy and integrity gained huge respect and loyalty from his players. I learnt so much from John's style.

After an FA Cup quarter-final tie at home to Aston Villa – we won 1-0 after a late Ray Stewart penalty – the dressing room was buzzing and John said casually to everyone, 'The press are going to ask whom we would prefer to play in the semi-final' – there were top teams left in – 'and I said, "We'll play any of them on their bad day."' I watched on in amusement as the question was predictably asked during the press conference and John said, 'Someone in the dressing room has just said, "We'll play any of them on their bad day, boss!"'

It turned out to be Everton and we beat them to reach Wembley after a replay. The replay had been at Elland Road, home of Leeds United, and the winning goal was scored by Frank Lampard Sr. We watched as he ran around the corner flag in delight after scoring. Many years later this feat was repeated when West Ham played Leeds United in a televised league game and Frank Lampard Jr scored in the same goal and repeated his father's celebration, running around the same corner flag. We played Arsenal in the final and a Trevor Brooking header secured a famous 1-0 win. We were a Second Division team at the time.

Once we were playing Watford at home and before kick-off John and I were in his little match-day office along the corridor from the dressing rooms, chatting about nothing in particular, when there came a knock at the door and in walked Elton John, who was the Watford chairman at the time. Apparently, he and John had become friends after John had sent Elton a goodwill message following Elton's mauling by the press over his private life. I got up and left them to their chat.

Another time, in December 1979, we were playing Nottingham Forest in the League Cup one midweek night and John asked if I would go to meet them and show them the quickest way to Upton Park. They were staying at the Bell Hotel in Epping. As I walked in, the players were just finishing their pre-match meal of scrambled eggs on toast. Peter Taylor, the Forest assistant manager, asked if

I would come on the coach in case I lost them in traffic leading in my car as had been my plan. I was happy to oblige. As the coach was about to leave there was still one person missing – Brian Clough. He didn't eat with the players and only got on the coach right on the designated leaving time. As we were travelling to the ground and got stuck in traffic, lots of fans would shout and barrack the Forest coach, at which point Cloughie said to the driver, 'Have we got a Nottingham Forest sign on the front of the coach?'

The driver replied, 'Yes, of course, boss.'

'Well take it down,' said Cloughie, 'and put a Notts County sign up. Nobody will want to know us then.'

When we got to Upton Park the car park attendant asked the driver if the coach was the players' or the directors' coach. Indignant, Brian Clough leant across the driver and said, 'This is the PLAYERS' coach and when the directors' coach turns up, don't let the b******* in!' The game ended 0-0 and we lost the subsequent replay.

John was always looking to improve players individually and would task the coaches to look at ways each individual player did things and whether he could be developed. Could he become better? Could he be taught something new? An example of John's approach to coaching and the detail he tried to go into was evident one Thursday morning when I was assisting him during a shooting practice. I was on the edge of the box setting up shots for the players. If a player missed the target, I said, 'Unlucky,' or 'Nearly.' John heard and rebuked me, saying, 'Don't comment on the outcome of the shot; coach the player on why he missed. Did he lift his head too early? Did he hook the shot instead of hitting through the centre of the ball? Coach what happened and try to improve the player with technical feedback.' This made me take notice of every pass, shot and piece of action from then on – and I'm sure it made me a better, more analytical coach.

Billy Bonds had told John that he was going to retire around this time and John had asked him to become youth team coach, moving me up to reserve-team manager. Ron Boyce and Mick McGiven would move up to first-team duties permanently and I would have sole responsibility for the reserve team. Billy was new to coaching and needed a little bit of guidance; he knew the game inside out but needed advice about simple organisational matters and getting his points across to young players. I used to coach the schoolboys in the sports hall in the evenings and Bill used to join in with the practices and watch the sessions just to see how I organised things. Bill was always very complimentary about the way I did things and was always very humble and respectful when we shared these evening coaching sessions. He was a little surprised by how much technical detail I used to give the young players: 'Move your feet here', 'Get on the half turn before you receive the ball', 'Head down and follow through', etc., etc. All very basic things but important.

I now had to deal with the reserve team and it was different to what I was used to. Youth team players are at the beginning of their football journey and are eager to please and to perform. With the reserves, you sometimes encountered a senior player who was not happy playing reserve-team football, so a different psychological approach was needed. It can be a tricky mix – on the one hand you have young players happy to be progressing into the reserves and on the other, diffident, unsettled senior players who are less than motivated. Tactically it's different to youth team games where there is more emphasis on individual performance and the result is almost meaningless. At reserve-team level, with more senior players, it's more about performing to win and ensuring players play with a desire and commitment – after all, it's only one step away from the first team. Most, if not all, got on with it and used it as one way of staying fit and sharp. It broadened my experience dealing with more senior players and I was happy to do it.

These days very few senior players play reserve-team football. It is called Premier League 2 and is an under-23 league mostly made up of nineteen- and twenty-year-olds. So it's really an extended youth league and is certainly not the stepping stone it used to be to first-team football. Another way must be found. A big step forward in this direction is that under-23 teams are now entered into the Papa John's Trophy playing against first teams from the lower divisions. I really believe that in the future the bigger teams will have B teams playing in the lower leagues as they do in Spain and other European countries. The advantages of this are fairly obvious: it means your young players are playing a competitive match with men each week in a league with similar pressures to their parent club's first team. Players need to be challenged and in my opinion, this is a far better way to challenge, prepare and develop young players than the present under-23 league. At present there is a lot of opposition to this suggestion, but in the long term I think there is a good chance it will happen.

Dealing with and developing young players is a difficult job, with the biggest problem facing youth academies being opportunity. Opportunity to play with senior players, either in the first team or on loan. As I said previously, the under-23 league does not prepare young players for first-team football. With a lot of clubs having split training sites, it takes young players even further away from the manager's eye. When I was coaching the West Ham youth team in the '60s, '70s, '80s and early '90s, all players trained at one site at Chadwell Heath and it was easy for the integration of players into the first-team environment. If the manager was short of a player or a player had to leave training because of injury, the manager would shout across and ask for a youth team player to be sent over, and this was their opportunity to show the manager what he was about. During my time as a young apprentice it was a regular occurrence that the youth team players were involved in first-team training, so it was easy for the manager to spot any emerging talent. My message was always: if you get the call to join in with first-team training, make sure you are ready. You may only get one chance, so get noticed!

This happened many times over the years, Ron or John integrating young players into first-team training, and a great example of this was when Harry Redknapp was manager and the youth team were training on an adjacent pitch next to the first team and one of their players had to pull out of training due to injury. Frank Lampard Sr came across and asked if I could send a midfield player over so I sent them a young Michael Carrick. This was around 1998. After training as we were walking in, Eyal Berkovic, our Israeli midfield player, came up to me and said, 'Who is this player you sent over?' I told him and he said, 'He is a good player and will take my place in the team one day.' Well, we all know the rest. I did not tell Michael this until many years later – I didn't want him to get carried away. This is just one example of what is lost at a lot of clubs today, including West Ham, who now have split sites, with the first team at Rush Green and the youth academy at Chadwell Heath and Little Heath.

This split-site strategy occurred first during Harry's time as manager in 2000. During one pre-season Frank Lampard Sr came to me and said that we were getting a bit short of space at Chadwell Heath and Harry wanted me to find somewhere for the youth team to train. I have to say I was a bit surprised and I went with Peter Brabrook, who was my coaching assistant, looking for places to train. We had no help from anybody at the club and went to places like the May and Baker sports ground in Dagenham, the Ford sports ground in Aldborough Road South, Ilford and ended up at Little Heath sports ground in Hainault Road. I thought this was a shabby way to push the youth team out of Chadwell Heath, with no help from anybody at the club, and at the very least we should have had a grown-up conversation about the alternatives for us. Little Heath was owned by the University of East London and we developed a good relationship with them. The pitches were very poor and the dressing rooms very basic, but we ended up buying the ground and I helped broker the deal. I think we paid around £350,000 for the site.

When we first used Little Heath, a team called Caribbean were using it, hiring it from the university. The pitches were being pre-pared by a volunteer groundsman who used to pull the springs of an old mattress up and down the pitch to even out the bumps and hollows! This was to be the home of the West Ham youth team after over 40 years at Chadwell Heath. It was disgraceful and I felt embar-rassed welcoming visiting teams there. They didn't take too kindly to the new home of the West Ham youth team and it took a few seasons to get it up to a respectable level. I am convinced that this had a really negative effect regarding the development and recruit-ment of young players. No young player would have been motivated or impressed by our new home but we had to get on with it and still produce players to progress into the first-team environment. Out of sight, out of mind! I never did find out if the lack of space was the driving reason for the youth team's removal from Chadwell Heath, but I suppose it would have happened anyway with the introduction of the Premier League's Elite Player Performance Plan and the expansion of the academy system.

One of the real enjoyments for the young players was to go on end-of-season or more frequently now pre-season overseas tournaments. One such trip in the early eighties saw us attend two under-19 tournaments back to back in Switzerland, the first being in Zurich for the Blue Stars Tournament. This is a tournament that goes back a long way – I even played in it for the West Ham youth team in the late sixties. Then it was on to Monthey, near Montreux. We played the tournament in Zurich and were going by coach the next morning to take part in the Monthey tournament. On our last night I allowed the boys a night out and set a curfew of 11.30 back at the hotel. I sat with our kit man, Stan Burke, in the hotel lobby counting the players back in, one by one. It got to about 11.45 and they were all back bar one, and to top it all it was our nineteen-year-old captain, Everald La Ronde. I was livid. Stan said to me, 'You go to bed and I will sit and wait here.' The players had said the last they saw of Ev, he was talking to a girl. It said it all. I went to bed and told Stan to let me know the moment he came back, no matter what time. Obviously, this was in the days before mobile phones. Well, I woke up at 8am the next morning and he still wasn't back and we were due to leave for Monthey at 11am. Most rooms had balconies overlooking the front of the hotel and at about 9.30 I heard a shout go up, 'He's back!' I immediately called him up to my room, read him the Riot Act and stripped him of the captaincy. I didn't need to know where he had been or any of the details. It was obvious what had been going on ... and if I could have sent him back to London, I would have. When we got back, I spoke to John Lyall and we fined Everald two weeks' wages, which was the maximum. This was the worst experience I have ever encountered when taking teams away to tournaments. It was quite worrying wondering where this boy was and what could have happened to him. I was responsible for the team and the consequences were huge if the player had had a mishap or worse. It is not an experience I would want to go through again. That was the last time I let players of any age go out unaccompanied.

John was always looking for new methods, always seeking gains and improvements in training. He brought in Angela Cannell. She was, I suppose, a sports scientist, although we didn't give her that title. She would watch training, warm-ups to full-scale matches and make comments on what she observed. She would point out players that looked fatigued and might become injured; she would also observe player behaviours and report things that the coaches may have missed, such as a player who constantly rubs his hamstring that could go at any moment. Many a time she would intervene in a subtle way to instruct John to pull a player out of training to avoid possible injury. She also brought in the requirement to hydrate during training, which was still unheard of. It's commonplace now. I can remember us having quite a serious debate about stopping training for a drinks break. The old view was that hydrating during training would give the players stomach cramps and would stop the continuity of training sessions, obviously all nonsense. I said to her that when I watched Wimbledon on TV, the players would drink during the breaks. What were they drinking? She said it was probably a supplement to boost energy called Isostar and she would like to introduce something similar with us – which she eventually did.

Angela was a keen hockey player so knew the energy and fitness levels required to play competitive sport. There are now many similar drinks on the market today, and the Premier League is sponsored by a Lucozade sports drink and you see it emblazoned all over the TV screens at every available opportunity. I found her very informative and she was probably one of the first, if not the first, 'sports scientists' to work in professional football. John had big ideas of how we could use Angela's expertise. He had plans to build a rehab unit and physio centre for the club and for outside organisations and players to use. It would be self-funding and would benefit the club's physiological and fitness regime at minimal cost. Of course, this all went out of the window when the club got relegated in 1989. John was sacked and Angela was forced to leave because of financial reasons but she left a lasting legacy in the way players trained and hydrated.

At the end of the 1980s things with the first team started to go wrong; after finishing third in the top flight in the 1985/86 season, the club failed to capitalise on this success. McAvennie (1987) and Cottee (1988) were sold to Celtic and Everton respectively and their replacements were not of the same goalscoring standard. Other signings were of average standard and after a couple of poor seasons finishing just above the relegation places, the inevitable happened. Lack of investment, poor form and performance led to relegation and John Lyall was sacked. Even a deadline-day (March 1989) signing of a returning Frank McAvennie from Celtic backfired when he got injured in his first game with us after a crunching tackle from Chris Kamara of Stoke City.

The sacking did not happen immediately. There was no knee-jerk reaction from the board, and in fact it was not until June, well into the summer. John, Ron Boyce, Mick McGiven and I were sitting at the training ground finalising pre-season training preparations and matches. The phone in the office rang and I got up to answer it. I answered, 'West Ham training ground,' and the voice at the other end said, 'Mr Len here (Len Cearns, chairman). Can I speak to John?' I said I would get him. John came back to the canteen and said the chairman wants to have a chat at his house in Chigwell. He left and we waited for him to return. About an hour or so later John returned and called us into his office. His demeanour had changed and it was obvious something was up. He said, 'I have spoken to the chairman and the board have decided not to renew my contract (his previous contract had come to an end).' We were all stunned, and after a few minutes John got up and said, 'That's it.' He got into his car and drove home.

In all my time at West Ham this ranks as the saddest day of my career. I owed everything to John and now this was the end of an era. John had been West Ham's most successful manager and basically ran the club from top to bottom and for it to end like it did was heart-breaking, even allowing for the fact that we had been relegated. John wrote me a lovely letter thanking me for my loyalty over the years, saying that I had the potential to become a very capable coach and not to be afraid to give management a try if that's what I wanted to do. The letter read:

7 July 1989

Dear Tony,

I am pleased things appear to be settled for the future. I am sure you must have been very concerned. It would be wrong of me not to write and thank you for your efforts and loyalty over the years. I do believe you are very capable and if you want to go all the way don't be concerned about trying. Whatever you decide for yourself I wish you every success and happiness.

Kind Regards, John Lyall

It gave me a lot of confidence. Once again it was typical of John to be thinking of others when he had just been put out of work. The club had decided to go in a different direction and with a new manager. It wouldn't work out quite as they had planned.

*

Recently, I spoke to Michael Carrick, who was a first-team coach at Manchester United, when they came to London to play a Premier League match. I thought it would be a good opportunity to ask him about his journey from the North East as a youngster to London and eventually settling in Manchester with his wife Lisa and young family.

**TONY:** What are your earliest memories of playing football?

**MICHAEL:** My first vivid memory really was when I was about four and a half and my dad and my grandad took me along to Wallsend Boys Club on a Saturday evening. It was like an all-comers night where you could just turn up and have a game, from about six years old to nine. I was only four when my dad and grandad took me. I still remember that because I cried before I went on to the pitch; it was a bit daunting for me. I had a little cry and they reassured me and encouraged me.

Then once I was on, I was off and away. I have quite a strong memory of that.

**TONY:** At what sort of age did you feel, *I'm not bad at this game? I'm quite comfortable with this*? And you felt you were as good as your age group or perhaps even better? Or did that not really enter your head at such an early stage?

**MICHAEL:** I think probably subconsciously – I'm quite quiet and reserved anyway, but I think probably I knew deep down I'm not bad at this. I was always one of the better ones, not necessarily the best but one of the better ones.

**TONY:** What age was that would you say?

**MICHAEL:** I went training at Middlesbrough when I was nine, so for that, maybe I was eight years old when I thought I was one of the better ones.

**TONY:** Obviously you are playing with players with like-for-like ability.

**MICHAEL:** Some lads were at Newcastle, some lads were at Middlesbrough at that boys' club at the time. So you get an idea. I didn't think I was the best, but I was decent enough.

**TONY:** And once you fall in love with the game, because you are good at it ...

**MICHAEL:** It works both ways, doesn't it? You get that because you enjoy it, you want to practise a bit more and all of a sudden you improve a lot quicker because you are enjoying it and then it just rolls on from there.

**TONY:** When did you feel that this could lead to something, or maybe even a career in the game?

**MICHAEL:** I don't feel there was a time. I started going to Middlesbrough when I was nine, going to West Ham when I was thirteen and then in between that I had gone to Newcastle and a few other clubs to look about. It was always what I wanted to do. Being an actual footballer at that stage seems worlds away really. If you asked me then, that was my dream.

**TONY:** So, you were dreaming of becoming a player, but not in a serious way?

**MICHAEL:** Serious in the fact that clubs were showing an interest. So you weren't just playing around for fun at that stage. There was a kind of, you have got to decide whether you are going to sign for this club or that club, so there was a serious element to it.

**TONY:** How did the move to West Ham come about? Obviously Dave Mooney was instrumental in it ...

**MICHAEL:** Dave Mooney and Bill Gibbs at the time were the two scouts in Newcastle. Because of playing for Wallsend Boys Club there were loads of scouts, like Senrab in East London. You get lots of scouts because everyone expects the better players to be there. They took me down to West Ham when I was thirteen with about five or six other lads, as a 'come and have a look'. A bit of a trial. You have a look at me, and I will have a look at the club type of thing. I remember Brian Nichols was the under-14s coach at the time. Jimmy Hampson picked me up from King's Cross Station and for two, three or four days looked after us. I just instantly felt comfortable. I had gone to other clubs, felt a bit uncomfortable and out of my depth a bit, not ready for it. But at West Ham straight away I just felt comfortable. That was the biggest thing.

**TONY:** A lot of players I have spoken to over the years, Joe Cole for example, were exactly the same. He said he just felt comfortable there ...

**MICHAEL:** It was the environment that you created as a group. Coming from you and Jimmy (Hampson) and all the coaches below that. The backroom staff, the kit men and everything – it was just a nice atmosphere. Jimmy Frith, Stan Burke, Peter Williams, Eddie Gillam, everyone comes into it to create that. It wasn't just me, it was my dad; he felt comfortable, not that he influenced me but that was a massive part of it.

**TONY:** That was the aim, that we always tried to create an environment where people could walk into the building feeling comfortable and not feeling intimidated.

**MICHAEL:** It was a smile as well; that was the biggest thing for me. I went to Chelsea – I say it in my book about going to Chelsea – I was treated in some ways like, I don't know, it was kind of straight and stiff. And my mum wasn't really treated great. That's the feeling it gives you. But at West Ham there was always that smile and welcoming me as part of the family; go and enjoy yourself, you'll have a great time here. It goes a long way.

**TONY:** What did you learn as an academy player that stood you in good stead, or was it just a matter of a process where you had the basic ability, the basic skills, and it was about developing year on year? Or was there anything that you think stands out?

**MICHAEL:** I think the development was the toughening up for me. I was quite young, maybe not immature, but I just felt I was a little bit intimidated. I'm a young birthday, at the end of July (youth age groups start in September through to August), so I always felt I was behind in some ways, socially maybe more than ... football-wise I felt on a level but some of the other lads seemed more grown-up than me and knew more than me.

**TONY:** Did you find the London boys a bit more streetwise?

**MICHAEL:** A bit more streetwise. They knew more about the world than we did in the North East growing up. There was more for them to know about down here. That was a big part of it, the lads and the group I came into. Other clubs I was going to, I was an outsider and they did not want me in, but the boys at West Ham, I felt part of it. It was a brilliant group. I was fourteen coming down sometimes and I trained with the youth team: Lee Hodges, Joe Keith, Lamps (Lampard). At the time they made me feel comfortable even though I was not at their level yet and I was training with them, a skinny lad from the North East.

**TONY:** Once they saw you play, you get that respect ...

**MICHAEL:** You probably get that respect, yeah you do. Even around the changing room, they did not belittle me, there was none of that. I just felt really comfortable. It is quite a big age gap from fourteen to sixteen, seventeen and eighteen. Again, that was part of it. I could see two, three, four years ahead and I enjoyed that.

**TONY:** A big part of Rio's and Frank's development was from a very young age they got pushed on very quickly and were basically playing with men at around seventeen.

**MICHAEL:** Going back to what I learned, for me, going away and growing up was a big part of it. Getting out of my comfort zone, even coming down between ages fourteen and sixteen during the school holidays and training with the youth team for a bit. I was pushed all the time and you get tested. Could I cope? For me, that was a big thing. Not technically or anything, just growing up and being tested in a different environment. Learning how to deal with the challenges. I think that was the big thing. Even in training, I remember doing the mile on Monday mornings. That sticks in my head. And full-time training with the youth team when I was not old enough to do it; it's a test. You are thrown in there and you have to find a way to deal with it. Obviously, listen, all your coaching through that time was massive. Rio and I always talked about third man runs. There was that discipline. There was doing your jobs, getting your jobs right. It wasn't necessarily just the football, as there was so much more to it than that. Living in Barking in digs, worlds apart from where I was used to. That was all part of the development.

**TONY:** Who were the managers and players in the first team when you first came down?

**MICHAEL:** Harry was the manager, and it was people like Ian Bishop, Trevor Morley, Steve Jones, Kenny Brown, Keith Rowland, Dicksy (Julian Dicks). I'm looking at when I was thirteen or fourteen – 1994 probably. Slaven Bilić might have also been there.

**TONY:** Did I ever tell you the story of Eyal Berkovic regarding taking his place in the team?

**MICHAEL:** Yeah, I remember you told me that. It's in my book actually. But you didn't tell me for a while. That is a skill in itself, because you don't need to be telling me that then. Talking about the younger lads getting ahead of themselves, it's quite a nice story.

**TONY:** How does a Tyne and Wear lad and a boyhood fan of Newcastle feel about playing against them? Do you still hold a candle for them?

**MICHAEL:** I was a Newcastle fan as a kid. My dad took me when I was really young, on the terraces and stuff. He was a massive Newcastle fan before I came along. And then as my football took over, he went less and less. But once I moved away I kind of drifted away from that fan-type feeling.

**TONY:** I remember you telling me many years ago that you enjoyed coming down to the south because you felt a little bit pressurised in the North East with all your pals and everyone supporting Newcastle.

**MICHAEL:** Moving away helped me. I had my mates like Richard Garcia moving from Australia the same day as me. I was in digs with Grant McCann (who until recently was manager of Hull City). I only met them because we were there to do that job, and there were no distractions for me then. We found a few distractions along the way at times but there were no mates going, 'Come out for a drink,' because we were all there doing the same thing. And there was not the pressure from people outside constantly wanting stuff. So it was a big part of it.

**TONY:** When not involved professionally, especially when you get injured, do you watch football? Do you like football? Or do you, like some players, say it is their profession but they do not really watch the game?

**MICHAEL:** I had spells in the early days when I'd watch any-thing and everything. As I kind of got older, towards the end of my career, I'd watch a bit less football because I'd be with the kids and feel like sometimes you just need an escape and relief from it all. When you are injured it's hard to watch. I would watch but it's tough to watch as you feel detached from it. As time went on, I was probably picking and choosing what I watched. In some ways, I preferred to watch other sports like golf to just kind of give my mind a bit of a rest.

**TONY:** As a player do you understand the fans' obsession with football?

**MICHAEL:** Yeah, it's their life. I always go back to what I was like as a kid, standing on the terraces at Newcastle, idolising Peter Beardsley or Paul Gascoigne or whoever it was. That is the feeling you go back to. It is a job and your livelihood, so there are times when, because it is what you do, you do have to have a little moment and think, if there are kids going mad for an autograph or a photo and you have just been beaten, there is a time when you pull yourself together and you have to do it. That is when I have little flashbacks to when I was eight or nine. I would have been doing exactly the same and that would mean a lot to me. There is that feeling, where you think that would have been me one day.

TONY: In some ways the platitudes are over the top when you have done well and win. And the criticisms are over the top when things are not going so well. How do feel about that?

MICHAEL: It's the extremes. That's always the test that I've found. The biggest one as a player, especially coming to United even more than before, was managing yourself and managing your own mindset of the ups and downs along the way. Fans or pundits, the extremes, you go from the best in the world to the worst team in the world. That's something you have to deal with as a player and be oblivious to and get on with your job.

TONY: You are climbing the ladder of success but sometimes you fall off ...

MICHAEL: You fall and sometimes you fall a good few steps. It was like when we got relegated at West Ham and playing for a year down in the Championship. It's something you have got to deal with and find a way of getting over it.

TONY: Crossing the white line, what does it feel like running out in front of 70,000 screaming fans on a Saturday afternoon? Once the whistle goes, how do the emotions change?

**MICHAEL:** You never lose that feeling of anticipation before a game. You learn to deal with it differently. Obviously comparing the first five games of my career and my last five games I would have been emotionally different going into the game. But sitting in the changing room, that anticipation stays with you.

**TONY:** Did you always get butterflies?

**MICHAEL:** I wasn't one for getting nervous so much. It's that waiting for something to happen, knowing you are going out there to perform. There is the pressure that comes with it that you try to block out, but it is there. You always get that excitement but I think probably the energy and enthusiasm when you are younger, you guide it a bit more when you are older. It's experience, isn't it?

**TONY:** Mentally, do you block out the fans?

**MICHAEL:** For me, I used them how I needed them to be used. If it's a big game and the fans are behind you, and the atmosphere, you go with it a bit and you manage it that way. If you play away from home and the fans are on your back, then you manage that as a motivation to think, *I'm going to enjoy this because they are all against us* and it motivates you more. If the ground is quiet or the atmosphere is dead, then you have to find a way of switching yourself on and motivating yourself. The odd negative shout wouldn't really affect you. If someone is on your back, you just use the emotion of the game to bring out the best in yourself.

**TONY:** You have played various positions, but how did you feel when the gaffer says, 'Mike, I want you to play at centre back today?'

**MICHAEL:** Until the youth team really, I was more of a striker, until you got your hands on me and moved me back when I was not scoring enough goals probably! I played a deeper role after that.

**TONY:** You played deeper, more of a holding role.

**MICHAEL:** Even before that in my first year as a scholar, Craig Etherington and Grant McCann played as two central midfielders and then me as a kind of No. 10 behind the two strikers. We played 5-3-2 or a 3-5-2.

**TONY:** Did you have a different mindset when you played at centre back?

**MICHAEL:** I always enjoyed the challenge. In some ways it was a lot easier because you see the whole game in front of you. And it's a lot easier when you are on the ball because you're not having to play 360, you're playing everything in front. But then at times I felt more vulnerable when you're defending, because you're the last man or you're running one on one down the channel, or the ball comes over the top and if you don't make it, it's a chance for the opposition. Whereas as a midfielder, you do not feel it is last-ditch. And you're constantly in the game as a midfielder. As a defender, you are out of the game or it's all on and you cannot make a mistake. Midfield, you can get away with making little mistakes in a game because there is so much going on around you it doesn't affect the game. As a centre back if you make one mistake or misjudgement, the chances are it is either a great chance or a goal. I always enjoyed that; I found a new challenge re-energising, like playing centre back. It wouldn't be one I wanted to play every week, but I did enjoy that different position, to kind of learn as well.

**TONY:** But you are learning at the highest level.

**MICHAEL:** Yeah, you're learning where there is no hiding place. I wouldn't have done it in training that much. It was only a case of literally in an emergency when needed. And you kind of learn to adapt.

**TONY:** What was your greatest moment on the pitch? When it all came together?

**MICHAEL:** Sometimes in myself, I've had a game where I feel like everything has come off and you feel at ease, in control. Everything is happening in slow motion and it's clear in your head; it's not necessarily the biggest win, it's just the games you feel content almost. That's not necessarily the games where everyone else will think, 'he was brilliant today'. But the things you wanted to do you have done. It is weird; it is just that clarity in your mind. You see things clearly.

**TONY:** Is there any particular game you can think of?

**MICHAEL:** The one game that sticks out in my mind was when Manchester United played Schalke away in the semi-final of the Champions League. We won 2-0 but it should have been more. That was a game where I just felt totally at ease. Not at ease where you take your foot off the pedal, but at ease mentally and physically. You read that pass early so you are in position and aren't chasing, or the pass was just the right pass. It is a magical place to be in. Even through some of my best seasons when I was playing well, I wouldn't have that feeling very often. You just wish you could get that feeling a bit more often.

**TONY:** And the opposite of that, what was the worst moment?

**MICHAEL:** The worst one for me was the Champions League final against Barcelona in 2009. That was the other way, where you feel like losing control. We lost 2-0 in Rome and you feel like you're losing control and the game is slipping away from you. You're talking about one of the best teams of all time. It's a horrible feeling to think that you're trying different things and you just cannot get hold of the ball and you haven't got the answers. You're reading that pass and you get there, but all of a sudden that pass is gone and you're too late and it's a struggle, a frustrating feeling. That was one of the biggest games as well, so to have that feeling in a big game was hard to take.

**TONY:** Captaincy – what did it feel like when you were captain? Did you feel extra responsibility? Did you relish it?

**MICHAEL:** Yeah, I did. I really enjoyed it actually. You know you see some younger players in the team quite early and you say they're a natural captain, but I don't think I was a natural captain, especially in my younger days. But towards the end at United I did enjoy that responsibility. I had seen the evolution of the players coming to the end of their careers and how they had adapted – Gary Neville, Paul Scholes, Ryan Giggs – and you actually think, well I'm one of the oldest in the changing room and it's my responsibility.

**TONY:** How did you do that?

**MICHAEL:** I think the important thing is to be yourself, but obviously still knowing what needs saying. I was probably more for looking out for the younger lads if anything, to try and speak to them and give them bits of advice, just little bits. That was more me trying to do things more by example, training well, looking after myself, rather than shouting or screaming. Because that's not really my style and if you suddenly change because you are captain now and start hammering players, you'll lose that respect. It's a balance that you've got to keep.

**TONY:** The role of captain in the dressing room, when things go well and when they go badly ...

**MICHAEL:** When it's going well, then it's easy. You don't have to do or say much. Just try to keep it bubbling. It's like a manager – when things are going well you just try to keep it bubbling along. Obviously when it's not going so well, that's when – it's like any player – you see people's real character and how they deal with it. Are they part of the team or are they not? Are they actually in it for themselves? That's certainly what I've found. The hard times find people out really and that's when you really know what you've got. And you find out about yourself. All the tough times that I've had are the times I've learned the most. The best times do not come easy, but it becomes easy mentally because you are winning. It's when you are having a tough time, that's when, as an individual, I've learned the most about myself, my teammates and the managers. And as a captain you have to try and deal with all these factors and try to set a good example and say the right things to your teammates.

TONY: Which players inspired you, and how and why?

MICHAEL: Early days, I would say Peter Beardsley or Paul Gascoigne were the ones who I looked at and admired. Just their style. Beardsley probably doesn't get the credit or get talked about for how good he was. He was an incredible footballer. With Gascoigne, it was the entertainment factor and his quality was scary at times. In a funny way, even in the West Ham days, even Lamps (Lampard) and Lee Hodges in the youth team because they were three, four years older and the pathway they were on is where you are thinking, *I want to be like them and where they are.*

TONY: They set good examples ...

MICHAEL: Lamps especially, the way he worked. Being in the gym and seeing Lamps, I used him as inspiration really.

TONY: Frank, in his autobiography, said he found youth team training a bit tedious. It was probably a bit easy and not challenging enough, and he needed to push on. He mentioned that most afternoons another young player called Martin Mullen would ask him to come up to the snooker hall and Frank wanted to do extra training in the afternoons and he said Martin would ridicule him for it.

**MICHAEL:** Mullen was the shining light at the time and great things were expected of him.

**TONY:** We all felt he had great ability but he did not have a great attitude to hard work.

**MICHAEL:** That is the difference. At that time, when the lads were talking, we were saying what a player he was. But obviously he didn't have the desire to become better. So you have that inspiration. Lee Hodges at the time was a great player but had many problems with injuries. After that, playing with Scholesy (Paul Scholes) was the highlight of my career to be honest. Just seeing him every day and learning from him every day. We had a good understanding on the pitch as well. There are other top, top players but playing with Scholesy, learning from him and having that relationship with him on the pitch, suiting each other's games, that goes a long way. And, to be honest, Rio. Even though he is only three years older, we had similar career paths. He was always one as time has gone on you looked to, because he was always that step ahead.

**TONY:** How did you find training at West Ham compares to a team like Manchester United where the expectation is to win titles?

**MICHAEL:** It was a massive jump, yeah. Going from West Ham, after losing the Championship play-off final, to Tottenham, I had two years there and we finished fifth on the last game of the season, so we were a good team. But then I went to United and it was an eye-opener to the levels, the culture, the training

COACHING FULL-TIME • 135

standards, the players' attitudes; everything was just a step up. That is when I realised; this is what it is like at the top. This is why they are who they are. That was inspirational as well because it challenged me to be like that. But it was a massive jump, probably bigger than I imagined.

**TONY:** Was Alex Ferguson the instigator?

**MICHAEL:** He was the instigator, yeah. He didn't let standards drop. Because he had been there so long, he obviously had the lads under him who were almost his lieutenants: Giggsy (Ryan Giggs), Scholesy, Neville (Gary) and Rio were there. Then you have got the lads like Wes Brown, Darren Fletcher and John O'Shea who had been through the ranks. So the mould was there. The manager just sat on top and came in when he had to. It was set. That is what stability brings.

**TONY:** I was at a Premier League conference in Manchester recently. Ryan Giggs spoke and said, 'Every day at United we used to kick lumps out of each other, but once you walked back into the dressing room, we were all mates again.'

**MICHAEL:** It was relentless, the desire from them to win every single day in training. Gary Neville said to me once when we were walking off the pitch – we used to do a fifteen-minute 10 v 10 on a smallish pitch the day before a game and that was it – he came off and said, 'That game is going to be harder than the Premier League game tomorrow.' And he was right. It was such a challenge because the standards were so high. You would go out the next day to play and it would almost be easy. This told the whole story.

**TONY:** What defines the Premier League?

**MICHAEL:** It's the excitement, I think. That's what it comes down to. The competitiveness and the excitement it brings. You could argue that technically or the skill factor in leagues like Spain are better, but for sheer endeavour and entertainment, as well as skill, the Premier League has just got that X factor, that something that attracts you even when the big teams are not playing.

**TONY:** Did you find as a player that as the Premier League developed and got quicker and technically better, as standards were raised and players were better physically developed and stronger, that it helped your game?

**MICHAEL:** It actually made the game a lot cleaner. The things that would go on when I first got in the team to towards the end; it was so much more sterile. Even the verbals you used to get from the old-school characters – that went out of the game as well. It was more technical, but ferocious and physical the speed and tempo of it. So from the start of my career to the end, the difference in the football was massive.

**TONY:** How did you feel you coped with that? Because if it got more technical that would suit you.

**MICHAEL:** It suited me. Obviously towards the end when you are getting a bit older, the game is getting quicker and you are getting slower, so it doesn't quite add up! But I'll be honest though, there is something about it I did like. I am not naturally that type of person, but I remember Patrick Vieira in one of my first games at Highbury, and you are having a right battle and have got each other's shirt, face to face. There is that fighting your territory, fighting that war, winning the battles. That battle now is different to what it used to be. Dennis Wise, you have got him pinching you, nipping you, standing on your toes, giving you verbals and trying to put you off and intimidate you as a young kid. Whereas I don't see that any more; that type of intimidation is of a totally different ilk.

TONY: Glory, dominance in the league, the FA Cup, the Champions League, playing for England, which is the most important and satisfying and why?

MICHAEL: From my experience, my best thing was winning the Champions League in Moscow against Chelsea when we won on penalties. That topped everything else for me. That was by far my number one. Funnily enough though, the year after was the biggest disappointment against Barcelona. That was the extremes from year to year. The Champions League, the sheer emotion, buzz and sense of achievement.

TONY: The Champions League is so tough to win ...

MICHAEL: It's the history and prestige and how tough it is to win.

TONY: Was that a better feeling than winning your first cap for England?

MICHAEL: Different, it was very different. It wasn't quite the buzz and excitement, it was the inner satisfaction, being proud with Mum and Dad there. It is more sentimental, whereas the

Champions League was more of a team effort, and the buzz of winning it on penalties. And you are getting your hands on that famous trophy. It was a totally different feeling. That is why it tops it for me.

**TONY:** All the managers you have worked for. What distinguishes the great from the good?

**MICHAEL:** There are so many things that go into it. It is tough. The thing about me going into coaching or managing later, whatever I do now, is that I have had the experience, from Harry Redknapp to Glenn Roeder, Trevor Brooking for a bit, Alan Pardew, Santini for a few months, Martin Jol, Sir Alex, David Moyes, Louis van Gaal, José Mourinho and Ole Gunnar Solskjaer. Not forgetting England managers Capello and Eriksson. There is such a wide range and some of them are up there with some of the best managers in the last 30 to 40 years. For me, Sir Alex was the biggest influence. Mourinho, obviously I only had right at the end. I was too old really for him to have that influence. Sir Alex just had that knack of getting the best out of players and doing the right thing at the right time, with individuals. That was the difference; he could treat every player as an individual at the same time as keeping the collective spirit as good as it could possibly be. He had that knack for me personally, of giving me a dig in the ribs when I needed it. But then giving an arm round the shoulder another time.

**TONY:** It is no surprise that Sir Alex has been one of the best you have worked with ...

MICHAEL: One of the examples ... He pulled me up one day, put his arm around me as we were walking off the 10 v 10 pitch the day before a Premier League game. We had played a game a couple of days before, in midweek. He said to me, 'That was your best performance of the season, that one.' Because I hadn't really been playing that well, I was thinking *Brilliant*. Then the next day, 'I'm resting you today.' So it was that management of, 'Well done, son, you're doing brilliant; you're on the bench tomorrow.' Even though he said he was resting me, I still felt ten feet tall. It wasn't as if I was walking out with my chin on the floor. I was like, 'Thanks, boss!' That is the magic of it.

TONY: Has your transition from player to coach been easy? What did you need to know when stepping from your playing kit into your tracksuit?

MICHAEL: The biggest thing for me was my last season of having the heart problem and not playing much. I was weaned off playing and I'd almost had enough of playing really. So I was ready to finish. I think that was the biggest thing: that I was ready to finish. To this day now, not one day has passed where I think *I wish I was still playing*. I have not missed it one bit, not even joining in training.

TONY: Was that because of your heart problem?

MICHAEL: No, it was just ... I was out for a bit with that, then I came back, and because I came back for a while and was 36 at the time I never really got back. And I knew I was finishing at the end of the season. I thought, *if I get two or three games left towards the end of the season, as long as I am going out on my terms then I'll be happy*. I was just coming to the time when enough was enough. So I've accepted that, which I think makes it easier. So I'm going in now fresh. It feels quite natural. The tricky bit now is dealing with players.

**TONY:** The players who were your mates ...

**MICHAEL:** But even that, because I am comfortable doing it, it's easier for me to get the balance. Towards the end of my playing career I was thinking more towards the coaching side anyway and I wasn't playing a lot, so there was a natural distancing of myself from being in the team. So that helped as well.

**TONY:** Which players could have been great, but ...

**MICHAEL:** Ravel Morrison is probably the obvious one, there are loads of names – you've probably got loads of names yourself.

**TONY:** Bertie Brayley, Adam Newton?

**MICHAEL:** Yeah, both talented, but you sometimes just need that break. Izzy (Iriekpen) with his knees that were a problem. There are all sorts of reasons players fail to fulfil their potential. I've written about Izzy in my book, when he was on the bench at sixteen for West Ham at Old Trafford and he could have gone on and become the youngest ever player to play in the Premier League. In the last few minutes he got the call to go on but he wasn't ready – he didn't have his shin pads on or his shirt on. It passed him by and the game ended and he never got on the pitch. A few years later he left West Ham having never played for the first team. It was a crossroads for him as his time never came again. And you think, that is a crossroads moment in someone's career and it could have gone either way. But yeah, Ravel was probably the one that sticks out. He had so much going on that he couldn't get it right. He was so talented that when he trained with the first team, he sometimes ran the show, amongst some world-class players.

**TONY:** Thanks, Michael.

# 7

## A NEW DIRECTION

After John's sacking, I was obviously left wondering about my own future. A new manager will generally come in and bring their own staff – and sack the present lot, including me! I was now managing the reserves, Billy Bonds was youth team coach, and Mick McGiven and Ron Boyce were with the first team. I applied for the manager's job and got an interview in front of the board. I have to say they looked as nervous as I was. They asked me how I would rearrange the staff, then Martin Cearns (vice chairman) asked me how I would deal with Frank McAvennie if he asked for another pay rise. My answers were: I would ask Billy Bonds to be my assistant; Mick McGiven would be asked to be reserve-team manager and Ron Boyce would be asked to be chief scout; the youth team job would be left open and we would discuss a suitable replacement for Bill. As regards to the McAvennie question, my reply was that he had only recently signed a contract and it would be out of the question to revisit it in the near future. Especially just after relegation.

I went on holiday with the family, in the course of which I got a phone call from Eddie Baily telling me a new manager would be announced later in the week and he wanted to meet all the coaching staff, which told me I hadn't got the job! Clearly the board wanted to go in a different direction. Lou Macari was announced as manager a few days later. This was the first time the club had not appointed from within – a complete departure from the Fenton, Greenwood and Lyall eras. The board was obviously looking for a new approach, a new style and philosophy. To be fair, Lou was as good as gold to the staff; he didn't bring any coaching staff with him and left Ron and Mick (first-team coaches) to get on with the day-to-day training. Bill and I carried on as usual and not much changed with the youth team under Bill and me with the reserve squad.

Lou's only real concern was with trying to get the first team back into the top division. I always felt Lou's main strength was his eye for a player. He brought in Luděk Mikloško, Trevor Morley, Ian Bishop and Martin Allen, and all these players gave great service to West Ham. In fact, Lou asked me to go with him when he met Martin Allen to try to convince him to sign for the club. We all met in a hotel near Reading and, without any warning, Lou asked me to give Martin a quick rundown on the club and how the bonus scheme worked. I didn't really know about the latter and said something along the lines of, 'It all depends on the team's league position – the higher you are in the league, the bigger the win bonus is.' Luckily – I had absolutely no idea about the exact figures – it seemed to deal with the issue. We must have been convincing as Martin signed a few days later. I was trying to support Lou whenever I could and at times he would confide in me about different aspects of the club.

Lou's biggest challenge was winning over the senior established players – Tony Gale, Alan Devonshire, Frank McAvennie, Mark Ward, Liam Brady, Paul Ince, Phil Parkes, Julian Dicks and the others. They were all John Lyall signings and, understandably, in their hearts remained fiercely loyal to John and his management style. They did not see eye to eye with Lou. Where previously training had been tactically and technically based, Lou's was largely based on fitness and diet; he was verging on paranoid about what players ate or drank. I'm not saying one way was right and the other was wrong, but Lou had trouble winning over this group of players who he felt were not fit enough. For my part, it wasn't about fitness – it was about gaining the players' respect. Whoever succeeded John would have had the same problem. A different approach was needed but not one that constantly antagonised the players. None of this is an indictment of Lou; he was more than capable of recognising where the problems lay, but he needed to introduce a more subtle, longer-term process that would have given him the time to slowly rectify what he felt needed changing.

It was Saturday night and I was at home when the phone rang. It was Lou.

'What are you doing tomorrow?' he asked.

'Nothing,' I said.

'Well, meet me at the Swallow Hotel at Waltham Abbey (now the Marriott) at 8am. We are going to Denmark, scouting.'

*Why was chief scout Eddie Baily not going?* I wondered.

Lou said he had asked him but Eddie had point-blank refused, saying it would be a waste of his time. I found this an astonishing thing for the most senior scout at the club to say to the manager. I'm sure Eddie would never have spoken to John Lyall like that. But then, it was also typical of Eddie's 'don't beat about the bush and say what you think' personality. So off we went to Denmark with an agent in tow called Tommy Lawrence. We arrived in Copenhagen and were driven to an afternoon game at Lyngby FC where we were to watch a striker, who we both agreed later was not what we were looking for. In the evening we went to watch Brøndby FC.

During the game, and without any formal information from the club about the players on the pitch, Lou turned to me and said, 'What do you think of their goalkeeper?'

Here I was thinking we'd travelled to look at strikers so, in my surprise, said, 'He looks the part. Big, imposing and has done little wrong up to this point.'

Lou replied, 'Not sure about him ... throws the ball out too much for me.'

The goalkeeper was Peter Schmeichel who two years later signed for Manchester United and, as they say, the rest is history. Peter Schmeichel, goalkeeping legend who threw the ball out too much ...

To be fair, Lou signed Czech keeper Luděk Mikloško who would go on to play 300 times for the club and in the process gain his own legendary status at West Ham, most memorably when he almost single-handedly stopped Manchester United from winning the league with a stunning performance in the last game of the 1995 season at Upton Park.

As Lou had been appointed in July, the pre-season schedules and matches were already organised and a first-team tour to Norway had been programmed that included games in Tromsø, Narvik (or Áhkanjárga as it is also known) and Kirkenes – which, for those of you who aren't familiar with it, is a small town in the north-east of Norway, right on the Russian border and inside the Arctic Circle ... There would be, as you can imagine, a lot of travelling involved and Lou asked all the coaching staff to go, except Billy Bonds who stayed behind to work with the youth team. It was a good opportunity for

A schoolboy at St Paul's Way School where I played my first organised team game of football. The picture was taken in 1965/66.

*Private collection of the author*

A pleasing memory, a hat-trick that put East London in the final of the English Schools' Trophy.

*Private collection of the author*

East London team with the English Schools' Trophy. The picture was taken at Daneford School, Bethnal Green. Players: back row, L to R: John Hanning, Billy Gardner, Brian Busby, Micky Spinks, Steve Bowtell, Stephen Moody, John Scanlan; front row: Bill Bailey, Pat Holland, Kevin Smith, Tony Carr, (Mr Cormode), Malcolm Jeffrey, John Brewer. The two men on the right are Mr Hurley and Mr George, manager and assistant.

*Private collection of the author*

Scoring against Oxford during the English Schools' Trophy final
at Millwall FC's ground The Old Den, April 1966.

*Private collection of the author*

A letter of congratulations on signing as a professional in 1968 from Wally St Pier, chief representative (scout) of West Ham. Wally was appointed club chief scout by manager Charlie Paynter and was responsible for the discovery of John Lyall, Bobby Moore, Geoff Hurst, Martin Peters, Pat Holland, Frank Lampard Sr, Paul Brush, Alan Curbishley and Trevor Brooking through his scouting network. He retired in 1976 after 47 years' service to the club and died in 1989.

*Private collection of the author*

Telephone: 01-472 0704

## West Ham United Football Co., Limited

*Secretary:*
E. CHAPMAN

*Manager-Coach:*
R. GREENWOOD

REGISTERED OFFICE:
**BOLEYN GROUND
GREEN STREET
UPTON PARK
LONDON, E.13**

Your Ref. _____

Our Ref. _____

6th Sept 1968.

Mr Tony Carr,
3, Northleigh House,
Devons Road,
Bow. E. 3.

Dear Tony,

    I thought I would like to congratulate you upon signing professional for this club.

    Needless to say, I am delighted Tony and I do hope that you will have a long and successful career with this club.

    Dont forget Tony, if you ever want any advice from me, please do not hesitate to come along and see me, will you. I am always at the lads service.

    Please convey my very best wishes and kindest regards to Mum, Dad, and all at home.

            Yours sincerely,

            Wally

With Pat Holland on the day we signed as professionals in September 1968 – my eighteenth birthday. Pat would go on to make 245 appearances for West Ham.

*Private collection of the author*

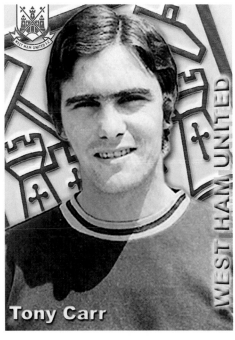

Tony Carr

A little while after you signed as a professional, the club would have your picture taken, because they hoped and believed you would one day make it into the first team. To me that still felt a long way off!

August 1966, one week away from the start of my first season with West Ham.
Players: back row, L to R: Geoff Hurst, Eddie Presland, Martin Peters, Dave Bickles, Ken Brown, Colin Mackleworth, Jim Standen, Alan Dickie, Paul Heffer, Bill Kitchener, Trevor Brooking, Roger Cross; second row: Bob Glozier, Ron Boyce, Trevor Dawkins, Johnny Byrne, John Sissons, Frank Lampard, Bobby Howe, George Andrews, Trevor Hartley, George Walker, Barry Simmons, David James; seated on bench: Doug Eadie, Peter Brabrook, Alan Sealey, Harry Redknapp, John Charles, Jimmy Bloomfield, Dennis Burnett, Bobby Moore, Eddie Bovington, Jack Burkett, Brian Dear; seated on ground: Trialist, Micky Glumart, Stevie Death, Stevie Lay, Tony Carr, Steve Knowles, Jimmy Lindsey; front row: Kevin Bliss, Micky Westburgh, John Scanlan, Ray Templeman. Present at the shoot but missing from this picture were Peter Bennett and Keith Miller.

I flick the ball through to a player making a forward run during a club summer youth tour to Zambia and Malawi on 18 May 1969. The trip was organised by Tommy Taylor's dad who worked for a mining company in Zambia, who supplied West Ham with the invitation. Sixteen players went, along with a staff of John Lyall, Bill Lansdowne Sr, Albert Walker and Wally St Pier. I recall we won the Peter Stuyvesant Trophy that we competed for during the trip.

*Private collection of the author*

Pre-match photo at Plough Lane before a
Wimbledon vs West Ham reserve game.

*Private collection of the author*

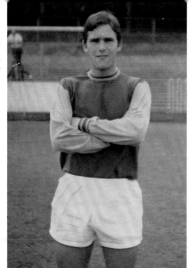

The only match I played in with Bobby Moore.
It was a charity game in the mid-eighties.
In the team were Martin Peters, Pat Holland,
Trevor Lake, Harry Cripps, Kevin Locke,
Mick McGiven, Ron Boyce, Trevor Brooking,
Frank Lampard and Bobby Moore.

*Private collection of the author*

Peter Brabrook and I meet
the great Pelé in 1997. It was in
Minneapolis–St Paul at a youth
tournament during which we
were invited to a 'dinner with
Pelé' by the sponsors Umbro.

*Private collection of the author*

Javier Mascherano was the subject of one of West Ham's most intriguing signings in 2006, making five appearances before moving on to Liverpool. Six years later, he arrived back at the Rush Green training facility as part of the Argentinian side ahead of an international. He was a Barcelona player at the time. The first thing he said to me was, 'Tony, are you still here!?'
*Private collection of the author*

*Below left:* Coaching at the Spurs training ground at a Premier League event in May 2013.

*Below:* A typical coaching pose around 1995!

Walking out onto the Boleyn Ground pitch at the start of my testimonial match, Wednesday 5 May 2010. It was a surreal moment and to this day I remain deeply grateful to the 14,000 fans and the ex-academy players who attended.

*Private collection of the author*

A moment to catch up with Frank Lampard before a West Ham vs Chelsea game. Frank had gone from an up-and-coming youth player at West Ham to a top England international with Chelsea.

*Private collection of the author*

Bumping into Rio Ferdinand in the corridor at Upton Park prior to a West Ham vs Manchester Utd game. Rio was super-talented and was always destined to achieve great things.

*Private collection of the author*

In September 2021, I was given an Honorary Doctorate of Science for development of some of Britain's greatest footballers from the University of East London (UEL) at their School of Education and Communities. I had to make an acceptance speech and said, 'Learning is a lifetime's journey. Make sure you choose something you love. Remember, we all have to be part of a team. It's all about character, attitude and a work ethic.'
*Private collection of the author*

Her Majesty the Queen pins on the insignia in recognition of my MBE on 21 October 2010. Such a proud moment and something you can only dream of. Who would have thought it!
*Private collection of the author*

After the ceremony, this picture was taken in the quadrangle at Buckingham Palace and I am showing off my MBE. It was wonderful to be able to share the occasion with my family, Louise, Dean, Brenda and Neil.
*Private collection of the author*

the manager to get to know his players and staff and vice versa. But it didn't get off to a great start.

As is the case with a lot of these sorts of games, the club were given an appearance fee – sometimes it would depend on the size of the crowd the game attracted. We're only talking about a few hundred pounds. Lou decided, as a way of motivating the players, to give the fee to the 'man of the match' as determined by the coaching staff. Normally the fee would be shared among the squad and the players felt as it was a team game that was exactly how any fee should be divvied up. But Lou ignored them and went ahead with his man of the match policy anyway. He did it for all the tour games, which added nothing to the team's harmony. Meanwhile, the vice chairman of the club, Martin Cearns, who was also on the trip, felt the *club* should retain the fee and thoroughly disapproved of it being used in this manner. Lou's motivational tactic had, therefore, managed to annoy both the players and the club's hierarchy in one deft move.

Once the season got under way the priority was promotion back to the First Division – at the first attempt if at all possible. The general feeling was that with the current squad, this was an achievable aim. We *had* experienced players who only needed to be won over – and then to focus on the task in hand.

Alan Dickens had attracted attention from Chelsea, whose manager Bobby Campbell was the father of an ex-player of ours, Greg Campbell, who knew Alan very well through his time with us. The clubs could not agree a fee so, as Alan was out of contract, the fee had to be decided by tribunal at FA headquarters in London. Lou asked me to attend the tribunal on the club's behalf as he did not know Alan very well, whereas I had coached him as a youngster and had seen him develop into the first-team midfielder he now was. West Ham chairman Len Cearns would also attend to keep an eye on proceedings. A committee was convened which sat to listen firstly to the player, then Chelsea and finally West Ham. Each party was heard independently and remained unaware of the other party's reasoning and arguments. I gave evidence on behalf of the club, saying that Alan was a very talented player who was yet to reach his full potential – so Chelsea were attempting to buy a player who could only get better. I likened the situation to West Ham's Trevor Brooking who only established himself as a player in his twenties. I felt Alan's development would follow a similar timescale. Eventually, we were all summoned back to hear the adjudication. The panel of experts determined that the fee should be £635,000, which by today's standards doesn't sound a lot but in 1989 was a considerable sum. Chelsea were none too happy, but Len Cearns went home with a big smile on his face, which was something you didn't see very often.

Around the same time, and having played only one game for the first team under Lou, Paul Ince became a target for Manchester United and made it clear he wanted to go. Paul had been unequivocal in his condemnation of the way John Lyall had been treated and, as I have previously stated, Paul still considered John his greatest mentor. He felt he owed him a huge debt for the way he had developed both as a player and as a person. The whole saga was a mess. No one blamed Paul for wanting to go to Manchester United – after all Alan Dickens had just left for Chelsea for similar reasons – so long as the club got a fair fee and everything was conducted openly and above board. At the time, Paul was only 21, but had an agent who was pulling the strings on his behalf. When Manchester United come calling, as an agent you want to get the deal over the line as quickly as possible; there's the potential of a big payday in it for you.

Paul was somehow persuaded to pose for a photograph in a Manchester United shirt *before* the deal was done with the promise 'they would keep it on file' until the deal was completed. Naturally, the photo found its way into a newspaper while he was still a West Ham player and, equally unsurprisingly, the fans went mad, turning Paul into a hate figure overnight; a feeling of enmity that exists to this day. Ironic really, given that a few months before, the fans had voted Paul the 1989 'Hammer of the Year'. The deal broke down when Paul failed a medical and Manchester United announced they only wanted to pay a fee based on appearances. My reading was that the medical thing was a smokescreen and was being used to barter down the price. Until now, Paul had only rarely been out through injury.

Eventually the deal was done – and Paul never did suffer medical issues … I can't blame Paul for the shirt fiasco – the worst I could accuse him of was being naive. Throughout, he was being manipulated and the newspaper concerned had gone ahead and published it when they had 'promised' to hold off until he had officially signed. That all said, I feel proud to have been involved with Paul's development. He would go on to have a fantastic career and was the first black captain of England, gaining 53 caps for his country. I know for a fact that had John Lyall still been the manager at West Ham, Paul's transfer would have been handled in a far more dignified way, perhaps leaving Paul with the eternal admiration of the West Ham fans – recognising and remembering his achievements as a great player and not vilifying him for mistakes that should never have happened in the first place.

The first five games of Lou Macari's management regime brought two wins and three draws – a reasonable start. But all was not well. Mick McGiven resigned and went to Chelsea. Mick, as a very principled man, could not work with Lou. He would later team up again with John Lyall, who was managing Ipswich Town, gaining promotion and taking them into the Premier League. At West Ham, form was patchy and winning over the players was proving to still be some way off. We remained in the top half of the table but the real push for the promotion places looked increasingly beyond us. As Christmas approached, a run of six defeats in seven games culminated in a disastrous exit in the third round of the FA Cup, losing 1-0 at Torquay United. This was relegation form not promotion-chasing form.

Our form was, in fact, utterly unpredictable and we were having a good run in the League Cup – reaching the semi-final. Our opponents were Oldham Athletic in a two-legged game with the first leg to be played on their notorious plastic pitch that every team hated playing on. We had won our previous two games so were confident going into the first leg. By now rumours were circulating that Lou was being investigated for betting irregularities while at Swindon, which didn't help with any positivity within the squad. The atmosphere was, if anything, getting worse.

The game at Oldham on a cold February night was a disaster from start to finish. At the hotel, prior to the final team meeting, Lou had spoken to Theo Foley on the phone. Theo was Arsenal's first-team coach, Arsenal having lost to Oldham in a previous round of the cup. He said they should have played 3-5-2 and this made Lou's mind up: we would play 3-5-2. With no previous training ground preparation, he announced this to the squad two hours before kick-off. The players were unsure how to implement this change of strategy with some of them asking, quite reasonably, what their role *was* in this unrehearsed formation. The uncertainty produced a pathetic performance. We looked disorganised and lacking in belief and lost 6-0. The second leg looked a formality for Oldham. Of course, the players must take some of the blame for their part in the debacle – as must the manager and coaching staff. It was a collective failure and reflected badly on everyone connected with the team that night.

It was the beginning of the end for Lou. The next game was in the league away at Swindon – Lou's previous club where the betting investigation was centred. The team and staff met up on the morning of the game at the usual Waltham Abbey hotel. Once the team were on the coach with the coaching staff of Ron Boyce, Billy Bonds and me, we were left waiting for Lou. Word came through that he would meet us at the hotel in Swindon where we were to have a pre-match meal. No one thought much of it as Lou still had a house in Swindon and it seemed entirely feasible he might have stayed there overnight. While we were travelling, players kept asking if Lou had resigned as they were hearing rumours from their contacts in the press that he had done so. We arrived at Swindon and Peter Storrie, West Ham's managing director, was on the forecourt waiting. He told the staff to stay on the coach and asked the players to go in for lunch. He came on board to say that Lou would not be coming to the game, he had in fact resigned, but the board were not yet prepared to accept his resignation and would try to get him to reconsider later after the game. Our job was to tell the team Lou was ill ... We did as we were instructed but none of the players believed a word of what was said. And to top it all, it was Luděk Mikloško's debut. He didn't have a clue what was going on as he didn't speak a word of English. Well, that's not entirely true. We had somehow managed to teach Luděk a little English and told him when coming for crosses to shout 'keeper's!' so the defenders would have some idea of his intentions. At the time it was pretty much the sum total of his English. We drew the game 2-2. A good result in the circumstances.

We never did see Lou after the game. He stuck to his guns and resigned and the board could not convince him to stay. The betting irregularities were all over the papers and he was eventually fined £1,000 by the FA for betting on Swindon Town, his club at the time, to lose an FA Cup tie against Newcastle United. He told me later that he'd done it to cover the club's expenses for the travel to Newcastle for a game they were odds-on to lose. Had they won, Swindon would have benefitted from the prize money for proceeding to the next round. It was a shame the way it ended. Lou was a good man and I seemed to get on well with him. All the staff and coaches had a lot to thank him for, for staying faithful to them instead of bringing in his own team of coaches and staff.

Once Lou's exit was confirmed, there was a huge club and public clamour for Billy Bonds to take over. The players wanted Bill and he was a popular choice with the fans after being the club's all-time record appearance holder, two times FA Cup winner and four times 'Hammer of the Year'. Bill was unsure whether he wanted the job or was even ready for it. But he eventually accepted the board's offer and was appointed manager in February 1990. The pressure was immediate and unrelenting and, at first, he wasn't entirely sure it was what he wanted in his life. However, typical of Bill, he threw himself into the role. When the players were told of his appointment in the dressing room at the training ground, it was greeted with cheers and a round of applause. Martin Cearns, who delivered the news to the players, looked a pleased man and obviously was hoping for a quieter period ahead!

For the remainder of the season there was a noticeably positive vibe about the place. Eighteen games remained to be played and Bill achieved eleven wins, three draws and two defeats, missing out on the play-offs by two points. Included in the sequence of games was the second leg of the League Cup semi-final against Oldham at Upton Park. Already 6-0 down, we knew it was mission impossible; we weren't going to score seven and win the tie, but the players gave it a good go. On a March night, we totally dominated the game, winning 3-0. We also hit the bar and post twice. It was a bad case of what might have been. We played the last game of the season against Wolverhampton Wanderers at Upton Park. It was Irish international Liam Brady's last game before his retirement and he scored a great goal in a 4-0 victory. So, after such a traumatic season, it ended on a positive note. The big lesson of the season was how the power rested with the players: we had a squad more than capable of getting automatic promotion, but sadly too many squad members simply wouldn't play for Lou Macari, and through a combination of circumstances and poor form, the players had got their way with Lou's resignation. Billy was now in charge and the players were back onside.

# 8

## BILL BRINGS IN HARRY

Billy Bonds was in charge and the 1990/91 season saw a real surge of form as we aimed to get back into the top division. The team remained unbeaten in the league until losing away at Barnsley 1-0 on 22 December, a remarkable run of 21 games unbeaten. The season ended with promotion as runners-up to Oldham Athletic. Another noteworthy statistic was that we finished with the best defensive record in the league, conceding only 34 goals from 46 games. We also reached the semi-final of the FA Cup, losing 4-0 to Brian Clough's Nottingham Forest at Villa Park. We played the majority of the game with ten men after Tony Gale had controversially been sent off.

Bill's first season as manager had ended very successfully and it proved, if proof were needed, that if you gain the players' respect, get them onside and unified and treat them as adults, even if you lack the experience to be a top-flight manager, as could be argued was the case for Bill, you can still be successful at the highest level of the game. Training had been quite basic, fun and serious all at the same time. Tactics had been bordering on the one-dimensional but the players had responded to Billy's management splendidly. There would be a twenty-minute warm-up of jogging, twisting, turning, bending to touch the ground, and jumping, normally in pairs, followed by a possession game of one or two touch for another twenty minutes or so. After which the group might split into forwards and defenders for specific training before finishing off with an 8 v 8 two-touch game. Every aspect had to be done with a match tempo and some of the games could get quite fiery but never went over the top.

The following season was the complete opposite. Despite being back in the top division, the club made little investment in the team, which resulted in the team only winning nine games from 42, ending in predictable relegation. We had finished bottom; we were back to square one. It has to be said that the introduction of the controversial financial bond scheme during the season didn't help the atmosphere between the club and fans: it was designed to raise millions in investment and the club offered supporters the 'opportunity' to purchase bonds in three price bands – £500, £750 and £950, ownership of which would confer the right to buy a match-day or season ticket for a designated seat for 150 years. Notwithstanding having purchased this 'right', the club said the fans would still have to pay for their season/match-day tickets. The not-so-subtle implication was that only those who paid the bond would maintain the right to buy season tickets in future.

All this had come about after the ruling – following the recommendation of Lord Justice Taylor after the Hillsborough stadium disaster – that First Division clubs would have to convert to all-seater stadiums. This would mean West Ham having to spend millions on the ground – money the club didn't have. However well intended, the scheme enraged the fans. At every home game there were demonstrations, pitch invasions and generally a bad feel about the place. From pitchside I can tell you it wasn't the best atmosphere to play competitive football in. Bill was asked by Peter Storrie and the West Ham board to publicly back the scheme and to mollify the atmosphere between the club and fans, but he disagreed, siding with the fans saying the bonds effectively ripped them off. So they turned to Trevor Brooking, who said he would back the club's plans. But the damage was done; only around 800 of the intended 19,000 bonds were bought by fans. Unsurprisingly, not long after, the idea of the scheme was dropped altogether.

During that season of struggles and ultimate relegation I had an offer from Peter Stewart, the editor of weekly football magazine *Shoot!*, to take a team to compete in the Dallas Cup in the USA. It would be an all-expenses-paid trip and on the face of it looked good and worthwhile from our point of view. I had a friend in Dallas, Clark Hunt, whom I had met a few years earlier when he came to the UK as youngster and trained with the youth team during a couple of summers. Clark's father was Lamar Hunt who many years earlier had arranged for West Ham to play a friendly game in the Houston Astrodome in an exhibition match vs Santos of Brazil. The Hunt family were from an oil and mining business and were also big supporters of sport and Clark, who now runs the business, owns the Kansas City Chiefs (NFL), the Columbus Crew (MLS) and also FC Dallas, so his sporting knowledge was second to none. I wrote to Clark and his reply was that he would recommend the Dallas Cup as a widely supported and well-run tournament. I accepted the trip and arranged to meet Clark in Dallas.

Paul Hilton took charge of the team, which had some notable players such as Kevin Horlock and Matt Holland. It was a well-organised tournament, which we won, beating Tahuichi of Bolivia 2-1 in the final. We were the first English club to have won the title.

I met up with Clark Hunt for lunch and he took me to a Tex-Mex restaurant for my first taste of Mexican chilli with a taste of Texas. He also came to the final with me and cheered us on to victory. It turned out to be a very successful tour and a great experience for all concerned. Soccer, as they insist on calling football in the USA, was certainly on the up and the standard was very good.

Post-relegation and during the summer break, Bill held a meeting with Ron Boyce and me and said that he felt he needed a bit more experience on the coaching staff. I was still coach of the reserve team and Ron was Bill's first-team coach. Bill had given Paul Hilton the role he himself had relinquished as youth team coach when he moved into the manager's role. Now he was looking for an assistant with more experience coaching senior players or a former manager who could bring that experience to assist and advise him. He told us all to think about it over the weekend and come back Monday with ideas.

Come Monday and Bill announced he had had a long conversation with Harry Redknapp, Harry finally saying he would be happy to come to help and be Bill's assistant. Ron Boyce and I both knew Harry from his time as a player at West Ham and when he used to pick me up for training at Bow Church with Colin Mackleworth. It seemed like a sensible appointment, and a good fit given Harry's past association with the club. Bill and Harry had been great friends during their playing days. In fact, Harry had been Bill's best man when he married Lynn. Bill felt Harry would give us the experience that was needed – he had been a manager of Bournemouth and had been coaching a long time. The fact that he was an old friend was a bonus. The combination was an immediate success and we achieved promotion as runners-up to Newcastle United, thus gaining entry to the recently formed FA Premier League (20 February

1992). Harry's arrival had sidelined Ron Boyce as first-team coach and later on down the line Ron was asked to be the chief scout, which he accepted.

The following season Bill asked me to return to the role as youth team manager with complete control of academy operations. I have to confess that at the time I was a bit disappointed and saw this as a thinly disguised demotion. However, the club, through Peter Storrie, felt in the longer term this was in the best interests of me and the club. They felt this was the role I was best at – and a very important one at that. The club even gave me a pay rise for this perceived demotion. Paul Hilton was promoted and made reserve-team manager. Jimmy Neighbour had been appointed as youth development officer after Len Hurford had resigned.

I threw myself into the youth academy to try and get things back on track after a fairly lean spell as far as West Ham youth development was concerned. Bill and Harry consolidated the first team in the Premier League with a mid-table finish and things looked on the up. We all came back for pre-season training and everything seemed perfectly normal. One morning, a few days into pre-season training, we set about the usual squad run in Epping Forest to build up fitness. Harry and I were jogging at the back of the group pushing on the stragglers with Bill, as always, leading at the front. The group ahead stopped to rest and Harry and I started to walk towards the main group when Harry turned to me and said, 'I don't know what to do. Bournemouth have made me a fantastic offer to go back as manager and be part of the board. To basically run the football side of the club.'

I didn't know what to say and so while collecting my thoughts I said, 'Have you told Bill?'

Harry said he had, and Bill had said in return, 'If that's what you want to do, I won't stand in your way.'

'Only you can make that decision, Harry,' I offered.

Nothing more was said that day and we got back on with training.

The board didn't want Harry to leave. They took the view that he had been instrumental in the previous season's success and were loath to break up what was obviously a productive partnership with Bill. It is my understanding that at some point Peter Storrie said to Harry, 'Would you leave if you were manager?'

And Harry had replied, 'No, but you already have a manager.'

So the board floated the idea that Billy would become a paid director and Harry would become manager. It backfired badly. Bill rejected the 'offer' out of hand. In fact, he told them where they could stick it and immediately resigned, feeling all this had been cooked up behind his back and being a man of principle would have nothing to do with it. Bill walked out and that, I'm afraid, was that. Bill called me a couple of days later and told me the club had paid him in full the remaining period of his contract, so at least in that respect, and in the board's embarrassment, Bill had been treated fairly. He told me he felt I would be okay, but to be careful when dealing with Storrie, although I felt that up until this point my relationship with him had been fine. Billy had already moved on and did not mention one word of what had gone on between him, Harry and the board. I know that as of writing, Bill and Harry have not spoken a word to each other – which is a sad thing to report. It took me back to Harry's first day with Bill: Ron Boyce and I were having a cup of tea before going out to start the training session when Harry suddenly turned to me and Ron and said, 'You think I'm here to take his job, well I'll tell you the day he leaves – pointing towards

Bill – is the day I leave.' Well, it didn't quite work out like that, did it? Circumstances, especially in professional football, have unique ways of upending things. Harry obviously wanted to be manager of West Ham one day, but, and to be fair to him, perhaps not under those circumstances.

Harry seemed genuinely upset that Bill had left and expressed serious reservations about accepting the role of manager – but by the end of the week had accepted. His first move was to bring in Frank Lampard Sr as his assistant; they had played in the first team together in the 1960s and were brothers-in-law after marrying sisters Sandra and Pat.

Unleashed, Harry set about changing things at the club: he was critical of the way we lost out on promising local schoolboys to rival clubs and demanded our recruitment system become more aggressive, more proactive, more effective when scouting schoolboys. Jimmy Neighbour, who took all this personally, argued it was such a big job he needed a full-time assistant to cope. Jimmy Hampson was approached and appointed, and it turned out to be the ideal appointment. He had previously been at Charlton Athletic as youth development officer and had been responsible for a very successful scouting programme. Scott Parker and Richard Rufus are just a couple of his successes. And from this point on we started to recruit some very promising youngsters.

Scouting schoolboys has changed over the years. When I first started back in the 1970s, clubs could only sign schoolboys on their fourteenth birthday through associated schoolboy forms. This was the very form I had signed as a fourteen-year-old in the 1960s. It meant you could train at a club from a young age but you still played your football with your school and local youth club (your Sunday club). The nonsense this resulted in was that the most talented boys were training at Arsenal on Monday night, West Ham on Tuesday night and Tottenham Hotspur on Thursday night. And as they approached their fourteenth birthday, there was an almighty ruck by the clubs to sign the most promising boys.

Now the system has changed. Academies have evolved and you can sign boys at the age of eight and clubs can also run teams at schoolboy level from under-9s through to under-16s. It means these talented boys cannot play for their Sunday clubs or school, but only for their chosen professional clubs at the weekend. Now obviously there are pros and cons for both systems, but it was felt that the very best players would benefit from training and playing with their equals and would make quicker and better progress. I'm not convinced it works in the way it was intended.

We have to be careful we don't 'professionalise' schoolboy coaching too early and take away some of the fun element that goes with playing the game. We must let the kids be kids, however talented. The clamour to sign the best schoolboys now takes place at eight and it is almost impossible to predict future development at that age, so in some ways we are creating potential 'superstars' far too early and the disappointment of being released or not progressing can be a massive shock to some parents – and the young boys fall out of love with the game before they are twelve.

While writing this book I gave a lot of thought to this and looked back at the players the club had produced before the change of rules that allowed signing up boys as young as eight was introduced. I tried to think about how they had developed their skills, before they were subjected to 'organised coaching' and Joe Cole sprang to mind. (Other player interviews on this subject are randomly distributed throughout this book.) Joe was a player who when first 'spotted' already possessed outstanding ability. I spoke to Joe just after he had retired and asked him about his earliest memories of the game and how his career developed. You can read the interview at the end of this chapter.

Ron Boyce, a good friend of mine during our time together at West Ham, had been made chief scout and, after a couple of seasons, was called into the office by Storrie to be told his services were no longer required. When he'd been offered the role of chief scout I had the suspicion that it was only a matter of time before the club got around to dismissing him. Ron had given his whole working life to the club as player and coach – 36 years – and had been a great servant of the club. Paul Hilton had also left the club in similar fashion. Roger Cross was brought in as first-team coach and to take the reserves on match days. Roger had been first-team coach at QPR and Tottenham Hotspur with Gerry Francis and brought with him a wealth of experience. I had played in West Ham's youth team and reserves with Roger, so with Harry and Frank and now Roger with the first team, they were a group of people whom I had known for a long time. Harry also brought in Ted Pearce as chief scout to replace Ron Boyce, but Ted's main role was to scout our future opposition and to file reports on them. He did this very well – presenting complete and thorough dossiers on opponents to Harry ahead of match days. Ted had previously been the manager of Farnborough FC who, as it happens, we had played in the FA Cup not so long before; they conceded home advantage and played their 'home game' at Upton Park, earning a creditable draw.

It wasn't long into Harry's reign that Jimmy Neighbour had a big falling-out with Harry and promptly resigned. It was inevitable,

I suppose, after Jimmy had made critical remarks about Harry to a scout of another club. The scout had rung Harry and told him what had been said ... After Harry had confronted Jimmy, Jimmy did the honourable thing and left the club. It was with much sadness that some years later in 2009 I learned that Jimmy had died. He was in hospital after having hip replacement surgery and during recuperation had a heart attack and died. I had known Jimmy since we were fifteen-year-old schoolboys playing for London; he was only 58 and a good man taken too soon. Jimmy Hampson was given full control of schoolboy scouting and he brought in Jimmy Tindall with whom he had worked at Charlton. As mentioned earlier, Jimmy Tindall had been my manager at Senrab FC and was very experienced in spotting and recruiting talented schoolboys. Jimmy H also appointed a number of new scouts and we widened the catchment area to include South London, where we had not had much success in the past. The three main scouts in this area were Paul Senior, Mike Dove and Dave Goodwin who, over a period of time, brought a number of good players to the club.

Dave was manager of Blackheath district football team and had knowledge of the best players in this area, one such being Rio Ferdinand. I spoke to Dave while researching this book and he told me the first time he saw Rio play he was watching Nigel Quashie (later of QPR and West Ham) who had been recommended to him, and thought this highly promising young player was Nigel. Straight after the game he approached the player and said, 'Hello Nigel, would you like to come and train at West Ham?' The player replied, 'I'm not Nigel. My name is Rio.' I asked Rio about this incident, but he swears he can't remember it ... It often happens with scouting – you go to watch a player that has been recommended and another player catches your eye. I'm sure there are countless examples of players being spotted in this way.

Paul Senior was a scout that Jimmy H brought in to specifically work the South London area. Two players that they brought in were Liam Ridgewell and Kieran Richardson, and while both were signed on academy registrations with West Ham, both left at age fourteen for other clubs. Liam signed for Aston Villa and Kieran signed for Manchester United. Kieran's move came as a surprise to me as I had no idea he was being targeted by United. The first we knew about it was when our under-14 squad was playing in the renowned Milk Cup youth competition in Northern Ireland. The tournament had finished and early on the day of our departure, one of our staff members was sitting in the lobby of the hotel when Kieran came out of the lift with all his bags and when asked where he was going said he was going home with his family and then going on to another tournament with Manchester United. The sheer cheek of it. We ended up getting a fee for him via a compensation agreement set up by the Football League but it never compensates for the loss of a potential first-team player. In the same way as Kieran, Liam left to go to Aston Villa and we received a similar compensation fee for his 'transfer of registration'.

While on the subject of players leaving, a few years earlier a certain John Terry left West Ham at the age of fourteen. At the time no such compensation system existed, so John could leave for nothing. He was a talented midfield player during his spell with us and Chelsea signed him as a midfield player in 1995. But trust me when I say no one at the time could have predicted what a stellar career lay ahead for John as a centre back! John became a world-class defender and would spend 22 years at Chelsea and make 78 appearances for

England. It shows just how difficult talent spotting and future player development is. Losing players in this way is the worst thing of all; it's different if you are trying to sign a player and he chooses another club. By way of an example: we tried to sign Tony Adams who was a Barking schoolboy defender and obviously in our traditional catchment area, as was Steve Potts. Tony chose Arsenal while Steve chose West Ham. You win some, you lose some, but when they have already signed for you, it's a hard thing to take when they suddenly announce they're moving on.

Among the prominent players Paul, Mike and Dave brought in and signed were Anton and Rio Ferdinand, Glen Johnson, Junior Stanislas and Gary Alexander, as well as Ridgewell and Richardson, the two that left. All were South London boys and a superb group of players. It has to be said that when Goodwin, Dove and Senior left the club, none of them, nor their scouting roles and abilities, were adequately replaced. It proved the point that youth recruitment was the single most important factor in a successful academy. The more a club is prepared to invest in good scouts, the better players the club will recruit – and it follows that this will mean coaches are supplied with better players to work with and so on, to improve their playing standard such that some, if not all, will be good enough to play in the first team.

As far as the staff were concerned, the club now seemed settled and I had signed my first ever contract as a coach at this time. After Ron Boyce, Eddie Baily, Paul Hilton and Jimmy Neighbour had either departed of their own accord or were sacked, I asked the West Ham board if I could have the security of a contract, as up until now, I had never been given one. During the release of staff, another senior member of staff told me my position had been a point of discussion, so it was reasonable that I felt somewhat vulnerable. It was reported that Storrie and Redknapp had discussed my position but felt there was nobody available *at the time* they had the sufficient confidence in to replace me! In fairness, when I spoke to Storrie, seeking some form of assurance, he couldn't have been more obliging, offering me a three-year contract, a company car and a mobile telephone. At least this was some measure of job security in a very insecure business. I kept my company car for a few years until the tax regime made it pointless and I gave it up. One morning I exited my front door to drive to the training ground and I immediately saw the car was minus its wheels. The car was jacked up on bricks and all four wheels had gone. I couldn't believe it – right outside my house on my own drive and I hadn't heard a thing. I rang Paul Aldridge, by now the club's MD, and told him what had happened and would he arrange a pick-up truck. 'Yeah, nice try! April fool, huh?' It was 1 April and no matter how much I pleaded otherwise, he wouldn't believe me.

Sometime later I bumped into Ron Greenwood at a match at Upton Park and we got on to the subject of contracts. He told me that all the time he was manager of West Ham he never had a contract, only a handshake from Reg Pratt, the chairman. How times have changed. Ron also asked me about how I was finding coaching the youngsters. I replied that I was still enjoying it and working hard. He asked whether I was still coaching 3 v 3s. I replied that yes, er, yes, I was. And below head height, he continued. I had to say yes. But it wasn't something I did as often as Ron had done. For the next few weeks 3 v 3, below head height, was back on the agenda. The master had spoken.

Stuart Prossor, a coaching friend from New Zealand, often came to the training ground, when he was in the UK, to watch the youth team training and to pick my brains on all matters coaching. This was during the time when watching training, first team or youth team, was as easy as just walking in the gate; there was no security and the club had a very liberal open house policy. Fans, coaches, agents and press could just come in and watch. It stayed this way until the incident between Eyal Berkovic and John Hartson was filmed by a fan on his phone: Hartson had kicked Berkovic in the head as he was bending down during training. It was all over Sky Sports that evening and Harry Redknapp, manager at the time, stopped the open house policy immediately.

It was Stuart who had suggested I should write a coaching book on my methods used at West Ham. I was not keen at first because I didn't feel I had the time to put it all down on paper. Stuart was insistent and with his help and over a period of months we started to get some stuff down and before long we had a formula and a draft outline. Now we set about getting a publisher interested and we had a call from Deborah Taylor of Cassell plc. Cassell were based on the Strand in London. Deborah came down to the training ground to meet us and after a lengthy chat agreed to publish the book. It was to be called *Youth Soccer Coaching*, which took two years from start to finish and I was very proud of the finished book. I asked Trevor Brooking to write the foreword and got endorsements from the director for youth at the Premier League (Dave Richardson), and England internationals Paul Ince and Tony Cottee. One player who featured heavily in the action pictures was a young Rio Ferdinand; his technique performing the skills in the photographs are as near perfect as you can get and that's why he featured so prominently.

A few years later I wrote another book, with Jon Hayden, called *How to Coach a Soccer Team*, published by Hamlyn. This time Rio, who was by now playing for Manchester United, wrote the foreword. Both books were well received and sold very well, particularly in the US.

A West Ham tradition was that ex-players would often come to the Chadwell Heath training ground for a chat during the season – mainly with Harry or with John Lyall when he was manager. One former player who started coming in more and more was Peter Brabrook, the ex-Chelsea and West Ham winger. Peter was always good company and liked a chat. He was now working for Ovenden Papers in Hainault and I asked him if he would like to do some coaching with the schoolboys in the evenings, to which he readily agreed. After a couple of seasons, Tommy Taylor, another ex-West Ham player, had taken the manager's job at Cambridge United and asked Peter to join him as full-time youth coach. I spoke to Peter about this and asked if he was going to be given a contract. He told me the club had promised him a two-year deal, so he agreed to join Tommy at Cambridge. It was what Peter had wanted for a good while – a full-time coaching role. My concern for Peter was that his contract had been promised but remained unsigned before he decided to leave West Ham. Things didn't work out that well at Cambridge for Peter: the two-year deal was never signed, and I started to see Peter more and more back at the Chadwell Heath training ground. When we spoke, he would only say, 'It's a day off today,' or 'We are training later on this afternoon.' It became obvious things were not what they seemed and shortly after Peter lost his job.

Harry, being a good friend of Peter's, gave him a job of assisting me during the day and scouting for Harry in the evenings and at weekends. I have to say Peter and I were a good partnership. We bounced ideas off each other and he had a good eye for talent. He was never afraid to give his opinion and would often make training or tactical suggestions – and more often than not, he was right. The youth programme was getting stronger and we had some really good players. We won the South East Counties League for the first time in the club's history, and we also got to the final of the South East Counties League Cup where we played Chelsea in a two-legged tie. The first leg was at Upton Park and Chelsea blew us away, winning 5-2; the second leg, played at Stamford Bridge, would be seven days later. We were going to be minus a couple of players who had gone on a first-team tour of Australia to celebrate the club's centenary (1895–1995). Without a moment's hesitation I brought in a young schoolboy to play in the second leg – a tall, gangly Rio Ferdinand.

The build-up to the game was quite subdued. The players couldn't help but feel the second leg was a mere formality and Chelsea would win the tie. My job was to lift the mood and tell the players that maybe Chelsea would feel the job was already done – which could work to our advantage. So I set about making training as enjoyable as possible and tried to take the pressure off the players. We were heading to Stamford Bridge to have a real go at recovering our respect and having a crack at winning the second leg at the least.

Now bearing in mind we were 5-2 down from the first leg, we had the worst possible start when Chelsea scored in the first minute, taking a four-goal lead on aggregate. However, from that moment on we were brilliant. Rio was playing out of his skin, looking every bit a great player in the making; young Frank Lampard was making surging runs from midfield and we pulled two goals back before half-time, reducing the deficit to 6-4 at the break. The second half started as the first had finished with us on top, and we scored again, 6-5, and to top it all we scored with minutes to go so the score was tied at 6-6. Unbelievable from our perspective! Extra time was a stalemate producing no more goals. So after a breathtaking 120 minutes of football it would all go to penalties. And it came down to the last penalty. Frank Lampard had to score to win the cup for West Ham – which he did! Football is full of ironies and how ironic is it that Frank won the cup for West Ham against his future club Chelsea.

Harry rang me the following morning wanting the complete run-down on the game – and was especially anxious to hear about this young player called Rio Ferdinand. Harry's dad, Harry Sr, had been at the game and was raving about Rio after the game. I confirmed what Harry's dad had said and told Harry that Rio had been, without doubt, the outstanding player on the night.

The following season we reached the FA Youth Cup final with a two-legged affair against Liverpool. In our ranks were Rio Ferdinand and Frank Lampard, the two players who had really pushed on over the last couple of seasons. Both lads were already in the manager's plans for the future. Liverpool lined up with Michael Owen and Jamie Carragher in the team and a young Steven Gerrard on the bench. We all know what our boys and theirs went on to achieve in the game as future England internationals. Steve Heighway, an outstanding winger for Liverpool in the days of Bill Shankly and Bob Paisley, was head of youth at Liverpool and I had always got on well with Steve during heads of youth meetings at the FA and the FA Premier League, so I was looking forward to a good encounter with them.

The first leg at Upton Park was really disappointing from our point of view, as Liverpool were quicker to the ball than us, played better and we ended up losing 2-0, with the second leg back at Anfield due a few days later. We went to Anfield and I slightly changed the way we set up. I played Rio Ferdinand in midfield and tried to play a more attacking formation. Lee Hodges, on the left-hand side, was instructed to come infield more and Frank Lampard encouraged to get forward more. I felt we needed to take the game to Liverpool, ask more questions of their defending and try to get them on the back foot. We hadn't done this in the first leg, so we had to be a little more adventurous and try to claw back the two-goal deficit. We couldn't have started better, scoring in the first minute with Frank Lampard half-volleying a ball from just inside the box. 2-1 and game on! Harry told me later he missed the goal, arriving in his seat a little late after chatting in the boardroom. We pushed for the equaliser and Lee Boylan, our striker, had two great chances to score, both of which he put wide unfortunately for us, one when he was clean through and another after a flick-on at the near post from a corner. Michael Owen scored just before half-time to give Liverpool back their two-goal advantage. They scored again in the second half and Liverpool won the FA Youth Cup 4-1 on aggregate.

After the game, while we were still on the pitch, I spoke to Steve Heighway and he put things into perspective when he said that even before the game, our jobs had already been done with both teams having three outstanding prospects for the future. How right Steve was.

The organisation around youth football was changing. Howard Wilkinson, who was technical director at the FA, put forward a plan for the future of youth football, titled 'Charter for Quality'. Its basic remit was to allow clubs more coaching time with their schoolboy players and to run teams from under-9s through to under-19s. The schoolboy groups would no longer play for their

Sunday youth clubs; instead, they would play for their respective clubs on Sundays and the club would take sole responsibility for each player's development. At the older end, it would change from under-16s and under-18s to under-17s and under-19s and also introduce an under-21 league. There was some resentment among other clubs who did not welcome change. Manchester United voiced their disagreement, arguing that they felt they had a perfectly good system in place with the Central and Lancashire Leagues, but even a powerhouse such as Manchester United could not sway opinion and it was voted in. This was fine with us as Peter Brabrook took charge of the under-17s and I took charge of the under-19s and we continued to have great success on the pitch and produced several players for the first team.

Towards the end of the following season Peter Storrie had arranged for the youth team to go to Minnesota, USA for an end-of-season tournament, the USA Cup, sponsored by Umbro in Blaine, Minneapolis–St Paul. The team, along with Peter Brabrook and me, stayed in the University of Minnesota dormitories. The room I shared with Peter was the hottest room I have ever stayed in, with no air conditioning and the showers were down the corridor ... So here we were, both of us in the middle of the night having cold showers just to cool down enough to be able to sleep. The next day we went to a Target store to buy a couple of fans. We bought the biggest fans we could carry and while they cooled down the room brilliantly, they sounded like fast revving aeroplane engines, which still made sleep an impossibility. But we did well in the tournament and reached the final, losing 1-0 to Brazilian side Corinthians.

Peter Storrie, who had come out for the first few days of the tournament, provided us with the trip's highlight, inviting us to

'Dinner with Pelé', sponsored by Umbro, at a downtown hotel. The great man himself had opened the tournament after being paraded around the stadium in a convertible car (only in America). We were told to make our way to the hotel by cab. Kit man Pete Williams, along with the physio, would stay with the players. While we were waiting for the cab, a mighty thunderstorm appeared from nowhere causing us to make a run for cover. As we reached the opposite side of the road, the telegraph pole we were standing next to was struck by lightning – which felled the pole. Peter and I stared at each other with a look that said we knew how lucky we had been. All this meant we missed our cab and consequently arrived late for the dinner. Once at the hotel we learned the guests had gone upstairs to take their seats to wait for the arrival of Pelé. As we were tidying ourselves after our mad dash, a large white limo pulled up and out got Pelé, who marched straight towards me and Peter. This was an opportunity not to be missed, so we both asked him to sign our invitation cards and posed for a photo with him. To say we were thrilled would be an understatement. To this day Pelé remains one of my all-time heroes – and here I was in the US and in conversation with him. It's a photo I have always treasured. Peter announced that he had played against him for England in the 1958 World Cup in Sweden. Quick as flash Pelé replied, 'Yes, I remember it was a 0-0 draw.' And off he went to the dinner with us trailing behind like a couple of gleeful schoolboys in his wake.

Peter Brabrook was always good company and used to tell some really funny football stories: one concerned the time he broke into Chelsea's first team at the age of seventeen. He used to travel to Stamford Bridge with Jimmy Greaves and the two of them would meet up and travel in on the Underground from Beckton, East

London. Before they got on the Tube, Peter and Jimmy would have pie, mash and liquor (an East London delicacy made from the water the eels are stewed in and no, it has nothing to do with alcohol!) and then travel to the game. Pete would say Jimmy would have double pie and mash and a couple of hours later score a hat-trick for Chelsea. Another of Peter's classic stories, and he always swore it was true, was how Jimmy and Peter would, at the end of each season, go to see the manager, Ted Drake, to negotiate a new contract. On one occasion, Jimmy went in first and sat down with the manager. Drake said, 'Jimmy, you have had a great season, our leading scorer again. We can give you £80 a week and £80 a week in the summer (this was in the era when players would get a reduction of wages for the summer break).'

Jimmy walked out and said to Peter, 'Ted's given me £80 and £80. Just to let you know.'

So Peter went into the manager's office forewarned.

'Hello, Pete,' Ted said. 'Well, you have had a good season and the club are prepared to give you £80 a week and £70 in the summer.'

Peter replied, 'You have just given Jimmy £80 and £80 and I want the same.'

Ted sat for a moment thinking before saying, 'Look, lad, Jimmy is a better player than you ...'

'That may be true, but not in the f****** summer he's not!'

It goes unrecorded whether he got the same contract as the great Jimmy Greaves.

Peter died in December 2016 at the age of 79. He made 251 appearances for Chelsea and 167 for West Ham, scoring 33 goals for the club. He was also capped by England three times and I was glad to call him my friend.

Peter had got on really well with Joe Cole during his coaching days and below I spoke to Joe regarding his development as a young player growing up in London.

TONY: What is your earliest memory of playing football?

JOE: I remember playing in the playground just for fun. I was about nine or ten. My dad wasn't into football and I didn't even know there were leagues and a professional game. It wasn't until the World Cup in 1990, when we had it on the television at home, that I really got into it. Gazza (Paul Gascoigne) inspired me and I fell in love with football.

TONY: When did you realise you were good at it?

JOE: I knew I was the best in my school in the playground. I just got the ball and dribbled. The first time I went to a live match was when my friend's dad took us to a Chelsea game. We were living in the Edgware Road at the time with my mum's mum. Dad used to watch me play for my local team and at that time I was the best player. I was ten or eleven. Before that I just played playground football at school and from the age of about five up to ten we played with sponge balls. I don't know if that is significant or if that helped develop skills.

TONY: Do you think playground football helped you develop your skills? You were free spirits and nothing was being coached out of you?

JOE: I wasn't coached until I started going to professional clubs. I didn't have a position, I just did what I did in the playground. I'd get the ball from the goalie, dribble and try to score, play a one-two or square it for my mate to score. That's how it was, it wasn't coached.

TONY: People would say, 'Joe Cole's a talented player.' Where did it come from?

JOE: It was just how I expressed myself. I wanted to see what I could do with a ball. I used to play up against a wall and try things. I'd watched Italian football on TV on Sundays (this is pre-Sky Sports) and would copy some of the skills I'd seen. I did it because I enjoyed it. No coaching, no pressure.

TONY: You recognised early on that you were better than most in your age group; you could dribble, score and make goals. How did that make you feel?

JOE: I was embarrassed if people praised me; I didn't like it. With my Sunday team, if I scored two goals I would try not to score more. I would rather set my mates up for a goal. I didn't enjoy adulation. 'Well done, Joe. You were great today.' That embarrassed me.

TONY: When did you realise you could make football a career?

JOE: When I went to West Ham really, and realised I was one of the better ones in the group. You're exposed to a professional environment and it starts to ramp up a bit (the expectation).

TONY: You signed for West Ham at fourteen, shortly after you got picked to go to the FA School at Lilleshall, so in effect two years of your development was with the FA.

JOE: Yes, it was like a hybrid system really. Every three weeks I would come back to West Ham to play. At West Ham, I had two seasons with Brian Nichols and Peter Brabrook, two years at Lilleshall, then came back for a full-time apprenticeship with you. At Lilleshall, they always played you in your own age group but when I would come back to West Ham to play, you or Peter would push me up the age groups, which tested me physically. I enjoyed that.

TONY: We felt it was pointless playing you in your own age group; you were the best player and it wouldn't challenge you enough. So at sixteen you were sometimes playing in the under-19s.

JOE: Yeah, that really helped me, playing in the older age groups. It gave me a real challenge.

TONY: How did joining West Ham come about?

JOE: I looked at all the top clubs and, similar to Michael (Carrick), I just got a good feel for the place. We had so much success at the academy and people would ask me, 'What is it about West Ham? What do they do differently?' I would say it's about good people. I don't know what you did, but you must have had communication with all the staff. Someone would greet you, smile on their face, and offer you and your mum and dad a cup of tea. The coaching was good and enjoyable, very inclusive and everybody was made to feel at home. Once you attract good players, other good players want to join. It was a good environment for young players to learn the game. Everyone thought I joined West Ham for money but my dad wouldn't have any of that. He said it was like selling your son. We were offered money but my parents said, 'It's up to you where you go. You're old enough to make that decision yourself but don't go for the money – go where you're most comfortable.' It had to be the right club for me.

**TONY:** I remember talking to your dad (George), God rest his soul, after you committed to signing for us. It was before your fourteenth birthday when you could officially sign and I said to him, 'I would be a lot happier if you signed now and I'll put it in a drawer until Joe's birthday.' George said, 'Here's my signature,' and held out his hand. I shook it and he said, 'You don't need bits of paper.' He was true to his word and you and your dad signed on your fourteenth birthday. That was the attitude your family had, which rubbed off on you.

**JOE:** My dad was always up front with people and, as you know, football can be brutal at times, so that was not the usual way of doing things. Once I had decided to sign for West Ham, Manchester United asked me to go to the FA Cup final with them, on the team coach, out onto the pitch at Wembley and to spend the day with them. It was a dream for a thirteen-year-old kid. I sat down with my dad and he said, 'You have made your decision to sign for West Ham. You will only be stringing them along if you go.' So we rang up and said, 'Thanks, but no thanks.'

**TONY:** That's a testament to your family and that down-to-earth approach stayed with you throughout your career and all your successes.

JOE: It's a whirlwind for your families as well on that journey. They go from watching a kid play at Chadwell Heath, getting a cup of tea and biscuits to watching you play for England in the World Cup. After one England game, a FIFA World Cup qualifying match vs Wales which we won 1-0 and I scored the winning goal, we got in the car, my parents and I, after the game and while we were going down the motorway, the topic of conversation was which service station we would stop at to get a McDonald's. No one spoke about the game or my goal until after we had eaten!

TONY: Dennis Coxall was the scout who watched you and brought you to the attention of West Ham. You were playing in Regent's Park at the time?

JOE: No, it was Market Road, Islington, for my local team.

TONY: Okay, I know Market Road from my time teaching at Holloway School.

JOE: Did you? I used to train there for the district team – small world.

TONY: A trip down memory lane there. Let's move on. One of the first times you came to Chadwell Heath, we played an under-12 game on the railway pitch. It's an artificial pitch now, but at that time it was grass. Jimmy Hampson asked Harry Redknapp, who was the manager at the time, to stay and come out to watch you play. He said, 'We think this kid is a good player. Come and have a look.' Harry saw you do a few things and called for the gate man 'Big Dave', also known as 'Dave the

Gate', and told him to lock the gates and 'don't let this kid leave until I've spoken to his parents'.

JOE: Yeah, football was a lot less of a business then. You wouldn't see a Premier League manager watching an under-12 game now.

TONY: When you were seventeen you were asked to train with the full England squad by Kevin Keegan. What was that like?

JOE: That was like, wow! I didn't drive then and my mum drove me to Bisham Abbey where we had to meet. I had my boots in a plastic carrier bag. I walked in and was waiting for someone to greet me and Paul Scholes and Phil Neville walked past and said, 'Hi, Joe.' They knew who I was! I had played in the first team a few times, but I was amazed they knew me. It felt like I was in the squad. The next thing I am on the pitch training with England! There was Shearer, Ince, Tony Adams and others; it was unbelievable. It was a great feeling. There was nothing to be scared of – it was just football.

TONY: When you first broke into the team, you didn't like to talk to the media. Is that true?

JOE: Yeah, I didn't like to do media. I spoke to Frank Lampard (Sr) and told him I wasn't happy doing media interviews. I was young and would shy away from it. I did some because the press were allowed in the training ground and mingled with the players at this time and it was difficult to avoid.

**TONY:** At one time when you were at Chelsea there was talk of a possible transfer to Juventus. Is that true?

**JOE:** I did get a chance to sign for them and I didn't take it. I used to watch Italian football when it used to be on TV on Sundays, and I loved Juventus and especially Roberto Baggio. It's one of my biggest regrets. Carly and I had just had a baby daughter and I thought it was not right to move everybody to Italy at that point, but I do regret not going there.

**TONY:** What was it about Italian football that you loved?

**JOE:** The great technique of the players. I used to watch a player perform a certain skill and me and my mates would try to copy it in the playground. That's how I learnt, what is it? Learn through play. I was always trying to copy great players' skills. I remember one time when I was at Lilleshall, when we were all trying to copy that Roberto Carlos goal from a free kick for Brazil in 1997. We used to go down to the training pitch early and I ended up nearly breaking my leg trying to perfect that technique. The coach Keith Blunt went mad at us all because we hadn't done a warm-up beforehand!

**TONY:** Being a Londoner and living up in Shropshire at Lilleshall – that must have been strange?

**JOE:** Yeah, before they know you, they think you're just a flash Londoner.

**TONY:** You roomed with a boy from Liverpool, I believe?

JOE: Yeah, a talented player, a guy called Ian. As soon as we all left Lilleshall things didn't work out for him at Liverpool, football-wise. He didn't become the next Michael Owen. He then just walked away from it and stopped returning people's calls. I haven't spoken to him for thirteen or fourteen years. I lived with him in the same room for two years. I think football broke his heart. It's such a shame because he was one of my best mates.

TONY: So two boys from the FA Lilleshall School, sharing the same room, both with the same ambitions and dreams. You achieved most of your dreams and he gets disillusioned with the game because it doesn't work out ...

JOE: He was a really talented player, a real talent. He played professional at Port Vale and he quit at 25, I think. He was a steady League One player. I just think there was a lot of pressure on him to be the next Michael Owen or the next Robbie Fowler. The squad of boys from Lilleshall, with social media, WhatsApp etc. all still speak and meet up when we can, and he is the only one that doesn't join in. That's sad.

TONY: Do you understand the obsession of the fans. Do you still hear the crowd when you're playing?

JOE: You hear them but you become accustomed to it. It's just a noise. When I went and played in America, we played in some places where there was hardly anyone there and that was abnormal to me. I think I have always had a good relationship with the fans of all the clubs I've played for, because I think they can relate to me. I have always made a point of remembering how important it was as a kid. Because it's very easy when you get a bit disenchanted with it because of all the other stuff in football. Once you step onto that pitch as a kid, I would have given my right arm to have just played one game as a professional in front of a crowd. So you've got a responsibility to the fans.

**TONY:** That is very similar to what Michael (Carrick) said. 'Sometimes you have your ups and downs in football, when kids come and ask for a photo or an autograph, but I always try to oblige.' He remembered when he was a kid and if a player refused an autograph how disappointed he was. Do you see it in the same way?

**JOE:** It's heartbreaking for a kid. You try and you try, but there's always an occasion when you're in a rush, you've got an appointment or you have to pick up the kids. Very rarely, but life happens sometimes. But you must always remember how important those things were for you as a kid. When you're a footballer playing for West Ham, Chelsea, Liverpool or England, there is a massive social responsibility for people around the game. You are thrust into a position of being a role model, which most of us are not ready or equipped for and you don't always do the right thing and mistakes are made.

**TONY:** And then people make judgements, when you're not really trained for it ...

**JOE:** Exactly. I am very conscious, as a player, particularly the older I got, of the responsibilities. Even when I was at Coventry, for the fans there who travelled to matches, and this ain't me trying to do it because I want everyone to love me, but you have to appreciate what it means to them. I am always conscious of that. It's really important to me.

**TONY:** You were never one to court publicity or attention and there was a report somewhere you would prefer to be drinking tea with the London cab drivers than in a swanky West End restaurant. Is that true?

**JOE:** I don't know where that came from but my dad, George, had a minicab business and I would often be in the office drinking tea with the cabbies and talking all sorts of rubbish, so I suppose it's partly true.

**TONY:** Would you say you played football for the fun rather than the money?

**JOE:** Without doubt, without doubt. Looking back now, because I've got a fresh perspective having retired, the money has been able to change me and all my family's lives for the better. And you can never underestimate that. A more comfortable life, my kids are going to be comfortable, my grandkids are going to be comfortable. I'm in a fortunate position because of football but motivation has always been enjoyment before money.

**TONY:** What's your greatest moment on the pitch? The FA Youth Cup final 1999? No, I'm only kidding.

**JOE:** That would have been one of the most fun and the most memorable. People still talk to me about it now. People come up to me and talk about my goal for England against Sweden. Chelsea fans talk to me about the goal when we won the second title against Manchester United, when I scored a big goal at the Bridge. West Ham fans love to talk about that Youth Cup win. I don't know if it's an indictment that West Ham haven't won anything for the past twenty years or so. But the West Ham fans love to talk about it; they just love the club.

**TONY:** As a senior pro, what was the game that you felt was your best game?

**JOE:** It was at Chelsea when we won the League Cup, the first trophy we won together as a group. It was in Cardiff and it was an amazing game at an amazing stadium. It was electric. We played Liverpool and we won 3-2. I started the game and I think I came off after we scored the third goal and had seen them off. They were a good team but on the day we were better. You are always conscious you want to win trophies because that is the currency of success. You can't be a good player and not win trophies. Well, you can, but you want to. And that was the first one and that felt to me like winning the World Cup, similar to the Youth Cup situation. Frank (Lampard) I'd known since I was a kid, John (Terry), Bridgey (Wayne Bridge), Glen Johnson – we had all come through. Again, it felt like you had won it with all your mates. All the best teams I've played in, we've had good relationships off the pitch as well. Yeah, that was the best moment, because it was the first trophy. We had a league game on the Saturday, so we went back to an Italian restaurant on the Fulham Road and we all had a celebration meal – that was nice.

**TONY:** And what was your worst moment?

**JOE:** The worst moment was getting relegated at West Ham. Broke my heart, it did. That season I think I played some really good football personally. I felt like I was carrying the team. I was captain. Glenn (Roeder) made me captain at the age of 21 for the last eight games. You don't want to dig people out but there were a lot of senior players that went missing during that season. And then Glenn's trouble with his brain tumour and Trevor Brooking took over. I was playing like a man possessed; I felt a massive responsibility going into games. We did everything right towards the end. We turned it around and got 42 points – you're mid-table with 42 points these days. I just felt it was heart-breaking. But for a 21-year-old man, what a life lesson to come through. I came through it and it made me stronger.

**TONY:** As you say, Glenn Roeder gave you the captaincy at 21. How did that feel? Did you feel you were ready? Did you see it as a challenge? Were you daunted or concerned?

**JOE:** I wasn't concerned. I was more concerned about organising the tickets and things like that because that isn't my strength. Steve Lomas was great. I think he was injured at the time for a lot of the season and he helped me a lot. Some of the other senior players, I think it riled them a bit. I don't want to name names; but Steve was great and he helped me with all the stuff off the pitch. I remember going in to see Trevor asking what the team needed. What do we need? It was a very steep learning curve, but I loved it, I relished it. If you look back at some of the games, I played like a man possessed. I was centre midfield, right and left midfield, I was everywhere trying to make things happen. It wasn't enough in the end and it was a tough one to take.

**TONY:** You won 'Hammer of the Year' in 2003 and Chelsea 'Player of the Year' in 2008. Such accolades must be among your most cherished memories as a player?

**JOE:** Yeah, at the time I did love it, but as you grow older you realise that it's a team game. Those things are great, but I cherish more the things we won as a team. But as a youngster, all those things, all the little awards you win, the man of the match, the player of the month, they feel great but then you realise how special it is when you actually do get over the line and win something as a team – that's what it's all about.

**TONY:** Do you think the Premier League is the greatest league in the world?

**JOE:** Yeah, without a doubt. I've been lucky enough to have experienced the French league with Lille and that is also a good league.

**TONY:** I remember talking to you when you came back from Lille and you saying what a great player they had in Eden Hazard.

**JOE:** Yeah, I can't take any credit for that; even a non-footballing person could see this guy was a special talent. I said when I saw him that he would become the best player in the world and I think at one point he will become the best player in the world. I think he is getting better and better. Barring an injury, he is one of the best now; he is absolutely phenomenal.

**TONY:** Your move to Chelsea, new club, new facilities – what did that feel like? Did you feel you had to prove yourself?

**JOE:** We were at Harlington at the time and the facilities were just as bad as Chadwell Heath! It helped having JT (Terry) and Frank (Lampard), who I knew very well. Coming from a big fish at West Ham, I walked into a dressing room and about four or five of the foreign lads who were sort of on the periphery of the team, but big names, didn't even know my name. I know that because as I've come in, they were like, 'Who's that? What's that?' I'd already played four seasons in the Premier League and I saw it as a challenge. The first season I played around 50 games, 25 starts and 25 from the bench under the manager at this time, Claudio Ranieri. We finished second in the league and I played in the semi-final of the Champions League. So, by the end of the season I was in, which is what I had set myself. They then went about signing big-money players: Verón, Mutu, Duff and Geremi.

**TONY:** What was your fee?

**JOE:** £6 million. I was one of the cheaper ones.

**TONY:** Because of the fire sale at West Ham?

**JOE:** Yeah. West Ham were lucky that Chelsea were about because Chelsea paid an extra £2 million. The price would've actually been lower because everybody knew West Ham needed the money. That's why everybody was waiting and waiting, and Chelsea came in and went bang, bang. We'll take Joe and Johnno (Glen Johnson). Then you go into Chelsea with Roman

Abramovich, who wanted to win the Champions League and the Premier League. Not because Chelsea was massively bigger than West Ham at the time, it was just financially they were now bigger. And now I'd gone from West Ham to playing with the likes of Marcel Desailly, Seba Verón and the Jimmy Floyd Hasselbainks of this world. World-class players. The West Ham players were good, but these guys were like geniuses.

**TONY:** You had big success at Chelsea and eventually went back to West Ham. What did that feel like, going back to where it all began?

**JOE:** It was great to see yourself, Jimmy Frith, Pete Williams and others. It was great to see everyone. You still had that core. I was also very aware that the club had changed. So in some ways it was the same and in others it wasn't. The game had changed and moved on. I was 32 at the time and I think when I came back, I still had a couple of years left in me. I played here and there, scored a few goals, but at that time in my career injuries were curtailing my performances. Ever since I had my knee injury in 2009 it was a real struggle. I can look back now I've retired and say I wasn't the same player I was before my injuries.

**TONY:** You had a short spell at Aston Villa. Were they a similar club to West Ham?

**JOE:** Yeah, when Villa came in for me, I just fancied it. Again, a similar story: the injuries curtailed it. I didn't play enough. When I played, I was fine. It was similar at West Ham – good enough to play in the team but then you pull a hamstring and you are out for five or six weeks. Someone else comes in and takes your spot. It's not like I was 25; I needed to be on it to perform. I stayed professional, giving it my all, and tried to stick at it. You can't really complain with the cards you've been dealt because I've seen some fantastic players lose their careers before it gets started because of injury. My dad said, 'You always have to be happy with what you've got and be thankful for it.' I would have loved not to have done my knee in 2009 and I know for sure I would've had twice as many medals. But the road I was on was the road I was on. And just be thankful I've got all these great memories.

**TONY:** How many England caps did you end up with?

**JOE:** 56.

**TONY:** Did you find being with the England squads enjoyable? Were the tournaments pressurised?

**JOE:** The players who I played with, I'm very different to them. They would say how boring down time in tournaments was. I loved it, I absolutely loved it. I couldn't think of anything better. I loved the tournaments. You train in the morning, have a nice lunch together; you go to watch other games in the tournament or another day you played golf or played on the PlayStation. So, for me, I absolutely loved it. But to be fair I didn't have children at this time. My eldest was born at the 2010 World Cup and she was just a baby. Give me a World Cup or Euro tournament any day. I thought it was brilliant.

**TONY:** So you saw no negatives?

**JOE:** Not at all. But everybody else did.

**TONY:** Players in the past have said how tournaments can be boring, being locked up in a training camp and filling in time. I would often think, *You don't know how lucky you are.*

**JOE:** Exactly, and I'm sure these lads, ten to twenty years down the line, would give their right arm to be back there. Because I would do it all over again. I would give it all back to go and start again. All that excitement and the pressure was never a problem. I've played under pressure to perform from as soon as I set foot on a professional pitch. Nothing ever fazed me in terms of going out and playing. I've seen players melt in an England shirt. But one thing I can certainly say is my performances never dipped from my club to England. If anything, they raised a bit. I scored ten goals for England, and I just always seemed to perform when I played. I loved it; I loved the tempo of the games, the style.

**TONY:** What did it feel like to score that volley for England against Sweden?

**JOE:** It was a top goal. It got voted the second-best goal in English World Cup history, which I'm proud of. Straight after the game, I gave my shirt away to one of the Swedish players and JT said, 'Where's your shirt?' I said, 'I've just swapped it.' He said, 'Go and get it back; you will never score another goal like that!' So I sent my spare shirt into the Swedish dressing room and asked for my shirt back. I gave him the one I didn't wear and got the match-worn shirt back. I don't know where it is now, someone's got it somewhere!

**TONY:** You went overseas to play for Lille in France and also to play for Tampa Bay in the USA. How did you find the cultural differences, especially in France?

**JOE:** I loved it, I lapped it up. Years before, I spoke to David Platt. He was my England under-18s manager at the time, and I asked him about Italy and playing there. He said, 'If you ever get the chance to play abroad, make sure you do everything you can to live like the locals. Take up the culture.' Which is what I did. I tried my best with the language, and they appreciated that because the English are renowned for being lazy with languages. So I tried my best and there were some good comedic moments with me wrestling with the language. By the end of it, I did a couple of TV interviews in French, just the basics, but they appreciated it. I loved and enjoyed it. And for the first time in ten years I had an injury-free season. I played a full season in the team and was back at my level. I think I scored nine goals in 40 games, was making goals and playing well because I stayed fit and was playing regularly. I loved it and should've stayed.

**TONY:** Could you have stayed if you wanted to?

**JOE:** I could have done at one point, but Brendan Rodgers got the Liverpool manager's job and Brendan remembered me from our Chelsea days. We got in contact and he said, 'Listen, I know what you can do. We will get you right, we will get you fit.' Then the same thing happened. I went to Liverpool, I was in the team and had started Brendan's first game, a European game, started it, had a good pre-season and then pulled a hamstring, out for six weeks. Then someone else takes your place and I think it was the emergence of Raheem Sterling and you're fighting to get fit again.

**TONY:** What was the standard like at Tampa Bay Rowdies in the USA?

**JOE:** The standard is hard to gauge because the factors are so massive. You've got the heat for one, and the travel. I think in America they've got lots and lots of average players, because that's what the system produces. The USL I was in was a good standard. People have this conception that it's like it is easy. Some people ring me up and say, 'Get me out there and I'll play.' You need to be a decent player to play; you just can't turn up and play. You need to be fit. Everybody is very professional and the standard is rapidly growing. The differences between the top and bottom in the game are getting smaller.

**TONY:** And Wayne Rooney has recently been out there in the MLS ...

**JOE:** Wayne Rooney has been brilliant. No doubt about it, he is a top player.

**TONY:** He looked like he enjoyed it. He didn't go for a holiday, he took it very seriously.

**JOE:** Yeah, he loves his football. Once you are on the pitch, it doesn't matter where you're playing, you are going to go at it. But I loved America, I really did. And I loved the lifestyle and the anonymity which was amazing. I could walk about. I lived in a little town on a bay, in an apartment and the stadium was at one end and there were little bars and restaurants. You had the bay with all the yachts in front of us and I lived at the other end. You barely needed to venture out from that. It was good, it was a good life.

**TONY:** And the family were out there with you?

**JOE:** Yeah, I wouldn't do it without the family, and that was the main reason why I had to come back. Otherwise I would've rinsed it and played out there for another two or three years.

**TONY:** What distinguishes the great managers from the good?

**JOE:** I've had two great managers, at least. There are other great managers, but I will use the examples of Ancelotti and Mourinho. You couldn't meet two more different approaches to a team, but they were both great. The one thing that defines a great manager from a good manager is football instinct. There are so many ways to do it but the one thing you must have is the ability to see a player, read the game and just have that instinct. Sometimes there is no rhyme or reason. José would do something ... like we would be chasing the game and he would take off a winger and put a centre half on and play him up front. The centre half would end up getting his head on to the ball, knock it down and Frank (Lampard) would go and score. And you think, 'How has he thought about that?' But he just reads the game. Ancelotti was the same; he could read when it was the right time to put a player on, from the bench, or when it was the right time to pull a player out. I've had other managers, Harry (Redknapp), Roy Hodgson, English managers; they were great with what they did. They did things very differently, both probably the two most successful English managers of the last ten years, you could argue. Sam (Allardyce) – you could throw him into that. They were all very different, but they all had good football instincts.

**TONY:** Mourinho, who's very clear about the way he wants the game to be played and there is no diversion – did that ever conflict with you or did that motivate you?

**JOE:** He got me at the right time. I was probably at my peak and he put me into a system which I'd never played a lot, 4-3-3, which suited me. I played on the right coming infield and allowing a bit of space for the full backs or others to use. I can't really describe him; his public persona is very different to what he actually is. He is quite good fun, well he was at those times. He was quite young as a manager at Chelsea. He was close in age to the players compared to other managers. He pushed me, really pushed me, really put it on me. I was just one of his lesser-known players. He knew I had ability, he said some nice things about me in private and then publicly in front of the other lads he'd really demand more of me.

**TONY:** Did that motivate you?

**JOE:** Yeah, I wanted to show him, prove to him. The first thing he said to us, when he took over the first time at Chelsea, he called a meeting and he had us all in the palm of his hand. He said, 'I am a champion, I've won this, I've won that. You lot, no one has won anything, no one is a champion.' Then he gave us a date in April, and said, 'If you follow me, we will win the league on this day.' And it was like three or four weeks before the end of the season! He had a presence and the lads just ate it up. I thought, anything this guy says, I'm in. He promised us we would win the league on this day and I think we won it the week before. So, he started off, and his initial meeting was amazing. With the team he had me, Duff (Damien), and Robben (Arjen) so it didn't matter if he upset one of us – the other two were going to do something and win him a game or something. He was brilliant. And I think with Arjen, the reason he left was because the intensity of the league didn't suit his body and the intensity that José required didn't suit his body make-up. At the time, I could do anything he wanted: up, down, up, down, doing everything. Arjen was more of a pure winger and found that intensity hard, but what a talent, one of the best players I've ever played with. He's unbelievable.

**TONY:** Which player inspired you and had the most effect on you?

**JOE:** The one player I've always held in high esteem was Frank (Lampard). Being three or four years older than me, I always looked up to him. I played, in total, 714 games and scored 104 goals. Frank scored 300 goals! I watched him every day – practice, practice, practice. I tried that, I tried to do that, because I saw how hard he worked and how good it was. I always put Frank up on a pedestal for any young player I talk to; I say that's the way to do it. I was very aware of what I could and couldn't do. I saw Frank not only work on his weaknesses but also his strengths. So he's the one player I put up there. I wouldn't have scored over 100 goals if it wasn't for Frank. I wasn't a natural goalscorer. If I was starting my career now, I'd reckon I'd be like a Jack Wilshere type, getting the ball in midfield and connecting things and passing it and then arriving in the box. You look at the front three of teams now, everywhere there's electric pace. I never had electric pace. I was quick, so I think I would be a slightly deeper midfielder.

TONY: So what did you see your role as, when you were a player?

JOE: I was a goal maker, primarily. Someone who would get the ball, break the lines, find a pass and create something. I also tried to score when I could. I think if I was starting off in football now, the game is set up for players like me, playing through the lines consistently and finding pockets of space for me to exploit. There wasn't actually a role for me in English footballing culture when I grew up. I had to make myself something because I was so different; I had a different upbringing to so many other players.

TONY: Everybody was playing 4-4-2. In your youth team, we played three at the back and I gave you a free role.

JOE: That suited me. Look how well that worked for us. Teams couldn't get near us.

TONY: It was quite innovative at the time; teams didn't know how to mark you.

JOE: Yeah, and teams have gone back to that way of playing. I loved playing in that team and in that system. I didn't always stay up there. Sometimes I would come deeper to get the ball. Teams couldn't mark you, it was good. Look at it now. When

Conte was Chelsea manager, he played that way and it was like Conte had invented the system!

**TONY:** What players have you seen who, for whatever reason, didn't fulfil their potential?

**JOE:** Bertie (Brayley) could've been a top player. In some ways he could've been but in other ways his mind was frazzled. If it wasn't the Youth Cup, where he was one of the stars, it would have been something else. But talent-wise, his left foot was lovely wasn't it? I think Richard Garcia would have been unbelievable if it hadn't been for his knee injury – he had everything. He still had a good career, although cut short. Ian Armstrong who we spoke about was as good a finisher as I'd seen in youth football. But it's all in the mind. Look at Jamie Vardy, what he has done late on in his career. With 'Army' something might have clicked at 26 or 27 and he could have gone on and played in the Premier League. Sometimes you have to stick at it, keep going and keep going, keep believing, even when everybody else doesn't. So yeah, for many different reasons, those three players.

**TONY:** What about Izzy (Iriekpen)?

**JOE:** Yeah, I'm mates with Izzy. I put Izzy's one down to a mixture of both his horrific knee injury and his lack of guidance. We have talked about how lucky I was having the family around me, guiding me. Izzy didn't have that. I'm sure he wouldn't be unhappy with me talking about it, because we still talk today. He would have been an amazing player.

**TONY:** What about players that made it and surprised you?

**JOE:** There are always people that surprise you. I wouldn't have thought Glen Johnson would've had the career he's had when he was a youngster. He has done terrific, after West Ham, Chelsea, Liverpool and England. He's done well.

**TONY:** Who would have said that Frank (Lampard) when he was fifteen would have had the career he's had?

**JOE:** You would have been laughed at, wouldn't you?

**TONY:** It's having that mental toughness; it's one of the most important things.

**JOE:** It's about having a constant belief, being able to take the criticisms and staying focused. And don't get carried away with the highs and that's why having good people around is important, to keep you grounded.

**TONY:** What was the difference in ethos or philosophy at Chelsea?

**JOE:** Remember I was at Chelsea in the Roman Abramovich era, not straight away, but when José got there it changed a lot. In my first year, with Ranieri, we did great but we didn't win anything. So when José came in it was, 'We have to win the league.' A winning mentality was installed.

**TONY:** Finally, what's your view on Abramovich? Did you meet him?

**JOE:** Yeah, many times. Very quiet, a good guy, very hands-on with the running of the club; it's his club and he is very passionate about Chelsea. Since I've left, all my dealings with the club, they have really looked after me and are very welcoming. They are good at that, never forgetting the past. All clubs need to tip their hats to the past, because it's a community thing. Fans want to see the older players, coaches and managers involved. Ferguson at Manchester United was great with things like that, never forgetting past history and getting ex-players and staff involved one way or another. Certainly, if I ever go into management, I'll be looking to do that.

# 9

# A GOLDEN ERA OF PLAYERS

The rapid rise of Rio and Frank into the first-team squad brought to mind the efforts we made to secure them youth international recognition. Harry spoke to me one day.

'Tony, why haven't Rio or Frank been picked for England youth?'

I didn't know the answer. England scouts regularly watched our youth and reserve games but clearly the FA didn't fancy them for some reason.

'Who is the England under-18 youth coach?' Harry asked.

'Dave Burnside,' I replied.

Harry immediately rang him.

'Hi Dave, it's Harry Redknapp. We have two fantastic young players here at West Ham, Lampard and Ferdinand, and we feel they should be playing for the England youth team.'

Burnside said, 'We know about them, Harry, and have had them watched, but we feel at this moment we already have better players in the team.'

Harry was riled. 'Well, if you have better players than these two already, you must have a f****** good team!'

He slammed the phone down. It just goes to show that playing for England at youth level is not a perfect indicator of future progression in the game.

Frank would go on to win 106 England caps and Rio 81. And both of them captained their country at various times. I think I know who was right.

At the time, England youth team coaches and scouts would come to our youth games but rarely discussed players with me. All they did was ask for a team sheet and disappear to watch the game. That was then. The system now is much improved and there is a lot more dialogue between the coaches – especially when Kenny Swain, ex-Chelsea, Everton and Nottingham Forest player, was England youth manager. He would visit the training ground or ring me regularly to ask about our players. Was any player showing good form and could he be a potential England player?

Another story of predicting future player development occurred during a fans' forum when Harry was quizzed about Frank Lampard and why was he in the first team while another young player, Scott Canham, was being ignored. Harry went on the attack. He explained to the questioner that Frank was a great prospect, a top, top player and was destined for great things. I am not sure quite how much of his irritation-provoked prophecies Harry actually believed at that moment, but Frank, of course, would go on to exceed even this paean. I mention this now as the moment has been played on YouTube thousands of times and, although you cannot see the guy in the audience, I recognised the voice as Scott Canham's uncle who had approached me several times asking me exactly the same question.

I asked Frank some years later about his football development and the conversation went like this:

**TONY:** What is your earliest memory of playing football?

**FRANK:** My earliest memory is Dad taking me over to the local park in Gidea Park, Essex, where I grew up. He wanted to get me into the local team – Heath Park Rangers – and that was the team I ended up playing for. I think they started at under-6s but I was a year younger than that, but my dad threw me in – a sign of things to come – and he said, 'Go on. In you go ...' He started talking to the coach, a fellow named Chris Nocill, whose boy played in the team as well. He took me on, so I suppose I always grew up with a football in my hand. My story is different in terms of my dad being an ex-professional player. It's not unique but it's different from the norm. I grew up with nothing else on my mind other than to play football. From that age up to about eighteen or twenty I was not quite the best but probably in the running to be the best. I was never naturally outstanding, even at Heath Park, because they had a lot of players who, like me, were taken on at West Ham – Danny Shipp, Scott Moore, Michael Black.

**TONY:** Your dad put you through private education. Were you ever tempted to look elsewhere for a career?

**FRANK:** Yes, I had two sides to my life. The schooling at Brentwood where football wasn't the strong point, although I did play for the independent schools' team. Then I had my Heath Park weekends and, when I got older, training at West Ham, Arsenal and Tottenham, which had a different feel. So, it was two separate lives as such and as I've got older it's been a big strength I think, because I've managed to see both sides.

As I went through school, I wanted to do well, a bit like how I approached football I suppose. I was never quite the best but I wanted the teacher to be happy with me. When I went to do my YT (youth training) at West Ham, the school tried to get me to stay to do my A levels. They said what a good grounding that would be for my life. Dad said no because he said that if you missed the YT (which was a two-year full-time training programme) then you wouldn't make it as a player, which was completely true. I came out of school with decent GCSEs but nothing really smacked me in the face. There was only football, and cricket which I liked as well.

TONY: You've said you were never the outstanding individual. Did that drive you on – because of your character?

FRANK: Yes. I'm still the same, although you wouldn't always know what is going on in my head. I'm not an emotional person so it was always an inner thing. I was driven to the point I had a professional jealousy. I always wanted to be the best in the team, score the most goals, be the best midfield player. That never left me and my dad was crucial because he let me know from a young age what he saw were my weaknesses and things I needed to improve on. He battered away at those to the point it became natural for me to pick up on how I could improve.

TONY: I was quite close to your dad. I played in the West Ham youth team with him and in that respect he was never afraid to tell you, unlike a lot of parents. That probably stood you in good stead throughout your career.

**FRANK:** When I look back, I think I was lucky because, one, I was from a football family. Dad was the hard taskmaster because he let me know in no uncertain terms the work that had to be done ... my weaknesses, which were always speed and agility. And then my mum, who was a lovely buffer, would help me with the emotional side at school. Not many had that balance. I didn't like it sometimes. My main memories of playing football were not winning the Essex Cup with Heath Park but over at the local park on a rainy day with Dad crossing balls for me to head. Not enjoyable stuff. I was a bit of a chubby kid – I liked the chocolate and sweets, but he always tried to get me quicker and more agile.

**TONY:** He introduced you to spikes, didn't he?

**FRANK:** Yeah, I hated them. I was embarrassed to wear them. Again though, it helped me to train my brain in respect of work to be done. At Chelsea, in my first year, I wore them over the back of the training ground and I was really embarrassed by them because I didn't want Desailly and Zola seeing me wearing them.

**TONY:** Going back to when you were a schoolboy, we didn't have the academy system as it is now but we had the South East Counties League, which I still think was the best. Am I wrong in thinking you were training at other London clubs as well?

**FRANK:** There were two reasons for that: 1) to keep my options open – and my dad was savvy in that he knew I didn't have to sign and put all my eggs in one basket – and 2) just to get different coaching. I remember Johnny Martin at Tottenham, where we used to do very technical stuff; at Arsenal it was in between while at West Ham it was tougher, more simplistic in a football sense. They were different, which was great for me. I would go to school in the day and then three nights a week at West Ham, Tottenham and Arsenal, so I was getting overload. I think that I was never going anywhere but West Ham because of my dad and I was a West Ham fan. The training ground was only ten minutes away from my home and it felt the right club because there were good people that I liked and there was a pathway to the first team. Because I had a foot in the door because of my dad, it felt homely and I thought there was an opportunity there to get into the first team. Also, Harry was there and there was a big push for the academy then. It was not where they had wanted it to be for years and there were a lot of good kids around me. I remember Jimmy Neighbour coming around and sitting with me and my dad in the garden. I thought, at the time, I was being a little bit pushed out because other kids were being chased more than me, but I suppose they thought I would sign anyway. Anyway Jimmy came around and said the club wanted to sign me as a YT (youth trainee) and I was sold. The fact that he had come round to the house impressed me. It was a no-brainer.

TONY: Are you a fan of football? Did you watch football? Did you love football and, if so, was it because of your dad? Do you still watch the game now?

FRANK: Yes, I am a fan. There was probably only one year when I switched off a bit and that was when I went to America near the end of my career. I had probably had enough of playing. Up until that it was everything to me, watching my dad at West Ham every week, standing in the tunnel looking at Tony Cottee and Frank McAvennie who were my idols at the time. That's why now I always try to give youngsters the time because I was that kid myself, with the advantage of being behind the scenes as well. The only thing that being a professional player does to you is that it takes some of the fun out of it. I was so focused in the Chelsea years that the love of it went slightly. I loved winning but without the pure love for winning that I had at a young age.

TONY: Can you understand the fanaticism of the fans?

FRANK: I get it completely. I grew up as that fan and even when I was playing, if I was watching a game, I would get passionate about it. You do take on allegiances. I played at Chelsea for thirteen years and when I was at West Ham, Tottenham were not your favourites. That tribal thing is in you and you can't take it away. I would shout at the telly – so I understand the fans. As a manager now, when your team is playing it along the back and the fans are yelling, 'Play it long!', you can react to it inside, but I do understand it. When you are playing you feel the atmosphere, particularly in big games, but you go into the zone once the game kicks off. If there is any break in the game, you feel it again though.

TONY: Going back to your youth days when you were training with me, Harry asked me why you and Rio were not in the England youth set-up. I said I didn't know and he rang the then England youth manager, Dave Burnside, and gave him a blasting for not picking the pair of you. You never did get the recognition you deserved at that time. My general observation of you at that time was that I could never read you, your expressions – I didn't know what you were thinking. I thought you were impatient. You wanted to be with the reserves and then when you were there, you wanted to be with the first team. It was an inner drive, am I right?

**FRANK:** You're spot on. I haven't lost that, and it can be good or bad. Sometimes it's good to show your emotions and some people thought I was rude. I've tried to improve it as I've got older. You are right about the impatience and that's why Rio and I gravitated to each other, because of that drive.

**TONY:** I agree with you 100 per cent. We got to the FA Youth Cup final in 1996 against Liverpool. You scored in the first minute, but we lost 4-1 over the two legs.

**FRANK:** I remember that because I absolutely folded in the home game because I was so pumped up for it. It was a good lesson for me because they had good players including Michael Owen, Jamie Carragher and David Thompson. He gave me the runaround at Upton Park. It was a really good learning curve and that's what youth football is about; it's not always about the good moments. We got taught a good lesson. I can also remember going to Chelsea and winning the League Cup.

**TONY:** I was going to mention that. We lost the first leg 5-2. Peter Storrie had a real dig at me. He said, 'Who picked these players? Who scouted them?' I said we didn't play well tonight, but we are better than that. We went to Chelsea and they scored in the first minute to make it 6-2. The rest is history. I pushed Rio into a more advanced position and we won through. You scored the winning goal from the penalty spot. That was the first time the youth team had won anything for years. The following year we reached the FA Youth Cup final. You and Rio had moved up and I think you were invited by Terry Venables to train with the England Euro '96 squad.

**FRANK:** It's commonplace now but back then for Venables to do that was very unusual. We were miles away from the England squad but I remember it vividly, being in the hotel with them, training with Gazza. It was terrific and a good period for me. I actually remember getting some 'well dones' from the manager and a few of the senior players. That gave me massive confidence because I idolised Gazza. I was quite a shy kid in many ways and that probably inhibited me from within, but when I went there and then came back, I remember feeling bouncy. There were different parts of my youth career and I remember the cup finals and then going on loan to Swansea. I remember I was at home and Harry rang. When the manager rings it's a big deal, even though he was Uncle Harry. He said you're going to Swansea. I shit myself. I had just passed my driving test and I didn't know where Swansea was! I had a Ford Fiesta and he said he wanted me there in time for training tomorrow. I went there for two months and grew up in a men's changing room and a men's world where points are vital. It was long ball and we were fifth from bottom, probably the same when I left. I didn't pull up massive trees but in terms of my development it was huge.

**TONY:** What is the worst ever moment you've had on the pitch?

**FRANK:** There was the Champions League final against Manchester United, but we corrected that one. With England, we never did. I missed a penalty and we went out in Germany in 2006. I'd gone into the tournament as England Player of the Year and I'd scored quite a few goals in us getting to the finals. I'd also had a good year at Chelsea but when I was at the tournament, although I had the record number of shots, around 30, I couldn't score. I could feel the pressure from the media etc. and it was the first time I'd had that. I missed a penalty and we were out. That was probably the worst. It was a bit of a recovery period after that because the England players were getting booed wherever we went with Chelsea – JT, me, but not Joe Cole because he had a decent tournament. We went to Tottenham and they were chanting, 'You've let your country down.' It took about six months to subside.

**TONY:** What was your best moment?

**FRANK:** Winning the Champions League in Munich. There were others, like the first time Chelsea won the Premier League and I scored two goals at Bolton, a great personal feeling and my mum and dad were behind the goal. That was good, but the Champions League became the holy grail for us – and it was ten years in the making.

**TONY:** You have been described as one of the best midfield players ever to have played the game, with your scoring record and energy. You weren't one of the most naturally athletic players when you were younger but you worked on that yourself. I remember training with the youth team at Chadwell Heath. You were in the first team and you had put two markers down and you were running box to box. I stopped the youth team training and asked them, 'What do you see? And what about Frank over there?' They said, 'He's doing a bit of training.' I said, 'He's a first-team player on his day off and he has come in to work on his weaknesses, on his own. If you want to be a player, you need to take ownership of your own development.'

**FRANK:** You know what, that's the nicest thing anyone could say to me in terms of my development because I love that stuff. I wouldn't have done it without my dad because it wasn't the norm for a seventeen-year-old to be doing that. I quickly found a way though, and when I did extra, ugly stuff, I always felt it made me lucky at the weekend.

**TONY:** What did you see as your role: a goal maker, scorer or creator?

**FRANK:** At West Ham, when I made a bit of a name for myself, I saw myself as a goalscoring midfield player. I wouldn't be involved in the build-up too much, just try to arrive and nick a few goals. When I went to Chelsea the rules were different and I had to get more involved in play. I remained a goalscoring player, but I did get more involved and that suited me because I'm not a back-to-goal player. So hopefully an all-rounder. I played at the top of a diamond under Carlo Ancelotti and I didn't enjoy it much. It allowed me to be marked all the time. I played there and didn't score for about eleven games. I loved him, still do and he is a great manager, but I went to him and said, 'I know you want me at the top of the diamond, but I don't really like it.' I felt bad saying it because he had won the Champions League with AC Milan playing a diamond, with Pirlo and that lot. He took it, though, and put me back on the left side of a three and that year I scored 27 goals.

**TONY:** I looked back at your record. In your West Ham days, it was good in terms of goals and appearances. Some people think you were only there for a short time, but you made about 130 first-team appearances and for a young player your goals to games ratio was good. When you went to Chelsea that improved – with better players and more experience, you improved. So is the Premier League the greatest league in the world and, if so, what defines it?

**FRANK:** Yes it is, firmly because of the competitive nature and the quality, particularly now. In the last ten to fifteen years the Premier League stands out.

**TONY:** You have been manager of Derby in the Championship. How did you see the differences?

**FRANK:** There are a lot more similarities than differences. The Championship now has foreign managers. You can't compare it to the Premier League and then say the Championship is old school. Most teams like to play. Of course the quality is differ-ent and the game-changing players are not there to a degree, hence you win one, you lose one, so the consistency isn't there. That's it though; I don't see much else. I played in America for eighteen months and the story is similar although there is a defensive problem.

**TONY:** Is there a right and wrong way of training?

**FRANK:** I try and train to be as elite as we can be. One of the things I take from my time at Chelsea and Manchester City is not so much the detail but the attitude, how you approach things. You can over-complicate training, but the most important thing is how hard the players work, as individuals and as a collective. From a managerial point, I like to push the work ethic every day and like to think the rest can follow. I also try to stay open-minded. The detail is the cherry on the cake.

**TONY:** When you played, what did you see as the glory times? Dominance in the league or playing for England?

**FRANK:** In general, dominance in the league because we had two years under Mourinho where we thought we'd win every game and even if we didn't play well, we thought we would grind out a result. It was a beautiful feeling because we were quite young as a squad and Mourinho brought in this positive family thing and it was great.

**TONY:** Playing for England, is it different to pulling on a club shirt?

**FRANK:** Yes, it's different. I didn't feel more or less pride. When I pulled on a Chelsea shirt I felt pride because it became my family and when I ran out at West Ham for the first time I felt immense pride. The difference with England is that you're playing under an intense magnifying glass that outweighs the others and that can become the most beautiful thing you can experience, or the worst.

**TONY:** How were you when you were away from home, in camps for a long time with England?

**FRANK:** I suffered from that. I was never one for bouncing off the walls, going into everyone's room. I kept myself to myself and I found that tough. I can't say I enjoyed the major tournaments because we didn't do that well, although in the 2004 Euros we did have a good run and I personally did well. It was a great feeling before we got knocked out by Portugal on penalties. That was amazing and we never reached that again.

**TONY:** It could have been better in 2010 if your goal against Germany had been given. That was a disgraceful decision.

**FRANK:** It was and it could have tipped the game, but in the group games we were getting hammered. We drew with the United States and Algeria and beat Slovakia, so we sneaked through the group. We never really came to the party.

**TONY:** I always felt, in a quiet, understated way, you were a leader by example. Do you see yourself like that?

**FRANK:** It's different now I'm into management but as a player, I would agree with you. I was vice captain to John Terry for years and it suited me down to the ground because I didn't have to be that chest-thumping character.

**TONY:** Which managers have influenced and inspired you?

**FRANK:** Harry (Redknapp) is one because he gave me my chance in quite a difficult situation for him because I was his nephew. He had the confidence in me, even though when I got in the team – and I did take a bit of stick – I wasn't flying as Rio did. He stuck with me. In the Chelsea years Mourinho definitely because of the shyness in me. He changed me because his arrogant, self-confident way rubbed off on me. Ancelotti, in terms of personality and as a man, I really liked. I had a difficult time with Villas-Boas at Chelsea. Probably he was given a mandate to change the team and style, but when he came in he came up against me and a few others who were probably set in our ways. He tried to change things drastically and I found that difficult. He left me out for quite a few games. The ones you don't like, though, are just as valuable as those you do.

**TONY:** What is the toughest decision that confronts you day to day?

**FRANK:** Dropping players. I don't have a problem leaving out players who give me an issue in training, but those who give you everything and you still don't pick is difficult. You realise quickly that you need to win though, so the quicker you come to terms with that, the quicker you don't have a sleepless night worrying about the four you can't pick. I had to sit in front of a couple of players when I was manager of Derby and tell them that we're not going to need you here – and that's a tough one.

**TONY:** Have you looked outside football for inspiration?

**FRANK:** What I try to do is listen as much as I can. I read a fair bit on other sports because people management is a huge thing. I would look anywhere, to highly stressed workplaces. I know a couple of people at Chelsea who were in the army and would tell you stories of teamwork and suffering which would put everything in perspective.

**TONY:** Would you trade everything you have won in the game for a Premiership title as a manager?

**FRANK:** That's a tough one. I don't put my trophies out on display. I found a Premiership winning medal once in my shoe about three years after I had won it. Put it this way, what I've done in the game is a memory – so right now, I would take a Premier League title.

**TONY:** Which player inspired you during your lay-offs?

**FRANK:** I was a nightmare when I was injured, and I ended up getting injured again trying to get back too quickly.

**TONY:** Going back to your early days, what players have you seen who wasted their talent?

**FRANK:** It's a good question for you really. We had Lee Hodges and he was ahead of me at West Ham. He could do loads with the ball and to be fair to him he had some bad injuries. Manny (Omoyinmi) as well. We had a player at Chelsea, Mutu, who was Romanian but came from Italy. He was out partying every week and would come into training looking dreadful. He was moved on quickly. If you go off track, especially now, you won't like it; it's too intense. If I hadn't had my dad and I had hit a brick wall, who knows? We're much more attuned now with mental health and it's a better set-up now. That's where academies have done well. There are a lot of pressures and influences.

**TONY:** Academies vs South East Counties League. The South East Counties system developed you in a certain way, gave you a roughness and toughness, if you like. Academies meanwhile have been accused of making life too soft. How do we marry those two extremes?

**FRANK:** There's a book in that question alone! Personally there's something we all loved about the South East Counties, definitely the toughness. The cleaning of first-team players' boots. I remember you used to call us back in because Rio hadn't washed out the dressing room because he was a lazy so-and-so! It was great but it's cheap just to say they should be cleaning boots. I think there's a middle ground. There's a big case for saying players should have responsibility and respect, and that's lost. There was a period at Chelsea where we had a lovely pool built, where I would come in and see youth team players sitting in the jacuzzi on their phones as Drogba is just getting in. I remember thinking I wouldn't have gone near Julian Dicks at the dinner table, let alone sitting in the jacuzzi on Instagram! Hopefully now the academies are really well run, and I know Neil Bath at Chelsea and they have a really good mix. They really help the young players. It's a balance. I watched Jody Morris when he had the Chelsea youngsters and he did great marrying the two.

**TONY:** How was the communication with Abramovich?

**FRANK:** In the early years it was pretty close. He would always have an interpreter because he didn't speak the language and his visits to the training ground were pretty regular, as were his visits to games. Occasionally he would be upset if we were having a bad time but I didn't mind that because he is the owner. That became more subtle as time went on. It was never that close because there were always people in the middle. It changed through the years, but you always knew he cared and loved it. When we won the Champions League and Drogba was dancing around the cup, you could see in his eyes that this is what he had wanted for such a long time. I think he will remain there while it is his club. He has a real feeling for Chelsea.

*

I am often asked what I look for in a player, and obviously it depends on age: the older the player, the more things you are looking for, while, in a young player, it might be only the one thing you notice. It could be a good turn of pace or an ability to see and deliver a pass. It could be about character – a young player's attitude who has a genuine enthusiasm for the game and a natural tendency to encourage his teammates. Or he might show fantastic ability on the ball (Joe Cole springs to mind). Whatever it is that catches the eye, it is then a process of playing and coaching him with players of the same high quality. Playing and training with the best challenges the player and is the environment in which to judge levels of improvement.

The key to good performance is effectiveness, and by that I mean having an end product arising from what the player does: is the wide player constantly putting crosses into the box? Does the midfield player consistently make accurate forward passes? Does the striker hit the target frequently and score goals regularly? Do the defenders get to the ball first and are not easily beaten? Passing skills are important, especially forward passing skills that penetrate the opposition's defence. Scoring goals regularly. These are all skills to envy – as demonstrated time and time again by Jermain Defoe and Tony Cottee. Defensively, I like to see players who actually enjoy defending: making tackles, tracking runners and who are not easily beaten – and, most importantly, are consistent in their on-field performances. At West Ham we always looked for the consistency of the end product. Players who are reliable and who you know precisely what it is you are going to get from them (most of the time) are worth their weight in gold.

As a team coach within an academy, you have to look at the players as individuals, not as a team, and plan a coaching programme for each player. It might still be collective work but within it each player must have set targets: the forward must try to hit six shots at goal, preferably on target; or the midfield player must make ten forward passes, or six forward runs off the ball; defenders must not let forwards turn. All this would be during training sessions and in small-sided games. You might increase or decrease the target numbers depending on the time that the game situations are played. Obviously during specific technique practice time, the target numbers can be flexible and relate to how many shots, crosses, forward passes you can fit in during the allotted time.

These are just a few examples of designing programmes to develop the good habits that players need to become effective. And, as importantly, the player and or the parents/guardians must actively buy into the plan and take ownership of the (serious amount of) work the programme will entail. By this I mean that the player and their support group must understand the purpose of the training regime and direction, and willingly accept it as something that will be beneficial and commit to actively work to try to achieve the targets the coach(es) set. The targets for each player will change over time as the player progresses through the age bands, and the demands become greater as the level of matches becomes more challenging.

Let's take a young Tony Cottee as an example: his obvious assets were pace and goalscoring. He was small, but this did not hinder his effectiveness as a young schoolboy. Ron Gale, one of our local scouts at the time, had brought him into the club and had great faith in his ability, insisting a young Tony Cottee had a great natural goalscoring instinct. Our job was to try and add to his game without detracting from his innate and obvious talent. Tony went to a local school (Warren Comprehensive) five minutes from the training ground at Chadwell Heath and we constantly challenged him to improve his back-to-goal game and to bring other players into the game with better hold-up play. We encouraged him to play quick and early (one and two touch) to lose defenders; and most of all we tried to ensure he remained effective as different challenges presented themselves once he started playing at higher levels. Over time and in a manner obvious to everyone, Tony answered all our questions: he remained a consistent goalscorer for West Ham (twice) and on joining Everton scored a hat-trick on his debut! His goalscoring exploits continued at Leicester, Norwich, Barnet, Millwall and, in the ultimate recognition, he won seven caps for England. All in all, he played 712 games and scored 293 goals – a goal every 2.4 games throughout his career. What a terrific record.

With Joe Cole it was obvious what he was good at: he had truly great skill on the ball along with a good change of pace and the ability to beat players in tight areas. In and of itself, provided he maintained these skills as he progressed up the age groups, it would have been enough to become a *good* player. But what could we add to make him into a *great* player? It's a tricky thing and a delicate process. It's all about adding something while not coaching out a special talent.

Firstly, I asked what position he played. What is his role in the team? At West Ham I used to play him 'in the hole' – meaning in the space behind the opposition's midfield and on the edge of striker territory. Today we know this as the number 10, but, as I say, back then we called it playing in the hole. This gave Joe the maximum opportunity to hurt the opposition in an attacking role but gave him only modest responsibility in the defensive sense. When we played in a 4-4-2 or 4-3-3, where we played Joe wide on the left with the freedom to come in off the line to join the front players and play them in behind the opposition or to bounce balls off them with one-twos or wall passes, he had the defensive responsibility to get back into the team shape and to be responsible for tracking the opposition's right back. This was a way to teach the game and a player's role within it, in both in an attacking and defensive sense.

Coaching young players is about teaching good habits so lots of the training is repetitive. At West Ham our philosophy has always been about an attacking, open and fast-moving, forward passing style, and our coaching would be based around these principles: lots of one- and two-touch passing drills, introduce forward running drills like third man runs that I have mentioned previously, 3 v 3 in tight 20 × 20 metre grids or in long and narrower areas (40 × 10 metres). You can make this type of area larger or smaller depending on ability levels, but remember, the smaller it is, the more it becomes a technical practice with less running; larger areas mean more running will be involved so it becomes as much a physical practice as a technical one. It's the judgement you have to make. Finishing skills, crossing drills and combination drills encouraging one- and two-touch finishes like those of Tony Cottee and Jermain Defoe, all these skills to have to be practised regularly and repetitively and performed at match tempo, with and without opposition.

I am a great believer in unopposed practice with young players, introducing opposition as the players become more competent. At a very young age (eight- to twelve-year-olds) the game should be based on fun and the sheer enjoyment of it – still technically based and repetitive, but enjoyment is key. Lots of small games, 3 v 3, 4 v 4, 6 v 6 will improve players as each player will have more touches of the ball. As players progress (thirteen to sixteen years old), concentrate more on learning the game, be more position-specific and make practice specific for each player, focusing on their needs and the areas that need improvement. Each player should have his own programme within the team structure, always remembering that it is the individual player that you are trying to progress into the professional ranks, not the team. For sixteen years plus, as well as all the technical requirements, physical attributes become more apparent and important.

Developing a strong mentality, learning to win and consistency of performance become the targets for the player. Development into a first-team player is now a ten- to twelve-year programme; it can't be rushed, but there will always be the exceptions – Rooney, Owen, Cole, Cottee, Defoe, Lampard, Ferdinand and so on. But for the majority it takes a little longer. Constant repetition of the basics from a young age is the key to future success. So don't rush it!

It was in the 1998/99 season that Harry brought in Glenn Roeder. One evening coaching session with the schoolboys I saw someone walking towards me. Glenn approached and said, 'I've spoken to Harry and he has given me a role working with you ...' I already had Peter Brabrook as my assistant and suddenly felt quite uncomfortable. I told Glenn that I would speak to Harry in the morning and see what part he could play. Glenn had recently been working with Glenn Hoddle in the England set-up but was now out of work. The next morning I went into Harry's office and told him what had happened and he said his idea was that Glenn would work with players individually and coach the players who were not in the main training squad or coach young reserve players who needed a little extra work. It put Peter Brabrook's mind at rest as he thought Glenn was coming in to take his job.

It was during this season that the youth team had another terrific run in the FA Youth Cup. After losing to Liverpool in the final a few years earlier we were determined to go one step further and win it. Our team had an all-round good balance; we were playing 3-5-2, which Peter and I had developed after starting to play Rio Ferdinand in a back three a few seasons earlier. Stephen Bywater was in goal. This was a player that Les Sealey had brought to the club from Rochdale and swore by. Les (nephew of Alan Sealey, former West Ham winger) was a larger-than-life character and when Les said, 'This goalkeeper is the best and you must play him,' well, that's what you did. Les was so confident in his own judgement that you simply went along with it. The two wing backs were Adam Newton and Shaun Byrne. I used to describe this role as 'high energy positions' based on how they were asked to function: essentially they were asked to play high and wide. In the system we employed they provided width going forward. Their defensive job was nominally that of conventional full backs, hence the term 'wing backs'; so, primarily, they had to be able to get up and down the pitch with regularity.

This system of play is becoming more and more common in the Premier League. By way of an example, Chelsea won the 2016/17 Premier League on the strength of their then Italian manager Antonio Conte's use of this system of play, employing Victor Moses and Marcos Alonso as 'high energy' wing backs. For us, Adam really caught the eye during this cup run and had some outstanding performances, none more so than in the final. He played a couple of games in the first team but couldn't quite step up and stay there. That being said, given time I always fancied he could have made a decent career at West Ham. But he was at least an example of a player given the opportunity to play in the first team, even if his performances weren't sufficient to convince everyone he could consistently step up to the first-team level. Many of us thought he had the potential but as things turned out he wouldn't get another chance. Shaun was a similar player to Adam, giving us good balance on the left side, but unfortunately he got injured in the quarter-final and missed both the semi-final and final. Sam Taylor came in and did a good job as his replacement.

The three centre backs were Terrell Forbes (very quick and a terrific man-marker), Stevland Angus (again quick, good in the air and reliable; not many forwards got past him) and the third was Izzy Iriekpen, who was captain – a ball-playing central defender who on his day was commanding. However, the lad was dogged by injury throughout his time with West Ham. To be honest, I didn't think, deep down, he had the dedication or passion for the game to get to the very top. He was too laid-back and didn't do enough to make the most of the talent he had.

The midfield three comprised Michael Ferrante, a player we had signed from Australia after Peter Storrie had set up a sponsorship arrangement with clubs in Perth and Sydney, Joe Cole and Michael Carrick. Ferrante was a great passer of the ball and complemented Joe and Michael really well; he would play a more holding role, giving the other two licence to get forward. Joe was an exceptional young player who could do special things on the ball, beat players with sleight of foot, run past players with the ball and was a real team player. He was also a real crowd-pleaser with his audacity on the ball. Even at youth level he was always destined for great things. Michael Carrick was an equally outstanding player, a tremendous passer and receiver of the ball. He was two-footed, which always gives the player the edge, could play short or long and rarely gave the ball away. With our three creative midfield players and the two wing backs we created chance after chance for the two front men.

Bertie Brayley played up top. Initially he was on Aston Villa's books as a very young schoolboy but used to train with our schoolboys in the evenings with FA permission. He lived in Basildon, Essex and it made sense to train with us as the travelling time to Birmingham made it impossible to train regularly with Villa. He enjoyed his time training with us and developed a really good relationship with Peter Brabrook. After some time Bertie left Villa citing the travelling issue and signed for us. It was Peter Brabrook who kept on at me that we 'must sign Bertie' once he left Villa. He was a good player, mostly left-footed, and scored goals on a regular basis. He had so much confidence in himself and believed he could do anything, and undoubtedly was a really good all-round team player.

Up front alongside him was Richard Garcia. Another Australian, from Perth, he scored in every round of the Youth Cup run, was quick, good in the air and was good technically. The first day I saw him, when he had come from Australia on trial, I liked him. He fitted in really well and adjusted to the pace of the English game very quickly, becoming a real asset to the team. Richard and Bertie were a formidable partnership at youth level, scoring bundles of goals. The run to the final wasn't all plain sailing. We were drawn away in every round. I remember going to Stockport County and Stephen Bywater making a save right in the top corner to keep us in the tie. We also travelled to Walsall, York, Arsenal, had a two-legged game in the semi-final vs Everton and were, of course, eventually drawn away for the first leg in the final against Coventry!

The semi-final vs Everton was memorable for two reasons: the first leg at home saw us play really well and storm into a 3-0 lead to take to Goodison Park. Originally they had Francis Jeffers in their squad but he was not allowed to play because he was already in the first team, so we took full advantage of that! Peter Brabrook and I both felt that in the first leg Everton had given us big problems from free kicks and corners and we had been lucky not to concede from them. During the week between the first and second legs we worked hard on better organisation at set plays and felt as we were 3-0 up from the first leg we didn't need to chase the game. As long as we avoided the danger of Everton's set plays, we would have a good chance to progress to the final. We didn't play that well – maybe we were too concentrated on defending – and lost the game 1-0 after they scored in the last minute. We had defended their set plays well and did not concede from one; despite the loss, we had reached the final and we were pleased to have done so. After the game the West Ham chairman Terry Brown came into the dressing room to offer his congratulations and Harry Redknapp also came in with his assistant Frank Lampard Sr. To my and Peter Brabrook's considerable surprise, Harry chose not to congratulate the team but instead launched into a tirade, berating them for not playing well, failing to pass the ball well and playing without fluency. To say we were disappointed is an understatement.

The sequence of away games continued and the first leg of the final against Coventry followed this pattern. I have to say the night of the final at Upton Park was a night I will never forget: we were winning 3-0 from the first leg (after a great performance at Highfield Road, Coventry). It was a very wet, rain-sodden night and our passing was of the highest quality. On a wet pitch we zipped the ball around confidently and accurately. There was no problem of complacency within the team, and we were confident we were good enough to go on and win the trophy. Peter Brabrook and I were totally focused and knew we had to score first to kill off any chance of a comeback by Coventry, but I'll admit that what had happened at Stamford Bridge against Chelsea a few years earlier remained in the back of my mind. It was cup football after all, so realistically anything was possible.

One side of the stadium had been opened up for any fans wanting to attend, but as the game time drew close, thousands of unanticipated fans were milling about outside trying to get in. In the end sense prevailed and the whole stadium was opened. It forced the kick-off to be delayed but the wait was worth it. The stadium was full, we were leading 3-0 and all that was needed now was the team to deliver the trophy for our expectant fans. Well, we got off to a great start with a fantastic cross-field pass from Michael Carrick for the marauding Adam Newton to nod the ball into Bertie Brayley's path and Bertie duly slotted home. It's something of a cliché, but the crowd went wild! And it lifted the team to one of the best performances I have ever seen from a youth team. We went on to win the match 6-0 and the final 9-0 on aggregate, which is still a record. We had secured the coveted FA Youth Cup for West Ham. Peter and I could not have been prouder of the players, the team and its achievement.

Angus had a decent Football League career, playing over 130 games for Cambridge; Forbes has done even better, playing over 100 games for QPR and over 200 games for Leyton Orient and Yeovil Town. Iriekpen was plagued by injury but still played 123 times for Swansea City. Shaun Byrne did play twice for West Ham's first team but most of his career was in non-league. The same applied to Sam Taylor, who spent most of his career in non-league and now works for West Ham in their community department giving opportunities to the kids of Newham and surrounding districts. Adam Newton made two appearances for the West Ham first team before moving to Peterborough United and making over 200 appearances for them, as well as over 90 appearances for Brentford and Luton combined; he also represented England at under-21 level. Michael Ferrante left West Ham and went to play in Italy for a couple of seasons before going back to Melbourne, Australia, where I believe he was, until recently, still playing.

The two other midfield players Cole and Carrick need no introduction, as they both have had fantastic careers, Michael playing for Manchester United and coaching United's first team when Ole Gunnar Solskjaer was manager. In 2017 he rang me and asked me if I would like to attend his testimonial at Old Trafford; it was a 70,000 sell-out and all proceeds were given to Michael's chosen charities. What a great gesture. It was nice to meet up with Richard Garcia, who had travelled from Perth for the game and had remained good friends with Michael and his wife Lisa, and I also got to meet Richard's mother, who I had last seen in Perth in 1998 just after we signed Richard for West Ham. It was a good day all round.

Richard played up front and, as I've mentioned, came from our sponsorship of a club in Perth, Australia. He played sixteen times for the West Ham first team before moving on to Colchester United where he made 82 appearances, then Hull City, 114 appearances, playing in the Premier League with them, before moving back to Australia where he is now head coach of Perth Glory, for whom he played until 2017. Bertie Brayley, his strike partner, after showing so much promise, drifted into non-league where it has to be said he had a very successful career, playing for over twenty clubs in the Essex area, from Canvey Island to Concord Rangers and many in between. I felt Bertie under-achieved and could have done a lot better for himself, but that was Bertie, impatient and impetuous, but with a heart of gold.

When Peter Brabrook was in hospital in 2016, and shortly before he died, it was Bertie who used to visit him on a regular basis; as I said, he had a heart of gold. All in all, this was a very good all-round team as the FA Youth Cup win demonstrated. Gordon Strachan, the Coventry manager at the time, was quoted as saying about the West Ham youth team, 'They may not be the best players I have seen but they certainly are the best youth team I've seen.'

The following season saw us bring in Jermain Defoe from Charlton and Leon Britton from Arsenal. Jimmy Hampson had been tasked by the chairman Terry Brown to try to sign the best young schoolboys around. Jimmy knew Jermain from his time at Charlton and Leon had played against us for Arsenal and Jimmy felt he was one of the best midfield players.

We signed both players, but the system regarding compensation for the transfer of a player's registration had been revised and we were one of the first cases to be heard. Jermain's was first and a Football League panel decided that West Ham should pay Charlton £400,000 in compensation and shortly thereafter the same panel decided a similar fee should be paid to Arsenal for Leon. Both clubs had insisted on adding clauses for additional payments related to future performances. Jimmy Hampson had attended the hearing on the club's behalf (I did not attend) and we both felt these initial payments were harsh. In fact, Jimmy actually questioned the panel as to quite how they had arrived at these figures. Brendon Batson, who was sitting on the panel, told Jimmy, 'That's the game you play.' I am not sure whether he meant to suggest that no player should move clubs or, more sinisterly, was implying West Ham had done something underhand. Who knows? But I felt they were trying to make an example of us. We took it on the chin and paid up, but, of course, from our vantage point it could only put additional pressure on the players to 'make it'.

Jermain played almost 100 games for West Ham before being transferred to Tottenham for £6 million rising to £7 million on appearances, while Leon, who never played for West Ham's first team, went on to play over 500 league games, mainly for Swansea. He has played in all the divisions, including being a regular for Swansea in the Premier League. It does, I think, prove our judgement about the young players' potential was right at the time, although the initial compensation fees still rankle.

During Jermain's development he was loaned to Bournemouth, as was Rio Ferdinand before him. Jermain demonstrated he was a natural goalscorer, scoring in nine consecutive games and going for a record ten goals out of ten games in his next game vs Cambridge United at the Abbey Stadium, Cambridge. I went along to the game, as did the manager Harry Redknapp and his assistant Frank Lampard Sr. We spoke to Mel Machin, the Bournemouth director of football at the time, before the game and he told us how well Jermain had done. We were all hopeful that he would score that night and break the record. He, and we, needn't have worried: Jermain did exactly what he does best and scored – and won the game for Bournemouth. This spell on the south coast convinced everybody we had a 'real player' on our hands and not long after he was in the West Ham first team and scoring goals for us.

It was the second season of the newly formed Premier Youth League. We had beaten Sheffield Wednesday in the play-off final with a Gary Alexander goal the previous season and were the first club to be crowned Premier Youth League under-19 champions. The following season we reached the final of the play-offs to decide who would be the under-19 champions and were to play Arsenal in a two-legged game.

The first leg at Upton Park was a real roller-coaster affair. Playing Arsenal at any level is always a competitive business: we had gone into a 3-1 lead and looked in control when I made a substitution to bring on another defender to see the game out (bearing in mind we had a second leg at Highbury a few days later). Well the last twenty minutes saw Arsenal take full advantage of our change of tactics – scoring four goals to take a 5-3 lead! I have to take the blame for this. I had instructed the team to change formation to accommodate the extra defender; I had wanted us to change to a back three and play five in midfield to keep things tight but instead of making us tighter defensively it had the opposite effect and had opened us right up.

234 • TONY CARR

The players were too wrapped up in the game, which was being played at a very fast tempo, and my instructions were either not followed or not understood. I should have left well enough alone! I have to say the players responded to this setback magnificently and rallied to score twice in the final few minutes. The final score of 5-5 meant we had earned a 'get out of jail' card that night. *Mea culpa* and a lesson certainly learnt.

So now we had a second leg at Highbury to look forward to and with the scores even it was all to play for. Michael Carrick had been called up for England youth and would miss the second leg. A big blow for us. So I decided to start with the same formation with which we had started the first leg (4-4-2) and this time was determined not to change it. The second leg was a much tighter affair with the score 0-0 until the 70th minute when we scored with Richard Garcia heading home from a Steve Clark cross from the right. It stayed that way until the last minute when we had a free kick just outside the Arsenal box on the left. Peter Brabrook and I were screaming at the free kick taker, Michael Ferrante, to keep the ball near the corner flag and see the time out, but instead he lofted the ball straight at the Arsenal goalkeeper who comfortably claimed it before throwing the ball to Jermaine Pennant who ran down the right and crossed the ball for Arsenal to equalise. I was not best pleased with Michael. After extra time it stayed 1-1 so it went to penalties. Goalkeeper Stephen Bywater was fantastic in the shoot-out, taking his time, questioning whether the ball was on the penalty spot and generally unnerving the Arsenal penalty takers. It seemed to work as Stephen made a couple of fantastic saves and we won the shoot-out. For the second consecutive season we were the Premier Youth League under-19 champions.

Liam Brady, who was the Arsenal academy manager, was gracious in defeat, bemoaning the fact that they were never any good at penalties. The next few seasons saw debuts for many home-grown players: Joe Cole was already around the first team and Michael Carrick followed quickly. Jermain Defoe, Richard Garcia, Glen Johnson, Anton Ferdinand, Elliott Ward, Mark Noble, James Tomkins, Jack Collison, Freddie Sears and Junior Stanislas all debuted in fairly quick succession.

Stanislas was a player who had good ability but didn't always take the game seriously enough. He lacked discipline and I had plenty of run-ins with him. I was always having to demand more from him. With all his ability on display on the training pitch, I could see the potential. He eventually played 42 times for West Ham, which is no mean feat, but he could have done better. He eventually left West Ham and went, for an undisclosed fee, to play for Burnley, who were in the Championship at the time, where the manager was Eddie Howe, whose assistant was Jason Tindall – the son of West Ham scout Jimmy Tindall. When Eddie and Jason left Burnley to return to manage Bournemouth, Stanislas followed them a short while later. Junior is now having a great run of form at Bournemouth and is finally realising his potential.

A couple of years ago I bumped into Junior at a game, and he greeted me with a big grin and said, 'I wish I had listened to you earlier in my career, but I have a family now and have responsibilities and I now know you have to work hard and be disciplined to succeed in life.' It pleased me immensely and I watch Junior with pride – now that the penny has finally dropped!

There were many other debuts of players like Grant McCann, who would later manage Peterborough United and Hull City, Kyel

Reid, Tony Stokes, Zavon Hines, Chris Cohen and Jordan Spence, who only made a handful of appearances but it's still an achievement to debut for a Premier League team. Chris Cohen was a player who came to the club at the same time as Mark Noble at around eleven years old, and they both developed at a similar rate. Mark was a very technical player, a good passer with great vision and innate leadership qualities.

Mark is now captain of West Ham and is a rare example of a player staying at one club from a schoolboy to retirement (although he's not quite there yet, this season 21/22 being his last!). I caught up with him in a café in Brentwood to have a chat about his career:

**TONY:** What are your earliest memories of kicking a ball around and playing football?

**MARK:** My earliest memory was Cumberland playing fields and my dad cut a hole in the fence. He undid the screws for the fence and slid the metal bars across and we used to be in there all day long until we had to come home and go to bed really. A fella who lived across the road from me, whose son was a similar age, asked my dad would I come and play with his team. My dad thought I was quite good and agreed. The neighbour said that he had quite a few players but Mark could come over and train with them. It was Barking Colts. I turned up and remember finding it quite easy and the manager said, 'Right, I want to sign him tomorrow.' So that was it. Barking Colts at the age of nine.

**TONY:** You lived local to West Ham at that time?

**MARK:** Yeah, Plaistow, Jenkins Lane, just opposite the hospital and fire station. I started playing five-a-side tournaments and I got scouted by Millwall at the age of nine. I did one or two training sessions. It was on an AstroTurf pitch in a sort of a community programme. I then went to Arsenal just before I was ten and stayed there until I was eleven before I went to West Ham. The Arsenal attraction was because they used to train in the indoor AstroTurf JVC centre at Highbury. But by the time I got from East London to Highbury, with my dad taking me after he finished work, I was always late – every time! So, it wasn't fair. West Ham were always asking me to sign. My dad tells the story that he went to watch an under-12 game at West Ham vs Gillingham and West Ham won 9-0 but my dad thought the standard would be too high for me. I said I wanted to go to West Ham and that was it.

**TONY:** Jimmy Hampson told me that Arsenal were convinced that you would sign for them, so he and Jimmy Tindall came around to your house and wouldn't leave until you signed the registration form ...

**MARK:** Yeah! They sat in my front room and wouldn't leave. They were playing with my sisters. I think we actually ordered a Chinese takeaway and they weren't going anywhere until I signed. Arsenal was just too far for us to travel and as my one-season registration had run out, I signed for West Ham. The two Jimmys' persistence paid off.

**TONY:** So when you started training, did you think, I'm as good as these? Did you think quicker, were you more skilful, was your passing more accurate? Is there anything that you can put your finger on that set you apart?

**MARK:** Do you know what, I have always had – and will say it openly now, I am not embarrassed to say it – even now, I have always got nervous before every training session, and obviously it's a good thing. I am 33 years of age, you're interviewing me now, and I still get nervous before every training session – I have had thousands and thousands of sessions – and that is because I want to be the best player in training. That is from within, and you can't teach that. For me it was more like a pride thing. Listen, I would be telling lies if I said I didn't want fame or money. When you are eleven or twelve years of age, of course you do. But for me, I just wanted to prove to everyone that I could do it. It was my club and I just wanted to be a footballer really.

**TONY:** When I interviewed Joe Cole, he is still as enthusiastic about the game as he was as a young kid.

**MARK:** Joe says it all. Because he is someone who won the trophies and did what he has done in the game, to go and play at Coventry, Aston Villa and then go to Tampa and play. Someone asked me a question about Joe recently, and I said as fantastic a player as Joe was, he is as good a person as he is a footballer. That's what Joe is all about.

**TONY:** Obviously it is not only talent that sets you apart; it is all the other mindsets and characteristics that go into making a footballer. Is there one characteristic you could say has got you where you are now?

**MARK:** I'll tell you one of them, which people won't realise. I think I had a sort of maturity about me where I sort of knew what coaches wanted, and what people wanted to see. I felt I could change, not my game so much, but that I could adapt to different styles of play, with different managers and coaches at a young age. I understood what was required. Obviously, it goes without saying, graft and hard work is the first requirement. But, at this age now, kids coming through, my biggest thing for them is that football is a fantastic game, but if you think it's smooth, it's not. I remember coming through, and it was always me and Chrissy Cohen really from our age group coming through together. I was always ahead of him and then under Pards (Alan Pardew) he made his debut three or four months before me. It killed me inside. Chris and I still speak now and I was so proud that he had made his debut because we had got buses together and we had travelled with the first team together. But I really wanted what he had. I really wanted to play in front of the crowd, and to have that adulation. To have played for West Ham's first team.

**TONY:** For me you have always been a leader. And if there was something to be done, certainly on the football pitch, not so much the apprentice jobs, you would always go and do it and get it done. You were never shirking in the corner; you always took the lead.

**MARK:** That is me in my comfort zone though. I think it comes from a belief in your ability. Because I knew that if I did it, most of the other boys would do it anyway. I still speak to the other boys now, players like Darren Behcet, who was our youth team goalkeeper, and he says, 'When people talk about Mark this or Mark that, trust me, when we were growing up at fifteen or sixteen, he would still be out practising or in the gym when I had my tracksuit on ready to go home.' At the time I was never one of those who got stick for that, oh look at him, busy bastard or whatever. If anything, the boys wanted to do it as well. But people don't see that side of things, they just see you getting in the first team and think, that was easy, and it really ain't like that.

**TONY:** It's sixteen or seventeen years ago now from when you were an up-and-coming schoolboy and the thought of failure never entered you head.

**MARK:** That's what it was; the motivation was the fear of failure.

**TONY:** What pressures come with having to perform in every game?

**MARK:** Teddy Sheringham said something to me once when I was a young lad coming through, where everything is rosy and there is no pressure on your shoulders and it's all about fun. He said, 'Mark, enjoy the good moments because in football there aren't many of them.' And I thought, yeah, whatever, Ted. But he was right. The pressure comes with having to win every game, and when you don't win, especially me, the next week ain't the same. There's no enjoyment; it kills everything. You can't go out with your missus and have something to eat because the next game is on your mind, and you're constantly thinking *We have to win on Saturday or we are in a relegation fight* or *We have to win on Saturday because we are only two points off being in sixth place.* Individually the pressure is always there to perform well. You have to develop a strong personality to cope with these things that are always there. No matter what you do, you lose some of the enjoyment. It becomes an obsession of having to do well consistently.

**TONY:** Looking back on your career, have there been any periods of doubt? When you have questioned yourself?

**MARK:** Loads, yeah loads. Every step of the way. Look, I don't care what anyone says, every player has doubted themselves at some point. As I've said, it's not an easy ride. There was a time when I came into the team under Alan Pardew in the Championship and I was doing things on autopilot, playing just on adrenaline and playing really well. Pards in his team talks was saying, 'Look, we have to get the ball to Mark.' And I was seventeen years old. I remember sitting there and we had all these experienced professionals around me, players who had played three or four hundred games and he is telling them to get the ball to me and I'm only seventeen!

**TONY:** How did that make you feel?

**MARK:** I was buzzing at the time. I didn't really feel the pressure then. It was weird at that point that I didn't feel the pressure as it was all new. I got by on adrenaline. We then got into the Premier League, I played a few games and didn't do so well and you start to think, *Am I cut out for this? Can I do it at this level?* And I was left out of the team. But the determination was always in me. I just wanted to get back in the team.

**TONY:** In those periods of doubt, there must have been times, when you were left out of the team, you start to question, 'Why has he left me out?' 'Am I good enough?'

**MARK:** No matter who you are, whether you're Sergio Agüero or whoever, at some point you are going to lose form, you aren't going to be in the team. But it is how you react to that. That's probably one of the reasons why I am West Ham captain and I've been in the team consistently for fourteen or fifteen years, because if I did get left out, I wouldn't chuck my toys out of the pram and say I want to leave, and end up going somewhere else [where] my family isn't happy, my kids aren't happy, I'm not happy, not getting on with the manager – then you end up going somewhere else and your career just peters out. I wanted to create a little bit of history for myself at West Ham. And being here that long, captaining the club from Upton Park and into the London Stadium and playing the most Premier League games for the club, you start to do that.

**TONY:** Are you a fan of the game outside, other than playing? Do you watch a lot of football? Do you enjoy watching it?

**MARK:** In all honesty, I love watching football, love it. I love watching games on the telly. If I'm on a recovery day, I'll go in and watch the players who didn't play train. I'll go and watch the youth team train. A lot of times, I prefer watching than playing myself. I took my wife to Chelsea vs Liverpool when Joe (Cole) was playing in the Champions League, and it was the first time in five or six years that I'd actually sat and watched a live game. I thoroughly enjoyed it because I had nothing on it. It was just a game of football that I could watch and enjoy. That's when I enjoy it most.

**TONY:** I bet your missus enjoyed that date didn't she? Going to a football match!

**MARK:** I know! With Chelsea fans surrounding us as well.

**TONY:** When you're out on the pitch at the London Stadium do you hear the fans, or are you shut off from that?

**MARK:** There was a certain time a couple of seasons ago that you could see in the changing room that the atmosphere was terrible in the club and Slaven Bilić was under a lot of pressure. We played Liverpool at home and got smashed. I'll never regret doing it because it's the way I am, but it was one of the first times in my life when I would go and look for the ball – because I would always want the ball – and as I got it and looked up, I could actually see players shy away from it and not want it. Players making runs that you could never get the ball to them, calling for it and making runs away and I ended up getting loads of stick because I turned back and played it back to the goal-keeper. We were losing and the fans obviously weren't happy. That's one of the only times that I'd felt, for that night and for two or three days, I fell out of love with football. It left a terrible feeling that I was trying to play and make things happen and players were actually shying away from trying to play.

**TONY:** As captain, you obviously felt a responsibility to lead?

**MARK:** Of course, and that has served me well over the years. But times like that when you actually think fellow professionals ... and it's hard to play when the fans are on you like that, but to actually see it clearly that you don't want the ball, it hurt me inside for two or three days.

**TONY:** Can you remember what brought you out of that mood?

**MARK:** I have always said, no matter what happens, you have to lace your boots up and go out to train. Simple as. For me, it was the best way of getting out of that mood. In all honesty, I sat back and thought, at least I ain't one of them who are shying away from it. I might have got booed because I didn't play it forward when I got it, or because I didn't have anything on, but I could look myself in the mirror and say I didn't shy away from the ball.

**TONY:** What is your lowest moment in the game? You have had a couple of relegations ...

**MARK:** One, under Avram Grant. It was hard for me because I got a double hernia about six weeks before the start of the season, so I wasn't in the team at the time. I didn't go through all the emotion of losing games and getting relegated, because I wasn't playing and didn't travel to away games. The worst moment was the Burnley game, when the fans were running on the pitch and took the corner flag to the middle. When you love a football club so much and the fans aren't happy with what they are watching on the pitch it hurts. I know it was directed towards the chairman (David Sullivan) but to see your own people run onto the pitch, I was disappointed. Obviously, the fans pay their hard-earned money, so they have a reason, or an excuse, but not on the pitch. I was on the front page of every newspaper because I wrestled a fan to the floor, but that was just my emotions taking over.

**TONY:** On a brighter note, what's your best moment in the game so far?

**MARK:** I've had a few. One of them was my first Premier League goal, against Spurs at home at Upton Park. And the week leading up to that game, and this is football for you, the manager (Alan Curbishley) pulled me into his office and said, 'You're playing tomorrow.' We were playing Charlton away. Alan Pardew was the manager of Charlton. He had been sacked by West Ham and was now at Charlton. It was a Thursday I think, when Curbs pulled me in. I had scored in the cup about four weeks before against Brighton and I couldn't understand why I wasn't in the team; we were losing every week. I just couldn't get my head around it. Then to get told I'm playing on Saturday against Charlton away ... so I was buzzing. The Friday morning before the game, during training, a Spanish player we had called Kepa put his foot over the ball and caught my ankle. My ankle rolled and just swelled up. I tried to do a fitness test on the morning of the game but it was too sore so I couldn't play. I travelled with the team to Charlton and we lost 4-0. I remember Pards (Pardew) looking around, his wife was in the crowd and she looked round at our chairman and was dancing with delight. A bad day all round. The next week we were playing Spurs at home. I got fit and played. I scored on the half-volley from outside the box in the first ten minutes and that feeling was just like ... phwoar! It was a roller coaster of a game but we lost

246 • TONY CARR

4-3 and I started crying. So it shows, in one week, the emotions you go through as a football player. It was mental. And then you go on an amazing run and beat Manchester United at Old Trafford on the last day of the season to stay up – that was a fantastic day. The last ever game at Upton Park, when we beat Manchester United 3-2, was unbelievable. So, I've had some really historical days. And obviously the play-off final win. I had two of them, as much as they say it's the biggest game in foot-ball, but how it can affect your career is unbelievable. When you look back, if we don't beat Blackpool in the final you stay in the Championship and then if you don't get up again, all of a sud-den, if you don't get transferred, you stay as a Championship player for maybe three or four years. Whereas we got promoted and I've played in the Premier League for the last eight years.

**TONY:** James Tomkins had come into the team but since you there haven't been many. Declan Rice has come in and estab-lished himself and James has moved on to Crystal Palace. Do you think it's harder to break through now?

**MARK:** You had players come in like Junior Stanislas but who have had to move on.

**TONY:** That was the making of Junior. He's now at Bournemouth and he realises that it is hard work as well as talent that makes you into a player.

**MARK:** Look at Freddie Sears who got in the team, did fantasti-cally but had to move on to get regular first-team football, first to Colchester and then on to Ipswich. There are many players like that.

**TONY:** Even Chris Cohen went down to Yeovil and then on to Nottingham Forest.

**MARK:** And you think, Chrissy should never have played for Yeovil, never in a million years; he was better than that.

**TONY:** Alan Pardew should never have let him go ...

**MARK:** Why he sold him to Yeovil I don't know, and for that money it was ridiculous. There was a time I remember Pards took me into his office, when I came back from a loan period at Ipswich, and said, 'I'm sending you out on loan again.' I said I didn't want to go. You have to have that about you as a kid. At the time we had Nigel Reo-Coker and Christian Dailly playing centre midfield for us. We weren't playing well at all; we were third from bottom or something like that. I just thought, *No, I'm not going back out on loan.* To be honest, he was under a lot of pressure and in the back of my mind I was thinking he may not be there long. So, if I go out on loan for three or six months, someone else comes in and they are not going to know me straight away. So it was my decision to say, *No, I'm not going out on loan, I'll just train.* And that decision as a young lad paid off for me because Curbs came in and the great escape and all that stuff.

**TONY:** I vividly remember Chris going. Chris was still a young player and I didn't even know we had sold him. No one told me – I read it in the newspaper. I couldn't believe it.

**MARK:** I couldn't believe it either. It was incredible.

**TONY:** You're the captain of West Ham, the so-called leader. How do you see your role on the pitch; does it give you added pressure?

**MARK:** What I've realised is, as captain, a leader, or as a chief executive, or manager, when it goes wrong, it's on your head most of the time. You get the blame because you're in charge. A lot of the time when things go wrong, I've gone out, done interviews and press calls because I'd rather it be on me because I've seen how some players react to criticism from the fans and it can kill them. I've always thought, *I can handle it, it's not a problem.* So, I've always taken it upon myself to go out and front it up when it's gone wrong. A lot of the time, people get confused with leaders, as in shouting and hollering. And I do that at times. But for me the best ones I've seen are ... watching them train, watching them play and knowing that if he's playing next to me then I know what I'm getting. When you've lost three or four games in a row and everything is going wrong and the shit does hit the fan, you still have to put your boots on, go out and train 100 per cent. Because it's the only way. As soon as you say to yourself, this isn't for me, I give up, you're f****d.

**TONY:** Michael Carrick said that when he was at Manchester United, training on a Friday before a game, it was really fierce and competitive. It was driven by the players and the captain Roy Keane and they would be kicking lumps out of each other. It was sometimes harder than the game on the Saturday. But you were never allowed to put your feet under the table and that was the standard.

**MARK:** One hundred per cent right. That's changing in football a lot now. Especially with the influx of the foreign players. I have only met a handful who are like that, who have got that mentality. A lot of them sort of go through the motions of, 'Ah it'll be all right tomorrow.' And it might be all right tomorrow. But I think, especially when I was coming into the team at West Ham, players used to kick lumps out of each other in training. It was just natural. It doesn't happen now, because everybody is too worried about getting injured, but that was the way it was.

**TONY:** Who did you make your debut against?

**MARK:** Southend at home in the League Cup. I think I came on for the last 25 minutes and then walked home after the game. My mum and dad were in Cyprus on holiday, and they didn't know I was going to be involved. So I walked home with Carly, who was my girlfriend at the time and is now my wife. And then I played against Norwich in the FA Cup, I think. It was like a blur; I couldn't believe it. I had just turned seventeen and that year up to when I was eighteen was mental. I had made my debut, played in the Championship and then the Premier League; it was just mad. There was so much going on. I remember I was in the first-team squad and Pards wouldn't let me play in the FA Youth Cup. We were playing at home to Blackburn. We lost and I was sitting there watching, but I really wanted to play. Even then, I was in the first team, but I watched the boys getting ready for the game and I was gutted I couldn't play. I wanted to get the game changed to a later date so I could play but we couldn't do that. Chris Cohen was in the first-team squad as well and he was also told he couldn't play. So the youth team had to play without me or Chrissy.

**TONY:** How many times have you won Hammer of the Year?

**MARK:** Twice, and twice Players' Player of the Year.

**TONY:** How does that feel? It's the fans that vote, so that must be special?

**MARK:** Yeah, when I won it, it was incredible. Obviously, the Players' Player ones are also special because the players vote for it. Me and my school pal Sam Taylor grew up together, we supported West Ham, we used to go to the games, hang about outside, ask for shirts, get the players to sign stuff and within a year I was playing. I got Young Player of the Year in my first year, then I won Hammer of the Year and it was like, phwoar. If you look at the names who have won Hammer of the Year, for me, who grew up five minutes away from Upton Park and had been through what I had been through, to win Hammer of the Year was f***ing unbelievable. I was always hungry to win more, and I wanted to win it again.

**TONY:** It would be nice if you could win it again and make it a hat-trick ...

**MARK:** Ha ha, yeah! I don't think that's going to happen now, but you never know. Yeah, it was a special, special time.

**TONY:** Touching on your international honours, you played for England youth and played all the way through to the under-21s. Kenny Swain (England youth team manager at the time) has always got lots of good things to say about you, in terms of your attitude and your willingness to take responsibility.

**MARK:** Yeah, my first one was in a tournament in Sweden, under-17s I think. There was a massive selection process that you go through and eventually I was picked to go to Sweden. I played the first game vs Holland and it was shown live on Sky Sports. We also played Spain and Germany and I was chosen as Player of the Tournament. When I got back to school our PE teacher made us all watch the Holland game for 'How to be a Champion'. And because it was live on Sky, I got a lot of praise and they did loads of clips of me afterwards. All of a sudden I had a Nike contract, and agents were ringing. I won't say their name, but one agent rang my dad and said, 'Can you come and speak to us?' And Dad was like, 'Yeah, whatever, all right.' They turned up outside my house in Beckton in a big Rolls-Royce. And my dad said, 'We ain't getting in that, no chance. I'm not putting my boy in that. He's f*****g fifteen.' So he asked where the offices were and we got a train. You can imagine me, I was like, 'Ah, Dad, let's get in the car!' But he made us get a train, to Aldgate I think. You can't imagine anyone doing that now, because they would love to get in the car. I played England 16s, 17s, 18s, 19s and 21s. My under-21s time was fantastic because I had just got in the first team at West Ham. I was eighteen or nineteen and hadn't even thought about the 21s, who had a European Championship coming up, and I got picked in the 35 to go to Valencia in Spain for a training camp. I remember ... do you know when you can just tell you had trained well? And I got a letter to say I had been picked in the squad for

252 • TONY CARR

the European Championship. In the squad you had the likes of David Bentley and Leighton Baines – players who were playing in Premier League teams before I had even made my debut. We had a really good team. I was sub for the first game against the Czech Republic and we didn't play that well, and the next game in the group stage was against Italy. We all went into the team meeting. I had no clues and all of a sudden my name was up on the board and I was playing. I played really well and set up one of the goals. We won the third game 3-1 – I can't remember who it was against – and I played. I played all the way to the semi-final, and do you remember the penalty shoot-out when Anton (Ferdinand, brother of Rio) missed? It was like 12-12 or something and I took two penalties. After that tournament, because it was all live on Sky Sports and beamed all over Europe and was the only football on that summer and because I personally had a good tournament, it was a massive deal for me. I remember going on holiday with Carly to Cyprus and everywhere I went I was getting noticed. I had never had that before. I was walking down the high street in Cyprus and people were coming out of bars asking for photos. It was incredible. After that, I played for the under-21s, was captain of the under-21s and then we lost in a final against Germany. Half of that German team went on to win the World Cup: Özil, Khedira, Neuer, Kroos. They were much better than us, but we did have a few injuries; and then that was it – I never wore an England shirt again.

TONY: There was a clamour at one point, a few seasons ago, when people thought you should have got in the full England team, you were playing well enough.

**MARK:** If you look at it, I think I should have played that year, that final season at the Boleyn. There were a few opportunities before that, with a few players that got picked. But especially that year, I had scored eight goals I think, we were fifth or sixth in the league and there weren't many English midfielders who were playing better football than I was that year. I think it was just a case of someone liking someone better than me. Do you know what, and this is the truth, I don't regret it one bit. I really don't. I hold no grudges. Look, I've played over 450 games for West Ham. That is pride enough for me.

**TONY:** What makes the Premier League the best league in the world?

**MARK:** I just think it's so unpredictable every week; I think it is getting a little bit stronger now, especially with the increased TV rights money coming in.

**TONY:** There's a bit of a breakaway group?

**MARK:** Yeah, there is. But I still think teams can turn up and beat anyone on the day. Obviously [with] the money involved, the players that can come here ... if you look at anyone in Europe now, managers or players that are doing well, they normally end up coming to the Premier League, because the money is so big. Now if you look at Premier League football, you walk out of the changing room and in the media zone there are Chinese, Japanese, Indian and obviously European press. [Press] from all around the world, not just England.

**TONY:** How many managers have you worked under? Who was the manager when you made your debut?

**MARK:** Pards (Alan Pardew). Pards gave me my debut. But before that, when I was still at school, my dad got a phone call from one of the two Jimmys (Hampson and Tindall) and they said Glenn Roeder has asked if Mark can come in and train with the first team during this week's half term. Can you imagine it? A fifteen-year-old, still at school, training with the first team. I remember training in the big sports hall at Chadwell Heath with Monks (John Moncur), Joey (Cole), Carrick, Jermain Defoe, Di Canio, Trevor Sinclair. As much as I look back now, and I was so nervous at the time, I remember actually doing all right. I did a little bit of good play and clipped one over the top for Sincs (Sinclair) and he went on and scored. You could see the players knew I had a little bit of ability and that was obviously why I was called in. Yeah, that feeling was unbelievable. Then Pards got the job. I was doing really well in the youth team. I don't know if you remember the game when we played Gillingham away in the FA Youth Cup and we were 2-0 down and I scored a hat-trick. I scored a free kick, a penalty and I chipped the goalkeeper. Peter Grant, Pards's assistant, came to me after the game in the changing room. I'd just had a shower, and he said, 'Right, you're with us tomorrow.' It was mad. Under Pards I played in the Championship and two play-off finals; we lost the first one to Crystal Palace and won the second against Preston. I played a lot of games that year in the Championship.

**TONY:** You had three consecutive years at Cardiff in two play-offs and an FA Cup final. What are your memories of that time?

**MARK:** At such a young age travelling with the first team, Pards was really good with me, and he played me a lot. And then I remember getting up off the bench – we were playing in the play-off semi-final against Ipswich at Portman Road, before we played Preston at Cardiff, and I was sub. We were winning 2-0 after drawing 2-2 at Upton Park the week before. I remember thinking I badly want to come on. My schoolmates were there, [so were] my mum and dad and I just got up off the bench and Pards was standing there and I said, 'Gaffer, please put me on.' He looked at me and said, 'Get your gear off.' And he put me on for the last twenty minutes. I can't imagine a young lad doing that now. I was so desperate to get on the pitch. And he said to me as I was about to go on, 'I am going to fine you for every time you give the ball away,' just as an incentive for me to keep the ball. It was wicked. It was a nice moment that.

**TONY:** Who was after Pards, Curbishley ...?

**MARK:** Then Gianfranco Zola, Avram Grant, Sam Allardyce – we had been relegated and Sam got us back up – Slaven Bilić, David Moyes, Manuel Pellegrini followed by David Moyes again. That was one of the best achievements I've ever had. I've had all these managers, different cultures, different styles of play and I've started every season with all of them. You go through a pre-season which lasts six weeks, so the manager has time to assess his players and I've always started in the team.

**TONY:** What distinguishes the great players from the good?

**MARK:** I would say a lot of it is down to mental toughness, being able to cope, and to do things at the right time under pressure. A lot of it, now especially, is physicality, like power and strength. But what I will say is the mental side of the game for the top, top players that can produce stuff at moments that no one else can. Keeping cool at the moments when others might shy away, or not take that shot on, or not be in that position. But the best players always come up with it when you need it most.

**TONY:** I asked Wayne Rooney what makes a great striker, and he said staying calm when the chance comes, so you don't slash at it or rush or force it. Stay calm, here's the chance, put it away. When you analyse that, in that moment he's in full control.

**MARK:** And also, the best players – and I've seen some world-class finishers in training when there is no pressure, but put them in a game situation and it was a completely different kettle of fish – the best players can replicate that in front of 80,000 in a final. That is the difference.

**TONY:** Have you got any desire to go into coaching or management?

**MARK:** In all honesty I love the thought of it because I feel I've got a lot of experience and I've played with so many players and had different managers. The only thing with me at the moment is time.

**TONY:** What, getting your coaching badges?

**MARK:** Yeah, doing that sort of stuff, because at the minute I just love spending time with my family when I'm not training or playing. Also, when you are involved in football you realise you can't do anything at Christmas, you can't do anything at Easter, and you've only got certain times in the summer to go away. At the minute, because I've been involved in it for so long, for me, time enjoying yourself, as in social stuff and time with the family, is precious. I think I will do something, especially at West Ham. If you look at it, if there are kids coming through, who better to ask advice than me?

**TONY:** I was going to ask, when your playing days are over and you think what to do next, West Ham would be silly not to use you in some capacity.

**MARK:** My only thing is, I'm going to be honest here, I've said to myself for the last five or six years – because you do start to think what you are going to do after playing ... I do a lot of other stuff, I'm involved in a business. But what I will say is I'm going to do it on my terms. I'm not going to be told I've got to be here, I've got to be there. I would do it because I want to do it, not because I have to.

**TONY:** You're a one-club man. What's kept you there for so long? There must have been times when you could have gone elsewhere for a bigger contract.

**MARK:** In all honesty, I had the phone calls when I was younger about going to other clubs from my agent. But for me, what I've always found is that money helps but it doesn't really make you happy. It gives you a great life, but it doesn't make you happy. My wife Carly, the kids, I've got my mates here and the thought of moving them somewhere where I'm coming home every day and they're not happy, just for the money, it doesn't sit right with me. Obviously if the offer was too good, maybe to play in the Champions League ... Where would you leave

West Ham for? I've played in the Premier League fourteen out of fifteen seasons and me being the loyal person I am I have stuck with West Ham, even when we were relegated, where I had a fantastic year in the Championship, getting promoted. It's very unlikely at West Ham in the Premier League that you are winning most weeks. But in the Championship, we were winning most weeks and it was a good feeling. When I was a kid coming through, I wanted to be West Ham captain. I don't take it for granted now, but people think because I've been there a long time that's why I'm captain. You have to earn and graft for that. Captain of any club you are seen as that figure, that leader. But to captain the club you came through the academy with and lead the team out at Upton Park and then into a brand new London Stadium is a historical moment; you create a bit of history for yourself. It's all right going to other clubs and maybe earn £10,000 a week more, but you retire and you're sort of not really remembered anywhere. But at West Ham, that's never going to be the case for me, because I've been here since I was eleven and will probably finish my career here. There aren't many players that will do that any more, it's so rare. And I don't look back and regret one bit of it.

**TONY:** You've created that little bit of history for yourself. What was it like adjusting to the move to the London Stadium?

**MARK:** I don't think it really hit me until we actually moved. The last game at Upton Park was incredible and because we were on such a high, we came sixth or thereabouts that season. It was a bit of a blur with all the hype surrounding the move. We were all buzzing because we had done so well and then it was so different. Silly things like I used to want to make a tackle in the first couple of minutes of a game at Upton Park. I remember doing it all the time and you heard the roar at Upton Park. Whereas, I did the same at the new stadium and it didn't have the same effect. For everyone everything was new, everything was different. But you learn to get used to it because we aren't going back, so you have to get used to the new surroundings. It's a lot, lot better now, especially this season and I am just over the moon that I played so many games at Upton Park and was the last person to have a testimonial there. But the future is the London Stadium.

Chris Cohen was a great competitor, full of running and endeavour with a really good left foot. He made his debut aged sixteen in a 3-2 win vs Sunderland in 2003. He was West Ham's youngest debutant for over 80 years, then Alan Pardew picked him in a night game at Upton Park vs Reading sometime later. He played him at left back (when for most of his development he was a midfield player) and up against him was Reading's oldest and most experienced player Glen Little. For a seventeen-year-old it was a little too much and he struggled to contain him. I'm sure this convinced Pardew that Chris was not going to be part of his plans and shortly thereafter he loaned him to Yeovil and eventually sold him for £25,000.

This annoyed me as I felt there was much more to come from Chris and selling him so young was a mistake; and, to add to my frustrations, Pardew had not bothered to inform me of his intentions. I actually read the news on the club's website. Obviously, the final decision on player acquisitions or sales rests with the manager and the club's transfer department, but I was disappointed not to have been asked my opinion about a player still so young. By way of comparison, Harry Redknapp had the decency to ask my opinion whether we should sell a player, Daniel Sjölund – a young Danish international we had signed a few months earlier, after Liverpool had made an enquiry.

After one season at Yeovil, Chris was sold to Nottingham Forest in a combined deal with a Yeovil teammate for over £1.2 million. Recently Chris has completed eleven years at Forest and has decided to retire after a string of injuries. He held a testimonial dinner at a hotel in Nottingham that I am pleased to say I was able to attend. It was great to meet up with Chris again and reminisce about his youth team days while growing up at West Ham.

This period from the early to mid-nineties when Matthew Rush, Danny Williamson and Kevin Horlock were making their debuts, right up to 2010, was a really productive era for the academy. Thereafter, debuts of home-grown players became altogether more difficult. There are a number of reasons for this decline but it all boils down to Premier League survival. Clubs often tried to buy their way to success or out of trouble, with knock-on effects for youth development. The Premier League was getting bigger and richer; managers were constantly aware that their jobs hung on the next result; patience in boardrooms, where the fear of relegation and its financial implications made them ready to hire and fire repeatedly, was noticeable by its absence. Looking back, I also believe we were losing our edge at scouting young players. We had lost our scouts in South London that had been a rich source of young players. Jimmy Hampson, who had done a great job previously, was getting frustrated with the lack of talent we were recruiting and blaming the 'big' clubs for throwing money at the problem. He started to lose some of his passion and West Ham would not invest more into scouting schoolboys. It seemed other clubs had moved on and we were getting left behind.

Jimmy was spending more and more time with a football talent agency he was involved with. At the start we had felt this agency was a help to us in recruiting young talent but even this was drying up now. We still had good players in the system but were missing out on players that we should have been competing for. Frustratingly, we were missing out on players on our own doorstep who often we were not even aware of. Obviously, club managers were becoming more reluctant to debut young players and were reliant on established players brought in from all over the world. The space for young players to make their mark was narrowing year on year.

There are exceptions, but generally speaking, academies will find it increasingly hard to produce players for the Premier League and some clubs have started to doubt the value of their investment in academies. Perhaps the financial consequences of Covid-19, bringing so much of sport to a standstill and worldwide empty stadiums, will mean that the comparatively cash-strained Premier League clubs will begin again to look to their own academies for player talent. We may yet see more home-grown players coming through. Or is that wishful thinking, I wonder?

In 2001, we saw Harry Redknapp leave West Ham. He had a disagreement with the chairman Terry Brown and resigned. I had no idea what had gone on and it came as a big surprise to all the staff. Harry always spoke his mind and obviously this time things went a little too far. Frank Lampard Sr also left, which I thought was unnecessary. Frank Lampard Sr was West Ham through and through and I felt a role should have been found and offered to him.

Upset that his father had been 'sacked', Frank Jr made it clear he too wanted to go. After Rio Ferdinand was sold to Leeds United for £18 million a little earlier, Frank left to go to Chelsea for £11 million. The two most promising young players West Ham had ever produced in my time left for combined transfer fees of £29 million and were never adequately replaced. Now the search for another manager began.

# 10

# ANOTHER NEW MANAGER

Harry's departure in 2001 wasn't planned and there was no strategy in place to replace him. The board had no one lined up or a plan of succession. I had a few conversations with Paul Aldridge (the club's managing director) who told me the managers they had spoken to were either not interested, unavailable or the compensation to pay up their existing contracts made it prohibitively expensive. I next spoke to Paul in May and he told me they were going to appoint Glenn Roeder. He understood it might not be a popular choice with the fans but felt he could work with him and between them do a good job. I must admit I was surprised, as were most people, but Glenn was a genuinely straight guy, a good coach and I wished him all the best. My role as academy director was always to support the manager whoever was in the post, but Glenn's rise from a support coach to manager in a couple of years was a surprise. Nevertheless, I would do what was needed and offer him 100 per cent support.

His first job was to appoint an assistant and he went with Paul Goddard (his nickname was Sarge from his time in the Boys' Brigade!), an ex-QPR and West Ham player. Paul had been coaching at Ipswich Town, mainly working with the youth team. Paul was a knowledgeable coach with bags of enthusiasm and in their first season Glenn and Paul proved a good partnership. They had inherited an excellent squad from Harry and finished seventh in the Premier League, a very good position, with Jermain Defoe on fourteen goals and Frédéric Kanouté with eleven finishing as leading goalscorers. They won fifteen and lost fifteen games in the league. The following season was in complete contrast, with only three wins from the opening 24 games and at the bottom of the league for most of the season. Relegation inevitably followed. Glenn and Sarge were as perplexed as were the fans. After such a good previous season and with the training routines much the same, they couldn't get it right. Injuries played a part, but that doesn't account for such a dramatic tailing off of performance. With Kanouté and Defoe only scoring five and eight goals respectively, the team struggled all season.

It was all the more surprising given the quality of the squad, with players including David James, England goalkeeper, Michael Carrick, Trevor Sinclair, Jermain Defoe, Paolo Di Canio, Steve Lomas, Frédéric Kanouté, Glen Johnson, Les Ferdinand and Joe Cole. But, for whatever reason, the team could not reach the form of the previous season. Glenn had not changed much, training was the same, there was no obvious dissent from the players – except Di Canio, but that was not particularly unusual. Paolo was a perfectionist and expected everybody to be as dedicated as him. He had a short fuse and if something had upset him in training or in games he would explode with rage. I remember an incident from the previous season when Harry was still manager. During training Paolo was visibly annoyed with everyone and everything. The ball came to him and he picked it up and walked off the pitch saying,

'This training is s***' and off he went. Harry just ignored him, got another ball and carried on.

One notable moment came late in the season when Glenn was struggling to find a suitable right back for the team. He had tried various players but most of them were playing out of position and it showed. He came to me and said, 'Do you think Glen Johnson could do a job for us at right back?' My reply was, 'You will never know until you put him in.' He was another youth academy graduate who had been playing regularly for the reserves and had been on loan to Millwall, so now was the time to find out if he was good enough. His Premier League debut came in January 2003 where he came on as a substitute in the 4-2 defeat at Charlton Athletic. His energetic performance earned him a starting place in the next game, at home to Blackburn Rovers, which we won 2-1 with a late winner from Jermain Defoe. Glen never looked back after this and, in an awful season for the club, he was a breath of fresh air. It just goes to show that young players need an opportunity and if they are good enough, they will grab it with both hands, but unfortunately, as I said earlier, those opportunities are becoming more and more rare.

As a footnote, at the end of that season, after relegation, Glen Johnson was sold to Chelsea for £6 million. He came to me at the time and told me he didn't want to leave but I told him it was a fantastic opportunity, to be back in the Premier League, and in any case West Ham needed the money!

Glenn Roeder's season almost came to a tragic end. After the home game vs Middlesbrough, which we won 1-0, Glenn fell ill. The club doctor, Ges Steinbergs, immediately called for an ambulance. It turned out that he was suffering from a non-malignant brain tumour which needed to be operated on. Fortunately, Glenn went on to make a full recovery.

In Glenn's absence Trevor Brooking was appointed caretaker manager, tasked with the difficulty of trying to stave off relegation. His first game was away to Manchester City where his old England teammate Kevin Keegan was manager. Kevin and Trevor had been great players for England, teaming up together and scoring spectacular goals. They were both injured during the 1982 World Cup in Spain when Ron Greenwood was manager and I am sure they would have progressed further had they both been fit.

A Freddie Kanouté goal gave us victory, which was followed by a 1-0 home win vs Chelsea. The Manchester City game was notable for the head injury Les Ferdinand experienced which prevented him driving his car home from Stansted airport on the return journey. As I had gone up to Manchester with the team and had flown back to Stansted with them, I drove Les's car back for him.

We were down to the wire as far as relegation was concerned and on the last day of the season we had to better Bolton Wanderers' result. They were playing Middlesbrough at home and we were playing Birmingham away. It wasn't to be. Bolton won 2-1 and we drew 2-2 and so were relegated. As often happens when relegation looms, you sell your best players, so Paolo Di Canio, Joe Cole and, as already mentioned, Glen Johnson were all sold, as were Jermain Defoe and David James later. Trevor Brooking had had a tremendous impact on the team during his short tenure: his tactics were sound, players were motivated and training was once again enjoyable, despite the fact it was similar to Glenn Roeder's. It just goes to show how a different voice and approach can have an impact by lifting morale and thereby improving results. We fell just short of survival, finishing with 42 points. No Premier League team has been relegated since with that amount of points!

Roeder had recovered and would be able to start the new season as manager, but after only three games, he was sacked – following a surprise 1-0 defeat at Rotherham. The team had changed into their match kit at their hotel. It was suggested they didn't fancy the small confines of the Rotherham away dressing room and had opted to use their hotel rooms for greater comfort. As you can well imagine, this hadn't gone down too well with the opposition, whose pride was hurt, making them even more determined to put one over on the pampered players from London! I can only assume the West Ham board felt the same after the loss. Another new manager was needed.

The board chose Alan Pardew, who was manager of Reading. Reading dug their heels in and made Pardew effectively work his notice by putting him on gardening leave. Trevor Brooking was asked to take over again as caretaker manager. Trevor had ten matches in charge and did a fine job, losing only one game and winning seven. Trevor had no ambition to be a manager but his record from his two stints as caretaker would suggest that he would have done a great job if he had only wanted it on a full-time basis. But he repeatedly said it was not something he wanted.

I had a meeting with Alan Pardew while he was tending his rhubarb. He was keen to find out more about the club and was, I suspect, trying to find out a bit more about me. I told him that in all my time with West Ham I had always given 100 per cent support to whoever the manager was and it would be no different with him. He would have no problems with me, I told him. 'Music to my ears,' Alan replied. I was pleased with how the meeting had gone and felt confident that Alan would do a good job, which proved to be the case. He was enthusiastic, innovative and full of self-confidence. He brought in Peter Grant, ex-Celtic legend, as his assistant. He took over with the team in a healthy position in the league. But he had to wait until his seventh game in charge before he posted a win, a 4-0 thumping of Wigan Athletic. Too many draws, seventeen of them, saw us finish in a play-off position instead of gaining automatic promotion. We got to the final at Cardiff's Millennium Stadium where we would play Crystal Palace, whom we had beaten 3-0 at home and lost to 1-0 away. Still, we went into the game as favourites. It wasn't a great game; we played nervously, with too much at stake, and lost 1-0. We should have had a penalty late in the game when Michael Carrick was fouled in the box, but it wasn't to be. So it would be another season in the Championship!

It was the worst feeling I had ever experienced after a football match and we didn't hang around. I felt as if the club had been relegated all over again. As we travelled back to London along the M4, there was silence while we watched the Palace fans celebrating in their cars and coaches, waving flags and scarves as they passed us by. On the Monday Pardew called all the staff into a meeting at Upton Park where he struck a real positive note. How he was about looking forward and not looking back, despite the still-painful disappointment of not getting promoted. 'Next season starts today,' he said. I thought this was a very positive message for everybody. To not use the summer break to wallow in the 'what might have been', but to use it to be positive about the season ahead. I thought that showed real leadership qualities from the manager.

Pards, as he was known to staff and friends alike, was always looking to use psychology or other motivational methods to gain that extra edge. He even had his own publicist to get positive messages through to the press and other media channels.

Meanwhile at the academy, it felt like a low time for the staff. After another of our youth products, Michael Carrick, was sold to Tottenham Hotspur it seemed like any talent we produced would be sold. Tottenham had driven a hard bargain and took advantage of the club having financial difficulties arising from not being promoted and paid only £3 million for Michael. What an absolute bargain, considering how two years later Tottenham would sell him to Manchester United for £18 million! Having said that, we still had Mark Noble, Elliott Ward, Anton Ferdinand, Richard Garcia, Chris Cohen and Trent McClenahan in the first-team squad.

They didn't all go on to have long careers with West Ham, but the emergence of Anton (Ferdinand) and Elliott (Ward) were further examples of young players being given an opportunity. With promotion denied, limits on the manager's budget were inevitable, limiting the club's ability to buy out-and-out quality, so the club has to look at every player, including the younger ones, when team selection becomes problematic through injuries or suspensions. During the season Pardew had just this problem: he had injury and selection problems with centre backs and decided to play Ward and Ferdinand together as a central defensive partnership in an away game at Wigan. Wigan were going well and still today it's not the easiest place to play and to get a result. We won the game 2-1 with Teddy Sheringham and Marlon Harewood the goalscorers. Anton and Elliott both went on to play regularly in the team and played a crucial part in the play-off final win vs Preston, finally securing promotion back to the Premier League.

Obviously the number one target that season was securing

promotion but we never looked like making automatic promotion. We rarely dropped out of the top six, but never seriously challenged for an automatic promotion position. We duly finished sixth and ended up playing Ipswich in the play-off semi-final. We drew 2-2 at home after being two up, but won the second leg 2-0 to return us to the Championship play-off final at the Millennium Stadium where we would play Preston North End. Promotion was achieved with a 1-0 win via a Bobby Zamora goal. The feelings this time at the end of the game were the polar opposite of the previous year. We were elated and I went onto the pitch to congratulate Mark Noble, Anton Ferdinand and Elliott Ward, who were so much of the first team's spine. I felt real pride that three academy products had played such a crucial part in gaining promotion for the club. As I said earlier, the pleasing thing for me and all the academy staff was the emergence of these players. As Rio's brother, Anton was always going to find it hard to deal with the obvious comparisons, but he coped really well and proved he had what it takes to be a first-team player in his own right. Elliott was always a confident player and he and Anton had a good partnership, which was honed playing with the youth team for a few seasons before. Both were good in the air, Anton also having a good turn of pace which sometimes got Elliott out trouble. Both had good technical skills, both could pass out of defence quite comfortably and they coped well with the physical demands of first-team football.

Having, arguably, scraped into the Premier League, not a huge amount was expected of us the following season and some pessimists were predicting a rapid return to the Championship. However, we did really well, finishing a creditable ninth in the league and reaching the FA Cup final against Liverpool – back at our favourite haunt, the Millennium Stadium. It's a game we should have won as we were 2-0 up at half-time, but a Liverpool fightback in the second half saw the game finish 3-3, Steven Gerrard equalising for Liverpool in the 90th minute. The game went to penalties where we lost 3-1 in the shoot-out! A big disappointment, but not as bad as the feeling after losing a play-off final! Some said it had been the best final in years, six goals, the game swinging back and forth and a penalty shoot-out; nothing between the teams on the day. Great sentiments, but nothing beats winning!

*

John Lyall and Ron Greenwood both died within a few months of each other in 2006. These former managers of West Ham United had had a massive influence on me as a young player and as a developing coach. Both possessed a deep, profound knowledge of the game and were very good at passing it on: simple things, like, 'play the way you're facing', 'imagine there is a hoop a yard (metre) in front of the player you are trying to chip a ball into', 'just cross the ball into space on the near post' (for players to run into) and 'lively mind, lively body'. All the simplest of things but when routinely implemented, helped develop good enduring habits in young players. I owe so much to both men. But for them, I probably would never have had a coaching career; they were that influential.

At John Lyall's funeral in Ipswich, Alex Ferguson gave the eulogy, offering a fantastic tribute. He told how John had helped him settle into his role at Manchester United when he took over after leaving Aberdeen, giving him the rundown on the opposition they would be playing next. We should remember that a young Alex Ferguson was new to the English league after coming down from Scotland

and needed all the help he could get at the outset of his magnificent career at United. Sir Alex said, 'I would ring John on the Monday after a game and if we had won it was down to John and if we had lost it was down to me!' After the funeral we all went back to Ipswich Town Football Club for the wake and there were hundreds of people all wanting to pay their respects to John: ex-players, managers and office staff who all held John in the highest esteem. It showed what the fans thought of Ron and John that before the FA Cup semi-final vs Middlesbrough at Villa Park there was a minute's silence held for both of them. There were banners and flags bearing both their names and the West Ham fans spontaneously burst into song singing 'Johnny Lyall's claret and blue army' throughout the 'minute's silence'. It was a very moving and fitting tribute to both men, who are still missed.

My own father, Charlie, died around the same time and, to his credit, Alan Pardew attended the funeral. I didn't know he was coming and all our family felt this was a terrific gesture. Alan didn't really know my dad but all of us were pleased to see him there. After my mother had died a few years earlier, Dad started to take a real interest in my job at West Ham. He started coming to under-18 games on Saturday mornings and came to some away games on the coach; he really seemed to enjoy it. It pleased me no end and I was able to get a lot closer to him than I had done previously. My job was full-on 24/7, weekends and evenings at training or watching games, and now in the twilight of his life we spent a lot more time together and I could share with him what my life was like. I know he definitely enjoyed it as my sisters told me that it was all he used to talk about after a weekend of football! Again, he's sadly missed.

\*

One of the big stories of Alan's time at the club concerned the sign-ings of Carlos Tevez and Javier Mascherano from Corinthians. The story has been told repeatedly and was all over the news at the time. Kia Joorabchian, an Iranian-born, British-educated businessman and agent, brokered the deal for the club.

The signings came as a complete surprise to everybody at the club, including the manager. The impression I got was that the board did the deal with Joorabchian and then told Pardew, *I think we should sign these two internationals*, but left him with little option other than to say yes. It has to be said they were two great players and even from the word go the deal did seem odd, but sometimes the football world can spring surprises. Tevez ended up being transferred to Manchester United and Mascherano was transferred to Liverpool and eventually to Barcelona. Some six years later I bumped into Javier when the Argentinian national team were touring Europe and were due to play Croatia in a fixture at Upton Park. The Argentinians were looking to train the day before the game and we offered them our Rush Green training ground. They turned up in a large coach complete with security outriders leading them in. The squad went straight onto the main pitch where Javier spotted me and came over. The West Ham under-23s were just finishing their training and the first thing he said was, 'Tony, are you still here!?' We had a chat about general football things before he rejoined the squad. Tevez was also there as were Messi, Agüero, Perez and Zabaleta. It was such a privilege to watch these players train at such close quarters and to watch their match the following evening at Upton Park where Argentina won 2-1.

*

I, along with my academy colleagues, carried on trying to find and develop the next graduate into the first team while yet again it was a time of change. In late 2006 the then chairman Terry Brown and the board sold the club to an Icelandic consortium headed by Eggert Magnusson for a reported price of £85 million. The new owners had big ambitions and at the time money seemed no object. After only four games under the new owners Alan Pardew was sacked following a 4-0 loss at Bolton. I spoke to Eggert Magnusson shortly after Pardew's sacking and was left with the impression that he and his board colleagues simply didn't like the way Alan ran the team. Of course, bad results don't help. Overall Alan had a successful time at West Ham: two play-off finals with promotion achieved at the second attempt, an FA Cup final narrowly missing out to Liverpool and maintaining our Premier League status. In total he had a 41 per cent win ratio (only bettered by Billy Bonds with 43.6 per cent) which is good by any standard, but Magnusson had his reasons to sack him and the truth is you never properly get to know the real reasons behind these sorts of out-of-the-blue decisions.

Alan Curbishley was appointed manager 48 hours after Pardew's departure. Curbishley had been linked with the West Ham job previously but now felt this was the right time to take up the position. He brought Mervyn Day (ex-West Ham goalkeeper 1973–79, 194 appearances) with him as first-team coach and Keith Peacock as his assistant. Both of these had been with Alan at his previous club Charlton Athletic where they had done a terrific job. But by January we were in the bottom three and struggling against relegation. It was a battle to survive, but survive we did on the last day of the season with a memorable 1-0 win over Manchester United at Old Trafford. Carlos Tevez scored the winning goal.

The victory and consequential relegation of Sheffield United opened up a can of worms regarding Tevez's and Mascherano's registrations and eligibility to play. It had to do with the third-party ownership of a player's economic rights, a quite common practice in South America, where both players of course hailed from. Although mired in legal complications and interpretation, essentially third-party ownership of a player's economic rights was impermissible in the Premier League and it was West Ham's failure to have sufficiently disclosed the essential nature of the deals done with Joorabchian that got the club into serious trouble. Sheffield United took the nuclear option and sued. And won. West Ham were ordered to pay Sheffield United compensation – somewhere in the region of £20 million. What an unnecessary mess.

*

On a lighter note: the academy is routinely invited to tournaments and festivals abroad and it was on one such tournament in the USA, featuring teams from across the USA, South America, Mexico plus a couple of European teams including us, that a new nickname was bestowed upon us.

As is traditional, before the tournament commenced the teams were introduced to the crowd by name and the club's nickname – the Panthers, the Bulls and so on, all threatening-sounding and aggressive nicknames. And then it was our turn. Paul Heffer told the announcer we are West Ham United from London and the club's nickname was the Hammers. In the US it is quite common for the cockney accent to come across as Australian (I've lost count of the number of times I've had people ask me whether I am from the Antipodes!). Anyhow, the announcer says, 'And this is West Ham

United from London and their nickname is the Hamsters!' What a let-down and now we were stuck with it for the rest of the tournament. I wish I could remember how we got on, but I do recall we were all in fits of laughter. Another time we were in Atlanta, Georgia promoting the West Ham academy on a soccer camp. It was something we had done for a number of years in the summer with Global Image Sports, run by an English guy, James Abrahart. During a day off I went shopping, looking for a jacket. I went into a Macy's store that was having a sale and eventually found what I was looking for and approached the counter. So far so good. I tried to pay with my American Express card.

'Sorry sir, we don't take American Express ...'

I was puzzled; this was America after all. I gave her another card that was accepted. Now the hard bit.

'Your name, sir?' the clerk asked.

'Carr,' I said.

'Keer?' came the reply.

'No, Carr,' I repeated.

'Got it, Mr Keer,' she said enthusiastically with a smile as wide as Texas.

'No! Carr! C-A-R-R,' I say again, slowly and reasonably.

'C-I ...?'

'No. C-A,' I say, frustrated.

Unbelievably, once more she says, 'C-I ...'

'No,' I say. 'A as in apple.'

'C-I ...?'

At which point I lost it and shouted, 'Where in apple do you see the letter "I"?'

It was that London cockney accent thing again and I would

still be there now trying to complete the purchase if I hadn't resorted to writing everything down for the clerk, who remained mystified to the end.

Our relationship with GIS was growing and Paul Heffer and his wife Rae fully embraced our trips to Atlanta, getting closely involved in the running of the camps. George Cowie, an ex-West Ham player from the seventies and eighties, was living in Brisbane, Australia and was keen to set up similar camps with GIS in his home town. He asked me and Paul if we would come out to Australia with a couple of coaches to give the camp the same 'West Ham authenticity'. Obviously the cost of flights prohibited both of us going so we went alternate years to help George set up the camp and give it an authentic West Ham feel.

I stayed in a local hotel near the camp and was startled by signs in the hotel saying 'No thongs after 6pm'. I understood thongs to be swimwear that left little to the imagination and while I know Australia's dress code in general is pretty casual, I thought this 'no thongs' policy was overly dictatorial. It wasn't until days later that I found out that 'thongs' was the Aussie name for flip-flops ... I went to Australia twice for the West Ham international academy and GIS to help George and as far as I'm aware Paul and Rae are still going every summer to keep the West Ham international academy thriving. I should point out that these trips were at no cost to West Ham and were paid for by GIS. From our point of view it was an opportunity to spread the name and reputation of the club and at the same time cast an eye over what talent there may be in the region and for seven days a year at no cost to the club, it was a no-brainer.

It was getting harder to get young players through to the first team and split training sites didn't help either. The club's revenue from the Premier League television rights was increasing year on year, which in itself did not necessarily guarantee better financial security for the clubs. Rather it simply played into the hands of the players and their agents, who demanded better contracts. The knock-on effect was that clubs were saddled with massive wage bills and relegation would result in financial Armageddon. Unsurprisingly more and more clubs are now inserting relegation clauses in players' contracts as an escape route in the event of relegation.

It puts huge pressure on the clubs' directors that must subsequently and inevitably descend on managers' heads. The resulting pressure makes managers reluctant to blood young players who they aren't sure they can 100 per cent rely on. A first-team manager won't know the player and will have rarely or consistently watched them on the training pitch (one of the problems of split sites for training), let alone during under-16, 17 or 18 games on a Saturday morning. The response tends to be to buy 'proven talent'. Players – usually from abroad where the market can be cheaper than buying locally – who have played visible first-team football. Managers now can only plan for the short term, because a mere handful of bad results and they know the threat of the sack grows exponentially. Now a Premier League manager can be forced to plan only two or three games ahead and thus needs players with the ability and immediate league experience to get the minimum required results.

There are exceptions, there always will be, and James Tomkins was one who would debut for the first team during 2008 and eventually hold a place down, after loan spells at Ipswich Town and Derby County. Mark Noble, from the academy, was establishing himself as a regular. Chris Cohen had made his debut during Alan Pardew's tenure but was sold, much to my disappointment. He retired from playing and was a coach in Nottingham Forest's academy until his recent move as first team coach to Luton Town. Many clubs could quote similar successes, but it was getting harder.

The management merry-go-round was about to start up again with Alan Curbishley resigning after two players were sold without his consent. The two players concerned were Anton Ferdinand (another youth product) and George McCartney. Alan eventually won his compensation battle with the club. For the record Alan's win percentage rate was 39.44 per cent. Not at all bad!

Gianfranco Zola was appointed manager and brought in Steve Clarke as his first-team coach. Their association goes back to when they were both at Chelsea. In their first season the club finished in a respectable mid-table position, but the wheels were about to come off after the world financial crisis in 2008. The club's sponsor, holiday firm XL Leisure Group, were placed into administration on 12 September 2008 and the crash of the Icelandic banks meant the club's owners were themselves in severe financial difficulties – and this would have serious ramifications later.

During Zola's reign a technical director was brought in, a fellow Italian called Gianluca Nani. I had a couple of disagreements with Gianluca concerning his recruitment policy. For example, he proceeded to buy and loan out two young Italian left backs without any prior discussion about who and what we might have developing at the academy. I thought this was downright disrespectful and evidence of him failing to do even the most basic of homework. I've said it before but clearly times were a-changing and the academy was being ignored at every turn. Or so it seemed. The financial troubles obviously were not going away; the club were in a lot of debt, especially after having to pay Sheffield United £20 million in relation to the 'Tevez affair'. While there was talk of a takeover from an American consortium, it came to nothing.

A few months earlier I had had a phone call from Scott Duxbury, the club's managing director. I was sitting in my car at Barnet FC waiting for a reserve game to start – we were to play Arsenal, whose academy play their 'home' games at Barnet – when he said, 'Hi Tony, the club have decided to grant you a testimonial match.' I was speechless. He went on to say that the club would sort everything out and he'd speak to me again later. While this had come as a complete surprise, I was very grateful.

# 11

# NEW OWNERS

It was while I was at the Football Writers' Association Dinner at the Lancaster Hotel in London that I learned who were to be the new West Ham owners. The dinner was in honour of Frank Lampard Jr and I had been invited by Ken Dyer, a football writer on the *Evening Standard* whom I had known for many years, initially through his friendship with John Lyall. He was and is an ardent West Ham fan who began following the Hammers in the early 1960s and has been reporting on the club for nearly 50 years. He thought I might like to come along to the evening as I had coached Frank as a youngster and I was very happy to attend to celebrate this honour for Frank. He had done fantastically well for Chelsea and England and the honour was fully deserved. Harry Redknapp, Frank's uncle, was there and we had a chat. He told me he had just spoken to Karren Brady, another attendee, and she had told him that David Sullivan and David Gold had just completed the deal to buy West Ham. This was January 2010 and the club was about to change again.

Not many people like change because you get set in your way of doing things and feel comfortable, so when change comes along, as with new owners of the football club, people get nervous, edgy and wonder how it will affect them personally. I've never been like that;

change can be a positive thing and new ideas and a different perspective on things can be a source of good and must be embraced; it should challenge and stimulate you.

I was soon asked to attend my first meeting with Karren Brady, who had been appointed vice chairman. She had worked for Gold and Sullivan when they were owners of Birmingham City and I'll admit to being quite nervous, but I would remain open-minded. She had a reputation of not taking fools gladly and ruled her roost with a renowned steely determination. I needn't have worried. It was really about her trying to get an insight into how things worked at the club; what was this person's role? what does he do? and so on. She felt that the academy was overspending, and could I look into making savings – which would prove to be an ongoing and endless theme throughout our dealings. However, Karren stressed that in me trying to make savings they 'shouldn't harm the product'. We ran quite a tight ship anyway and making substantial economies would be difficult. I understood where she was coming from. The club had a massive debt and any savings in any department would help. The burning question I wanted to ask was: would the new owners honour the promise of the testimonial given to me by former managing director Scott Duxbury and the previous owners? Karren was fine about it. Yes, they would honour the promise given to me ... as long as it did not cost them anything! She told me to get on with the job and keep on producing players for the first team. All in all, it was a positive first meeting. In passing, I should mention that Scott Duxbury is now CEO and chairman of Watford FC.

I now set about trying to put together a game and opposition for my testimonial. I asked Dave Giess, my accountant and a former scout for the club, Tony Cottee, Alvin Martin and Keith Cosby, a good friend of mine who had a number of businesses in the Essex area, to form a committee and to my lasting pleasure, they all agreed to help.

A couple of weeks later I was at the Chelsea training ground with the academy. While I was watching a game, the Chelsea first team were jogging around the perimeter warming up for training. Frank Lampard and John Terry broke away from the group and came jogging towards me. We shook hands, said hello, and Frank said, 'I'll come back later and have a chat.' Later he said he had heard I was getting a testimonial and asked what I had planned. At this point nothing was certain but we had a number of ideas. Frank made a suggestion: 'Why don't you get an ex-academy team together? I've spoken to a few players and they'd all be up for it.' And that's where and when the idea was born. Now the biggest problem presenting itself was ringing around the various clubs getting their permission for each player to play. Inevitably some asked me to have insurance put in place for their players in case of injury. Such is the modern game.

We set a date of Wednesday 5 May 2010 and hoped all the players who had promised to play would actually turn up! Zola was really helpful and put out a strong West Ham first eleven and even donated the football boots he had worn during his last ever professional game. I auctioned them at my golf day and they fetched a tidy sum, with the purchaser asking if Zola would pose for a photo with him at the training ground, which I arranged. I suspect the purchaser was checking the authenticity of the boots. Gianfranco Zola, ever the gentleman, was more than happy to oblige.

As the day drew nearer, the inevitable happened. Glen Johnson, who was playing for Liverpool at the time, rang to say he had to

attend a Liverpool function on the same night and Liverpool manager Rafa Benitez would not let him come down to play for me. I
thought this a bit unfair. Jermain Defoe, who was with Tottenham,
had a rearranged game at Manchester City which prevented him and
Harry Redknapp attending – Harry was Tottenham manager at the
time. Michael Carrick's wife Lisa was due to give birth imminently,
so that stopped Michael coming down from Manchester and to top
it all, Frank Lampard, John Terry and Joe Cole, all from Chelsea,
were allowed to attend but not allowed to play!

The last Premier League games of the season were the following
Sunday and Chelsea needed to win the last game to win the Premier
League title (which they did comfortably, beating Wigan 8-0!) and
I asked them to attend anyway, get changed and join in the team
photo and sign autographs for the fans. To be fair they were brilliant,
although John and Frank were a little bit unsure of the reception
they may get when I introduced them to the crowd, but West Ham
fans are fair and knowledgeable and they both got a good reception.
They, in turn, were great with the fans; John even took his boots
off and gave them to a disabled fan. The only non-academy player I
asked to play was Paolo Di Canio. Always pure box office, I thought
he might put a few extra on the gate. Paolo was living back in Rome
at the time and through his agent he said he would love to come and
play and would not take any expenses for travel or accommodation.
What a fantastic gesture.

I thought it would be a good idea to try and get a sponsor for the
game and have their name printed on the shirts. It so happened that
the youth team had an invitation to take part in a tournament for the
Clyde Best Trophy in Bermuda (Clyde being an ex-West Ham player
from Bermuda). Who wouldn't want to go to Bermuda in February

on an all-expenses paid trip? We arrived in Bermuda and were met by Clyde with whom I had played in the West Ham youth team in the sixties, so I knew him well. He took us to the hotel and the guy I knew from our GIS soccer camps in Atlanta, James Abrahart, was also there on business.

The first day I had to go along to the local TV station to give some publicity to the tournament and James said he would join me. We jumped into a taxi and I mentioned to James that I was looking for a sponsor for my testimonial and with his business contacts he might know someone. No more was said until a few weeks later when James told me that Ricoh and his company Altodigital would sponsor the match. A few months later, he told me it was the most expensive taxi ride he had ever had! Umbro generously supplied the shirts in a one-off claret and blue style and had RICOH-Altodigital printed on the front with each player's name on the back and to finish it off my own unique badge with embroidered lettering on the front. I was really proud of the way they turned out. A big thank you must also go to the kit man, James Saban, for helping put all the kit together. James is still at the club after progressing from youth team kit man and he is now kit man for the first team.

The game was attended by almost 14,000 spectators, something I will always be grateful for, and it was their presence that gave the game a proper atmosphere. On the morning of the game, I had a phone call from Rio Ferdinand to tell me that while he was still in Manchester, Alex Ferguson had given him permission to play, but for only twenty minutes! 'I'm getting on a train. I should be at Upton Park around 4pm.' I would spend the time between the call and 4pm offering up continual prayers that the train would be on time. There were times when I was concerned that I would not

286 • TONY CARR

have enough players to put out a representative ex-academy side. I needn't have worried; I had 25 or so players who wanted to play and another eight or nine who were there for the game but couldn't or wouldn't play – players like Paul Allen, Bobby Barnes, Tony Cottee, Alvin Martin, Alan Dickens and Chris Ampofo.

Frank Lampard Sr agreed to be the manager of the Academy All-Stars, for which I was grateful. Frank was an academy product himself from the 1960s and I had played with him in the youth team at that time, so our friendship went back a long way. Paolo Di Canio told me before the game that he would play only half the game, which was fine as by now I had plenty of players to use. The game was a typical testimonial: low tempo and lots of goals. On the twenty-minute mark we were desperately signalling for Rio to be substituted (as had been agreed with Alex Ferguson) but the ball wouldn't go out of play. He ended up playing about 26 minutes and got a terrific reception as he left the pitch. I had also played Anton Ferdinand alongside Rio as twin centre backs; I thought it would be a nice touch as they had never played alongside each other since they had turned professional.

At half-time I said to Paolo, 'You come off and Gary Alexander can come on.' 'No, no, no,' he said. 'I play for ten more minutes. I want the adulation of the crowd when I come off ...' Typical Paolo, always the showman! Well, after ten minutes Paolo did come off to the desired crowd adulation. 'Paolo Di Canio, Paolo Di Canio,' the crowd were singing and as he left the pitch he gave me a great big hug saying, 'Thank you for this wonderful experience!' That's Paolo, always very emotional. That wasn't quite the end of Paolo. About ten minutes later, there was Paolo in the proper West Ham kit along with Gianfranco Zola; both came on for the West Ham team to give the game a brief cameo performance from two truly great Italian players. Gianfranco even scored. The game finished 5-1 in West Ham's favour, and it was a great night all round. I'm sure I missed somebody, so to the people I have missed offering my heartfelt thanks and to everybody who took part to make it such a wonderful night for me and my family, I say now and for the record a big THANK YOU.

If that hadn't been enough of a special day, the next day, Thursday 6 May 2010, will always stay firmly fixed in my memory. I was back at the training ground when during the afternoon my wife rang me to say a large brown envelope had arrived in the post addressed to me. Large brown envelopes usually mean a tax bill, trouble or expense. I thought it must be a tax bill but hellfire that was quick, I'd only had the testimonial the night before! (You pay 22 per cent corporation tax on testimonial games.)

When I got home and opened the envelope it was something very different and totally unexpected. It had come from the cabinet office, and the letter was telling me I had been nominated to receive the MBE (Member of the Order of the British Empire) and would I accept if the nomination was successful. You are sworn to secrecy and must return the form inside to accept or otherwise. Well, I was overwhelmed, of course I would accept, but who had nominated me? This is something you never find out, but whoever it was, another thank you! You wait for weeks to hear any more and the only person I told was my wife Brenda. I didn't even tell my children until, some weeks later, it was confirmed. A second letter confirmed the award and that my investiture would be at Buckingham Palace on 21 October 2010 and I was entitled to bring three guests. I have three children and a wife, so who was going to miss out? My wife Brenda gallantly said, 'I'll miss out. You have to take the children.' Er, 'children'? All of them were in their early and late twenties. Thankfully it didn't have to come to that. It turns out that there is a number you can ring at Buckingham Palace to talk to someone who deals with these matters. I rang it and they were very helpful. 'Not everyone takes up their full allocation on the day, so we may be able to send you an extra one,' they said. I had to confirm it was for a direct family member and the extra ticket eventually arrived. Panic over.

The day finally arrived. You are given a pass that allows you to park in the quadrangle at Buckingham Palace. As a family we drove through the gates of Buckingham Palace and parked up. I still find that an odd and stirring sentence to write. After they have put you into the various groups for the different awards (in my group were the physicist and TV personality Brian Cox, Vicki Michelle of 'Allo 'Allo! fame and Tamara Mellon, co-founder of Jimmy Choo shoes), you are taken to a side room to await your turn. I say side room – it was a room full of Rembrandts and Vincent van Goghs on the walls. It is in this room and just ahead of the ceremony that the officials tell you which member of the royal family will be making the investiture. To my great delight it was to be Her Majesty the Queen. They tell you exactly what will happen and how to perform: walk towards the Queen and bow. She will start the conversation and you initially reply with 'Your Majesty' and after the initial greeting it's always 'Mam' as in jam. Now it was my turn. They announced my name and gave the reason for the award: 'Mr Anthony Carr, for services to football.' Our conversation was along the lines of 'It must be so rewarding working with young children and watching them develop.' The Queen then pinned the award onto my left lapel, held out her hand for me to shake and that signified I was done.

I walked backwards a few steps, bowed and exited to the right. It was all over in about three minutes. But three minutes that will live with me forever. I was surprised to see that Her Majesty doesn't wear gloves for these occasions, which I was rather pleased about. My family and I went to lunch in the West End in a French restaurant called La Petite Maison to celebrate (there are no refreshments at the Palace) and drove home feeling very proud.

After the testimonial game on 5 May, we had one more Premier League fixture to play: Manchester City at home, which we drew 1-1, but our Premier League status was already assured. Two days later came the news that Gianfranco Zola had been sacked. I thought this especially sad as Franco was a genuinely good and likeable man with the all the right ethics. But in football if you don't win enough matches, the manager is always going to be vulnerable and it was obvious the new owners obviously wanted their 'own man'. Zola was a fantastic player and was new to management, but he was never afraid to ask his staff their opinion on coaching, team selection or tactics. He wanted his teams to express themselves and entertain. Steve Clarke was a great help and sounding board for Zola. He would always ask me about the young players and would often watch the youth team train. Steve went on to become first-team coach at Liverpool with Kenny Dalglish, taking Kevin Keen with him as assistant coach. He then went on to manage West Bromwich Albion, again taking Kevin Keen with him, and at present is the national team manager of Scotland. Zola was recently back at Chelsea as assistant to Maurizio Sarri but left the club after Frank Lampard's appointment in the summer of 2019.

To everybody's surprise, the Israeli former Chelsea and Portsmouth manager Avram Grant was appointed manager. The team did not improve. In fact, it went from bad to worse, culminating in eventual relegation from the Premier League. I always felt Avram was a decent guy who had football contacts all over the world and knew players from everywhere. He treated the staff well but I didn't think he was cut out to be a Premier League manager, especially with a team like West Ham. It was a different scenario and unlike his time at Chelsea when he took over mid-season from José Mourinho and had a team of top-quality internationals at his disposal. To his credit he almost won the 2008 UEFA Champions League, meeting Manchester United in the final in Moscow. The match was drawn 1-1 and only a slip by John Terry in the penalty shoot-out gave United the European Cup win. Notwithstanding such a near triumph, a relegation battle with weary players was more of a dogfight and would prove his undoing.

Following the final Premier League game of the season at Wigan, which we lost 3-2 after being 2-0 up, Avram was sacked and the search for a new manager began once more. In retrospect, Avram was a very laid-back type of character and this trait would necessarily be transmitted to the players. His management style simply didn't bring out the best in them and by rarely showing his emotions, let alone passion (which I'm sure he felt inside), he couldn't motivate them sufficiently. They needed to play out of their skins for a manager they would die on the field for. Never a hands-on coach, he left that to his assistant Paul Groves and between them the chemistry just wasn't right.

I suppose it takes all sorts of management styles, but this super-chillaxed variant was never going to work at West Ham. When he returned to the training ground to clear his desk and to say his good-byes, he sought me out to give me his phone number and to say that,

'Any time you need advice, you let me know.' This was thoughtful of him and much appreciated at the time.

During the summer of 2011, one of our academy strikers, Dylan Tombides, was playing for Australia under-17s in the World Cup finals in Mexico. After scoring a goal in one of the games he was called in for a routine drugs test ... and failed it. But then a later medical diagnosis revealed he had testicular cancer. Apparently he had been suffering pain a couple of months earlier and had gone to the doctors who told him not to worry, it was only a cyst. Dylan was understandably desperate to play in the under-17 World Cup so he accepted this, assuming his heavy training schedule was to blame and he should therefore carry on. At the club we were not aware of any of this until I got a call from his family telling me what had happened. To say I was shocked was an understatement. I immediately called Karren Brady and told her the news; she was brilliant from the word go. She told me to get her the numbers of Dylan's father and mother, Jim and Tracylee, so she could tell them that whatever treatment Dylan needed, and whatever it would cost, West Ham United would pay. I thought this was a marvellous gesture from the club.

I started thinking about Dylan a lot at this point and started to reminisce about how he came to the club. It was through a friend of mine who lived in Perth, Australia, Mike Leigh. Mike would do a bit of scouting for West Ham in and around Perth and tip me off if any talent surfaced. He spoke to me about Dylan and said the boy and his father were visiting the UK and could we give him a trial. He came over and did well so we offered him a scholarship, but he was an Australian national and there were rules regarding signing players from outside the EU. Dylan's mother worked for an international casino and was getting a transfer to work for the company in London, so as the family were moving to London for non-footballing reasons, that meant he was able to sign. He did well from the word go. He was one of those footballers who loved to train and would push himself to the limit. All in all, he was a great kid to work with.

At first the cancer went into remission and Dylan carried on playing and training as this was what he loved to do above all else. But the cancer returned. More treatment, operations, chemotherapy. Nevertheless, whenever Dylan came to the training ground, he always wore an infectious smile. He recovered sufficiently to make his first-team debut in September 2012 against Wigan in the League Cup. It was, for Dylan and his family, a dream come true. But once again the cancer returned and the last time I saw Dylan was one lunchtime at the Chadwell Heath training ground. I asked how he was doing and for the first time instead of the usual brave smile and typical, 'Yeah, I'm fine,' he shook his head and looked down at the floor. That moment will live with me forever. Such a brave boy with a zest for life, cut short by this terrible disease. The type of cancer that Dylan had was very aggressive and you can't help wondering how the universe arranges things so a seventeen-year-old athlete contracts such an awful illness.

Dylan passed away on 18 April 2014 aged just twenty. Alongside Bobby Moore, he is one of only two players who have had their shirt number retired by West Ham. I had the task of telling the youth team squad the news. I had a lump in my throat as I sat the boys down and told them that one of their teammates had died that morning. The room fell silent and I could see several lads were in tears ... as was I. Dylan's parents have set up a foundation in their

son's honour, helping to make youngsters aware of the signs of testicular cancer and encouraging them to forgo any embarrassment
and to get checked out quickly. They have used the tag DT38 using
his initials and his squad number. God bless you, Dylan, you are
sadly missed. It puts football into perspective.

About a month after sacking Avram Grant, the club appointed
Sam Allardyce as manager. His task was simple – to get the club
promoted as quickly as possible. He signed several players and one
of the most influential was Kevin Nolan. Kevin was a big personality
with lots of experience and was a massive presence in and around
the dressing room. He was an ex-Bolton player who I remember
had played for Bolton youth at Upton Park some years earlier in a
Premier League under-19 play-off game. We had won the game 2-1,
which I reminded Kevin about. He was unimpressed. 'Yeah, but we
(Bolton) were the better team!' Not entirely true, but at least he
remembered the game.

Abdoulaye Faye, Joey O'Brien and Matt Taylor, all ex-Bolton
players and known quantities to Sam from his time as manager
there (although Taylor had joined Bolton just after Sam had left)
were soon signed. Sam was bringing in players he knew he could
trust, and many others would follow as he went about reshaping the
team. After a season with a record number of away wins (thirteen)
and only eight defeats, we finished third in the league and were in
the play-offs. We played Cardiff in the semi-final and won comfortably, 5-0 on aggregate over the two legs. So here we were again, back
in the final, but this time it was at the new Wembley. The board had
given me the privilege of watching the game from the Royal Box
and furnished me with a meal before the game. I was surprised and
at the same time honoured to watch the game from such a lofty

position. The game ended with a nail-biting 2-1 win over Blackpool. Paul Ince's son, Tom, had scored the goal for Blackpool and Carlton Cole and Ricardo Vaz Te had scored for us. Sam had done what had been asked of him and at the first attempt. West Ham were back in the Premier League. A great job done.

It was after the game, up in the Royal Box dining room, that Phil Stant – our Football League club support manager who would regularly visit me at the training ground to check that we were complying with League regulations and offer support where needed – came up to me to offer his congratulations and to say that as we were now a Premier League club again, his visits would now cease. His parting gift was to present the match ball to me (one of six made especially for the game and positioned around the ground for the ball boys to use to keep the game flowing). It was inscribed with the teams, date and play-off details. I thought it was a nice gesture from Phil and thanked him for thinking of me.

At the same time as a promotion push, the youth programme was going through immense change. The Premier League were in the midst of implementing a method of categorising clubs through on-site audits. This was quite a daunting process. Each club would be assessed using twelve KPIs (key performance indicators) such as facilities, medical provision, coaching programme, staffing levels, etc. I have to say much of my time the previous season was taken up with preparing for this audit. It was carried out by an independent company, Double Pass from Belgium, who had been appointed by the Premier League. Our audit was over three or four days and it just happened to fall on the weekend of the play-off final with Blackpool. I managed to negotiate with them to audit for half a day on the Saturday (the day of the final) and the other half day on the

Sunday! It was a mad dash on the train to Wembley that day, but it was worth it. Not only did we win at Wembley but a few weeks later we were told that we had achieved Category 1 status – the highest level possible for any academy.

The dedication and hard work of the staff at the academy had paid off but there was a price to pay: my role as a coach to the senior youth team and managing the academy had changed for good. When I started out as a coach, the youth department had one full-time coach in me and one full-time scout in Eddie Baily. We didn't have a kit man or a physio and if a player got injured in training, he was treated by the first-team physio, Rob Jenkins. On match days 'treatment' was supplied by a part-time 'sponge man'. I drove the minibus back and forth to Upton Park on a daily basis and organised the next day's training kit with the youth players' help and packed the match kit on Friday afternoons. But now staffing levels within the academy had skyrocketed. These days we employed more than 30 full-time staff who needed managing. The roster included additional coaches, medical staff, sports scientists, fitness coaches, scouts, player welfare officers, educational staff and psychologists and I could feel how the burden of managing these disparate and at times conflicting departments was growing increasingly heavy. I also became aware that I was spending less and less time out on the 'grass'. Instead, my days were spent ensuring the audit criteria were being actively followed and endlessly sorting out departmental problems.

The competition to attract and sign the best players in and around London was to become even more competitive: the new rules – the EPPP (Elite Player Performance Plan) – brought in by the Premier League forbade any club signing any player under fourteen from more than one hour travelling distance. London clubs' boundaries necessarily overlapped, and this alone would intensify the competition and bring about obvious conflict. For players fourteen years old and above, clubs could scout countrywide as long as you had provisions in place to safeguard their education.

While we had evolved and developed all of the academy departments, we'd failed to revamp our scouting set-up for the new challenges ahead. I take some blame for this as I should have been more demanding of the scouting department and the head of recruitment Dave Hunt, whom I had appointed earlier. The one thing we couldn't change was the money being thrown at eight and nine-year-olds by the bigger clubs. We developed a relationship with a local school (Robert Clack) close to the training ground at Rush Green. The idea was that the players all enrolled into Robert Clack at the age of fourteen; they would spend two hours a day being coached and the rest of the day educated at Robert Clack. Some compromises around educational subject matter proved necessary, but I have to say that during my time, the grades the boys achieved were all better than the predicted grades they had arrived with. There were boys who were unsure about changing schools at such a crucial time and for them we made special efforts to negotiate extra coaching time with the relevant schools. In most cases the schools were very co-operative.

Sir Paul Grant was the headteacher at Robert Clack during this period. Liverpool-born, he came to Robert Clack in 1997 when it was a failing school and turned it around magnificently. I got on well with Sir Paul right from the word go and his love of football was a big help. We would talk about how the boys were doing and Sir Paul was always interested in their football progress. He had a nephew who was a professional player at Everton and knew of the problems and pitfalls of young players trying to make their way in the professional game. If I was having a problem with any of the boys, whether it was discipline or a lack of form, we would talk it through and see where and how we could help each other to solve it; it worked extremely well. The football element was a great incentive for the boys to toe the line and when their behaviour at school or during training became problematic, we found the mere threat of stopping them training or playing in matches usually did the trick! Sir Paul Grant retired in the summer of 2017 after doing a fantastic job at Robert Clack for twenty years. He now works as a consultant for the Premier League in their education department and I had hoped his successor would have as good a relationship with the academy as I had with Sir Paul. Sadly, shortly after I left West Ham, the club cut their ties with Robert Clack School and now have a new partnership with St Edward's School which is closer to Chadwell Heath where the academy is now based.

Sam Allardyce had four years as manager and I think it's the right judgement to say they were successful years: promotion at the first attempt and consolidating the team in the Premier League thereafter. He brought in tried and tested players, many who had played for him at his previous clubs. But there came a moment in the 2014/15 season when the fans began voicing their frustration about the 'negative' style of football being played. Banners were displayed at matches showing their disapproval and more determined fans even unfurled one outside the chairman David Sullivan's house. After finishing twelfth in the Premier League and within minutes of the last game of the season finishing, the club announced that Sam had departed, so the search for another manager was up and running.

Sam never dictated the way the youth team should play in order to fit in with his own playing philosophy. He only ever said to me, 'Play any way you want, carry on with what you are doing, but they must be able to do the things I demand at first-team level.' Which was fair enough and no different from most managers I worked with. At academy level we had problems with two of our promising youngsters, Ben Sheaf and Josh Pask, who had turned down our offer of scholarships. They had both been with us since the age of nine or ten and both attended our partnership school, Robert Clack. This was a new development for me as I had never had a situation where in their final year at school a player would turn down an offer of a scholarship. Quite obviously they had been approached by other clubs. I knew Ben Sheaf's parents quite well – both high-level sportspeople in their own right – and had various meetings with them to try and convince Ben to stay. They were adamant they would leave. I even offered them a guaranteed professional contract, which I hadn't done with Michael Carrick! But it came down to the money and we could not agree. He subsequently left and signed for Arsenal. He has subsequently made one 89th-minute substitute appearance for Arsenal in the UEFA Europa League but otherwise has been sent out on loan. And is now playing for Coventry City in the Football League Championship.

Josh Pask was different: he was a quiet lad with very supportive and straightforward parents. He was playing regularly in the under-18s, which is not something all schoolboys get to do, but he was still set on leaving. Arsenal had made him an offer and he was very tempted by it. We had tried everything to persuade him otherwise but I was resigned to losing him. I went on a week's holiday with this on my mind – not convinced he would sign for Arsenal, but unsure whether he would sign for West Ham.

I was in Monaco, where my son Dean lives with his wife Melissa and our grandchildren Blake, Indie and Sienna. On our second day, just as we were sitting down to lunch, I had a phone call from the club's youth scout Dave Hunt to say he had had a conversation with Karren Brady, who wanted an update on why Josh Pask had not committed to us. Dave had explained to Karren that we had tried everything to convince him and his parents to sign but until now they had not committed. Karren had replied that he and I should have another go at persuading Josh his future lay with West Ham. Dave mentioned I was on holiday for a week. Karren's response was unequivocal. 'Tell him to come back,' she said. I told Dave to book me on a flight from Nice to Stansted that afternoon, meet me at the airport and we would go to Josh's house to give it one more go.

Josh and his family lived in Manor Park, so it was only an hour from Stansted airport. I wasn't too confident this tactic would work, but Brady had insisted, so that's what we would do. We arrived at the family home around 6pm and went into the sitting room with Josh's father. Josh stayed in his bedroom, which was not a good sign. I told him why we were there and that I had broken my holiday to take this last opportunity to convince him to stay at West Ham. We stayed for about four hours and left without a commitment from the father either way. It was too late to get a flight back to Nice so I stayed overnight in an airport hotel and flew back to my family early next morning. It was some weeks later that I was told that Josh had turned down Arsenal and was going to sign for us.

Credit must go to Karren Brady for insisting we made the one final last-ditch effort to try to change Josh's and his family's minds. However, I have to say his reluctance to sign was based on football and not money. He liked the way Arsenal played and felt he could have been part of it. When the season began and I bumped into Josh's dad, he mentioned to me that the fact that I had broken my holiday to get Josh to sign was a big factor in him changing his mind. Watching the Chelsea vs West Ham game at Stamford Bridge on television a couple of seasons ago I noticed that Josh was on the substitutes' bench, but unfortunately that's as far as it went with West Ham and in the summer of 2019, Josh left and signed for Coventry City.

In June 2015 Slaven Bilić was appointed manager and, as is always the case in these situations, he brought his own staff with him – coaches that had been with him when he was manager of Croatia and Beşiktaş of Turkey. Bilić had been a West Ham player some years before under Harry Redknapp so the fans easily accepted him. He also brought in Julian Dicks as an assistant coach, Julian being a real fans' favourite from his time as a player at West Ham; it made sense and would help Bilić settle in. I had known Slaven from his time as a player and the same of course goes for Julian. It helped that I didn't have to build a relationship with a new manager.

At about this time my role had changed within the club, as described in Chapter 1, and I was less involved in trying to promote youth team players that the manager ought to be aware of. The club had qualified for the preliminary rounds of the Europa League but our adventures in Europe didn't last long when we failed to qualify for the group stages. It was also the last season at Upton Park before the club's historic move to the former Olympic Stadium, now named the London Stadium. It was a good first season for Bilić, finishing in seventh place with Dimitri Payet ending up as leading scorer, and the final game at Upton Park vs Manchester United was a fitting finale as we won the game 3-2 with Winston Reid scoring the last ever goal at the stadium. For me this was one of the greatest games ever seen at Upton Park, and there had been many, but for the pure nostalgic moment and the game's excitement it had everything. The team had ended up with 62 points (the club's highest ever).

Bilić's second season was a real test: a new stadium and unrest with Payet, the club's star striker. The team finished eleventh in the league and at the start of the following season, results did not improve and, after a run of poor results, in November 2017 Bilić was sacked along with his coaching staff. I had left the club before then but I'd like to point out that Slaven Bilić was the fifteenth manager the club had employed since 1900 and, including Slaven, I had worked for twelve of them!

\*

I was now out of work, but not ready or willing to retire gracefully, and I started to go to odd games here and there – youth games, under-23 games and the odd first-team game. Chelsea were very generous, with Neil Bath, their long-serving academy manager, inviting me to a pre-game lunch at Stamford Bridge and taking in the Premier League game vs Burnley. John McDermott, academy manager of Tottenham Hotspur, invited me to come and talk to their academy coaches about my 43 years' experience in youth development. Likewise, Fulham, Arsenal and Crystal Palace and further afield Sheffield United and Aston Villa did the same. Going around clubs like Tottenham, Chelsea, Aston Villa and others showed me how far behind West Ham were with regards to facilities and how important this is when recruiting young players. I know that recently West Ham have upgraded their facilities at Chadwell Heath and I hope this will help improve the standard of player the club can attract and recruit in the future.

With my footballing appetite still strong, and as I was still looking to get involved in the game somewhere, I received a phone call from Marc Canham, who is head of coaching at the FA Premier League, and he asked if I would be interested in coming for a chat about a part-time role at the Premier League. It sounded interesting and we met in London, and he brought along Neil Saunders who is head of youth development at the Premier League. I knew them both from my time at West Ham so it was a very relaxed meeting, nothing formal at all. Marc did most of the talking, outlining the role, which was basically supporting their programmes on coach development and creating a role at all clubs for a head of academy coaching.

There was a new programme being piloted around the concept of each club having a 'head of coaching' for the academy, funded by the Premier League. It was open to all Premier League and Football League clubs. The contract the clubs had to agree to was that if they accepted the funding, the head of coaching had to commit to a three-year programme of attendance at various workshops around the country – and it was at these workshops that the Premier League wanted me to attend as a 'consultant and coaching adviser'. Other consultants include Kenny Swain – former Chelsea, Nottingham Forest and Aston Villa player, where Kenny was a European Cup winner in 1982; and Steve Burns – former West Bromwich Albion, Wolverhampton Wanderers and Aston Villa academy head. Typically, I spend two days a month meeting with the heads of coaching at all the clubs, talking football, sharing football experiences and giving coaching advice. Since the pandemic, my role with the Premier

League has changed into one of mentoring coaches and future heads of coaching. I go to youth games at weekends or sometimes watch the Hammers. I get time to see my grandchildren – Blake, Sienna, Indie, Preston, Hudson, Harrison and Jenson – and I also get my 'football fix'. I am not a person to sit around and I want to be involved in football for as long as I can.

During 2019, the FA Youth Cup winners of 1999 held a twenty-year anniversary charity match, again against Coventry City, that was played at West Ham's Rush Green training ground. It was great meeting all the players again, now in their late thirties! All the old team showed up and it was a really fun day. Sadly, Peter Brabrook had died a few years earlier and his son Wayne filled in for his dad as my assistant. Coventry got their revenge for the 9-0 aggregate defeat in 1999 by winning the charity match 2-1. This occasion reminded me that the FA Youth Cup winners of 1981 held a similar get-together on their twentieth anniversary, having a dinner together to meet their old teammates. I attended and it was great to be invited to be with them and reminisce about their success all those years earlier.

Another big surprise came my way recently when I received an email from the Chancellor of the University of East London, Shabir Randeree CBE, asking if I would accept the honour of an Honorary Doctorate. This was completely out of the blue and I gratefully accepted. Being born in East London (Bow), and having spent most of my working life in East London I was completely humbled. The ceremony took place at their Beckton campus, close to London City airport in September 2021. And I was conferred as a Doctor of Science! It surprised me how emotional I felt on the day at such an unexpected honour; life is a journey and you never know where it will take you.

As I write, the country is still in the midst of the pandemic. It is more than four years since I left West Ham and I have had plenty of time to reflect on my career. Luckily, I have very few regrets and can look back on my 43 years as a coach and my earlier playing days with great affection and will always be thankful for being able to spend my working life at the club that I've followed and supported since I was a very young boy. The journey continues and football will always be a big part of my life.

# GLENN ROEDER – A TRIBUTE

During the writing of this book, we sadly learnt that the ex-West Ham manager Glenn Roeder had died of a brain tumour aged 65.

Harry Redknapp had brought Glenn to West Ham in 1999 when he was without a club after leaving the Football Association. His coaching role with the England team had come to an end when the England manager at the time, Glenn Hoddle, had his contract terminated.

Glenn was a very dedicated and enthusiastic coach and his role at West Ham was initially to coach the younger players individually and he struck up a good rapport with the players who were just breaking into the first team but not quite there. He didn't have the responsibility of running a team so he could help with the coaching of players individually, helping them improve their weaknesses as well as their strengths.

After Harry had left the club Glenn was given the job as manager and brought in Paul Goddard, an ex-West Ham striker, as his assistant. Their first season was very successful, with the team finishing in seventh place in the Premier League. Their second season was beset by injury problems to key players and the team struggled.

Glenn started to take a lot of flak from supporters and media as the team dropped further and further down the table. He took this very personally and the pressure started to mount, and after a home game vs Middlesbrough in April 2003, Glenn collapsed and was taken straight to hospital with what was later diagnosed as a brain tumour.

The inevitable happened to the team and the club were relegated at the end of that season. A few months later Glenn had recovered enough to take charge of the team for the following season.

Now some eighteen years later when the news came through of his passing, it came as a complete shock to me and my thoughts and belated condolences are with his wife Faith and his children, Will, Joe and Holly. Football has lost a good man.